The Soviet Legacy

THE SOVIET LEGACY

ROY D. LAIRD

Westport, Connecticut
London

Library of Congress Cataloging-in-Publication Data

Laird, Roy D.
    The soviet legacy / Roy D. Laird.
       p.   cm.
    Includes bibliographical references and index.
    ISBN 0–275–94558–8 (alk. paper)
       1. Soviet Union—Economic conditions—1985–1991.   2. Soviet Union—
    Social conditions—1970–1991.   3. Former Soviet republics—Economic
    conditions.   4. Former Soviet republics—Social conditions.
    I. Title.
    HC336.26.L35   1993
    330.947—dc20   92–41617

British Library Cataloguing in Publication Data is available.

Library of Congress Catalog Card Number: 92–41617
ISBN: 0–275–94558–8

First published in 1993

Praeger Publishers, 88 Post Road West, Westport, CT 06881
An imprint of Greenwood Publishing Group, Inc.

Printed in the United States of America

The paper used in this book complies with the
Permanent Paper Standard issued by the National
Information Standards Organization (Z39.48–1984).

10 9 8 7 6 5 4 3 2 1

For
Myra Frances, Ellen Michelle, Larissa Ruth,
and Martin Ross in their journey into the
twenty-first century

CONTENTS

PREFACE

This work is an attempt to accomplish two major purposes. The first is to produce an analytical discussion of the accelerating collapse of the Soviet Union, starting with the elevation of Mikhail Gorbachev to the post of general secretary of the Communist Party of the Soviet Union (CPSU) in 1985 and ending with the death of the Union in December 1991. The second purpose is to explore the legacy of the USSR as of the end of the first quarter of 1992. What is the heritage of the people of the newly independent states, economically, physically, and psychologically, and what does that bequest bode for the foreseeable future?

Part I is a descriptive analysis of the demise of the old Union and the birth of the new states, ending with a prognostication of what seems to be their destiny, at least for many years to come. Part II is a chronology, an internal documentary record of a deteriorating human condition, including the masses' reaction to a severe decline in the standard of living for the vast majority of the people. In that connection, special attention is given to the most serious of all the problems, declining production of food and a breakdown in its distribution. Also provided is a chronology of the changing thought patterns of both the people and the leaders. What was their mental response to the dying Union, and what are their hopes and fears for the future?

Some aspects of Soviet society were positive and beautiful—for example, achievements in the realms of art, literature, and science. Thus, in no way do the pages that follow present a total picture of the former USSR, even during the new time of troubles, a time of catastrophe, which resulted in the disintegration of the old Union. Since this work is about the multiple crises that culminated in the fall of the Soviet Union, however, the material offered is overwhelmingly negative. This is so for several specific reasons.

First, in the final years, the morale of both the leaders and the people was overwhelmingly grim. Intellectuals and leaders often used such terms as *crisis*, *catastrophe*, *deep depression*, and *anarchy* to describe the situation. Measures of the psychological makeup and health of society revealed a grim, increasingly desperate people.

Second, the work depends almost entirely on internal reporting and commentary—thus, it does not include evaluations by Western specialists on Soviet affairs, who, sometimes rightly, focused on the positive. Glasnost opened Pandora's box, and, with the unleashing of the demons of knowledge, the Soviet press (and other communications media) became extremely self-critical. This study, therefore, is a mirror of the increasingly depressing picture that was (and still is) presented daily within the boundaries of the Central Eurasian states that formerly constituted the Soviet Union.

Third, beyond reports on an economy in extreme depression, mounting civil strife, ecological disaster, political anarchy, and so on that have crowded the pages of the internal press since the introduction of glasnost in the mid-1980s, a plethora of negative reports on the opinions, attitudes, values, and expectations of the people has arisen. Public opinion polling surfaced and, if the polls' contents are at all accurate in reflecting the mentality of the citizenry, they reveal a desperate people deeply dissatisfied with their lot and extremely apprehensive about their future.

Thus, Part I is an analysis of the crises that culminated in the demise of the USSR and its legacy, based almost entirely on primary sources, including (1) a review of the Stalinist-Brezhnev base inherited by the Gorbachev leadership; (2) a discussion of the first several years of the so-called Gorbachev era, focusing on his unsuccessful attempt to employ perestroika and glasnost to correct the ills inherited from the past, with special emphasis on the major economic problem area (i.e., agriculture and food shortages); and (3) a probe into the beliefs, values, and expectations of the people (i.e., the opinion leaders, but especially the masses), which, surely more than anything else, will shape any future course of events in the successor republics.

Part II, on the other hand, is a topical-chronological catalog of the revelations of glasnost, a verbal panorama almost entirely devoted to citations taken from the Soviet and post-Soviet communications media since the mid-1980s. A grasp of that rhetoric is essential to any probe into the current state of affairs and what the future might bring.

Some, but far from all, of the material in Part II is incorporated in Part I. The particular value of Part II, however, is that, although the material offered is necessarily selective, it is much more comprehensive than Part I in its presentation of primary sources, and, since each of the topic areas covered is presented chronologically, it also provides the reader with a blow-by-blow insight into changing events and the evolution of the attitudes of the people and the opinion makers—intellectuals, journalists, and political leaders. For example, one of the major parts of Part II, ''The Soviet Mind-Set: Public Opinions,'' has a section the polls in chronological order dramatically illuminate the ever-deepening sense of desperation that gripped society, tearing the Soviet Union apart. The revelations also suggest what changes the people are willing to tolerate under the new dispensation, assuming that their wishes and desires are heeded.

Again, the sources for the work are overwhelmingly primary material drawn from the Soviet press and other communications media, both in Russian and in English translation. Although some of the material was taken directly from original Russian texts, the magnitude of the task (i.e., to do as wide as possible a survey of primary sources) dictated that most of the material be drawn selectively from the voluminous translation sources, such as the weekly *Current Digest of the Soviet Press* (CDSP), the weekly *Moscow News*, and, most especially, the very comprehensive U.S. government translations taken from many scores of periodicals, plus daily broadcasts by Soviet, and now republic, radio and television, and transmissions by such sources as the Moscow-based *Interfax*. Indeed, no single library contains all of the original Soviet sources that are covered in such translations.

Therefore, the author obtained, and has exploited to the fullest extent to which he is capable, all of the Joint Publication Research Service (JPRS) reports on "Soviet Political [and social] Affairs" and "Soviet Economic Affairs" plus translations from the CPSU journal *Kommunist* and the journal *USA: Economics, Politics, Ideology* and the daily Soviet Foreign Broadcast Information Service (FBIS)—now entitled *Daily Report: Central Eurasia*—translations from many Soviet central and regional periodicals, as well as transcripts from the broadcast media.

In the sources used, various alternative spellings of words and names were encountered, such as centre and center, tonnes and tons, Tatyana and Tatiana. For the sake of consistency, a common spelling has been employed.

As has been the case with all of the author's work over the past forty-five years, Betty A. Laird skillfully edited every line of this work before it was sent to the publisher. Of course, the errors that exist are entirely the fault of the author.

Part I

From Crisis to Catastrophe

The Soviet winds of change built to hurricane force. The new Soviet experiment in parliamentary government at the end of the 1980s failed. All of the republics declared themselves independent, destroying the old system. The winds also severely crippled the once all-powerful Communist party. Several score of lives have been lost in ethnic strife—for example, bloodletting in Armenia, Georgia, and Azerbaijan that threatens to escalate into major civil wars among the newly independent republics.

The Commonwealth of Independent States (CIS), formed at the beginning of 1992, is a precariously weak confederation, seemingly incapable of addressing the economic interdependence that must continue if total catastrophe is to be averted. Moreover, as of mid-1992, Georgia and the three Baltic states, Estonia, Latvia, and Lithuania, have counted themselves out of any new union, however weak.

Most serious of all, the economies of all the republics have fallen into a deep depression, far worse than any depression experienced by Western nations in the past. There are severe consumer shortages of nearly everything, including food. Skyrocketing inflation has taken hold. The old command economic system has seriously broken down and no new viable market system has taken its place. The word *anarchy* is often used correctly to describe the post-Soviet scene.

Reporting in the Western media has concentrated largely on the growing ethnic strife and the political breakdown that devastated the union, both of which contributed to bringing the country to the verge of anarchy, civil war(s), and, finally, dissolution. Although this is a correct picture as far as it goes, too often what is missed is a discussion of the forces (especially economic and managerial) that unleashed the ethnic and political turmoil. Key questions explored here are: Why? Why now? Why not ten or twenty years earlier?

A central theme in the pages that follow is that the cumulative forces that destroyed the Union were not primarily the result of an inevitable awakening of latent democratic sentiments and/or desires for self-determination by the various nationality groups. Such sentiments were there, and they reached revolutionary levels. The major fuel for the disintegration of the USSR, however, was the devastating deterioration of the economy, especially the quality of human life, to the point of being intolerable for most people. Tragically, those forces remain in place, promising even further deterioration of the quality of life in the future.

A central assumption of the study is that a primary determinant of the fate of nations is the mental health of the people and their psychological makeup, as inherited from the past, but profoundly affected by the quality of their evolving life experiences. Thus, the major focus of the analysis is not on the rise and fall of economic and political institutions or groups as such, but rather on the real-life experiences of the people in the former USSR.

Although the quality of life in the beginning of the 1980s was dismal compared to that in virtually all other modern industrial nations, from Stalin's time until near the end of the Brezhnev era, advances had been made and, bolstered by the official rhetoric, on balance, there was some reason to hope for a brighter future. During the Gorbachev era, however, not only did the hope for a better future vanish but also there evolved an increasing perception among the masses that things could get only worse in any foreseeable future. For example, in April 1991, 40 percent of the people who responded to a national poll indicated that they feared the possibility of famine in the future.[1] The respondents to another representative national poll conducted in September 1991 reflected a view that "just one-third of the population . . . believes that our life will improve." By way of commentary, a *Pravda* reporter asked: "What is there left for the other two-thirds?"[2]

Over the last several years, what the people personally have experienced and what they have read in their press and heard and seen in the broadcast media tells them that they are in the midst of catastrophe. Not only has the economy gone into a perilous decline but also there is a food crisis, a consumer goods crisis, a health crisis, an environmental crisis, and an alarming rise in crime.

The forces that shape the human mental condition are enormously complex. The mental health of people and nations is not shaped by tangible life experiences only, most of which can be measured to some degree—for example, the availability of consumer necessities, the quality of medical care, and the crime rate. The mental health of nations also is profoundly shaped by individual and collective beliefs and values, most of which are intangible and are often based on irrational considerations, and thus are most difficult to measure. Surely that is why, for example, even in democratic open societies, public opinion pollsters are often wrong in predicting the outcome of elections, especially when polls are taken a considerable period of time prior to an election.

In his classic study of politics, *The Web of Government*, Robert M. MacIver wrote:

[Myths are] the value-impregnated beliefs and notions [a combination of rational and irrational convictions] that men hold, that they live by or live for. Every society is held together by a myth-system, a complex of dominating thought-forms that determines and sustains all its activities. . . . Every civilization, every period, every nation, has its characteristic myth complex. In it lies the secret of social unities and social continuities, and its changes compose the inner history of every society.[3]

The imponderables in the human equation mean that social scientists' attempts to appraise the immediate state of any nation, much less forecast the future course of events, inevitably are imprecise at best. That reality, however, does not mean that all efforts to conduct such analyses should be rejected as fruitless enterprises. Indeed, one of the major benefits of such probes (worth the candle in itself) is that any serious attempt to make public policies must start with a careful inventory of available resources, material and psychological, tangible and intangible, which serves to sharpen the understanding of both the positive and negative aspects of the socioeconomic scene. Specifically, such efforts allow nations to sort out social and economic priorities, a necessity in a world in which there never are enough resources to do everything that seems desirable. Thus, politics has been best defined as both "the art of the possible" and, especially, "the authoritative allocation of scarce resources."

For example, take environmental legislation. Every law on protecting the environment, thus every regulation promulgated by the U.S. Environmental Protection Agency, is based not only on a forecast of what might, or might not, happen if specified actions are, or are not, taken but also on the resources available to carry out a specific course of action. Similarly, in the private economic sector, individual or corporate decisions (e.g., when to buy and when to sell) stem primarily from the decision makers' perception of the current situation, perceived future trends, and the availability of funds for investment.

Unfortunately, however, as suggested, the serious barriers to accurate analysis do not lie just in the great gaps in verifiable tangible knowledge. Human actions are motivated by a combination of rational and irrational (often unverifiable) considerations. Certainly, the whole record of the Soviet attempt to build communism is testimony that irrational convictions can often determine the course of national affairs. For example, by the end of the 1920s, Lenin's pragmatic (i.e., rational) deviation from Bolshevism, the New Economic Policy, had solved a major food crisis that had existed for many years. Yet Stalin (guided primarily by irrational considerations) turned success into failure. He forced collectivization on the countryside, resulting in the greatest human-made famine in human history. That tragedy cannot be understood without realizing that Stalin and company shared the myth that building communism required imposing socialism on the peasantry—that is, in practice, command-central management. Moreover, many of the value-impregnated beliefs, intangible cultural and historical influences that existed under the tsars, were incorporated into the Soviet experiment in building communism.

Just as the tallest mountains will crumble eventually, change in the affairs of men and women is one of the greatest of all universals. Fundamental change in individual and collective values and, thus, behavior, takes many years to occur, usually generations, however. Take, for example, the defeat of the South in the U.S. Civil War. The South was forced back into the Union, and the slaves were emancipated. Nevertheless, much remained unchanged for Southern blacks for many decades—for example, legally sanctioned segregation continued for nearly a century after the Civil War.

For nearly as long as slavery was a way of life in the U.S. South, state ownership and management of industry and commerce and state serfdom (the collective and state farms) dominated Soviet affairs, shaping attitudes and behavior. A distinct Soviet political culture evolved. Not surprising, then, as documented here, glasnost has disclosed that many, perhaps most, of the citizens of the former Soviet Union are not mentally prepared for an abrupt emancipation from authoritarian socialism. Many of the leaders now contending for power, and most of the people, express distrust of pluralist, open, democratic institutions and practices. Further, if the public opinion polls are a reflection of mass attitudes, the vast majority of the population rejects a market economy in practice, especially prices determined by supply and demand.

A *Kommunist* editorial posed this question: "[T]o what extent in our country today are there greater obstructions to perestroika: in real life or in the mind? Perhaps . . . we should agree to consider as equally important the reorganization of the economy and the 'perestroika' of our own minds."[4] On many occasions, Mikhail Gorbachev made essentially the same point, such as his statement in 1988 that perestroika must incorporate a "mobilization of the human potential."[5]

In his call for a perestroika of the mind, Gorbachev stated the need to create a Soviet value system akin to what has been identified in the West as the Protestant work ethic. Thus, for example, in agriculture, the most serious economic problem area, he repeatedly called for changes that would allow the peasants to feel that they are the masters of the land.

If a fundamental change in the mind-set of the people is required to end the crises in the newly independent republics, one needs to know first what their present thinking is. How, at the beginning of a new era, do the masses view their lot? What are their hopes and fears for the future? Most importantly, are they prepared to make the changes, often sacrifices, necessary to eliminate the social and economic crises that brought the Soviet Union to catastrophe?

In the pages that follow, an attempt will be made to answer questions posed in this introduction. Believing that the past is prologue, however, one needs first to look at the nature and health of the Soviet Union prior to the onset of the revolutionary convulsions now faced by the people and their new leaders.

NOTES

1. Tatyana Zaslavskaya, "When the 'Powers that Be' Err," *Moscow News*, April 1991.

2. Ye. Sorokin, "Our Commentary," *Pravda*, September 14, 1991. JPRS-SOV-91-183, September 20, 1991.

3. Robert M. MacIver, *The Web of Government* (New York: Macmillan, 1948), pp. 4, 5.

4. "Socialist Idea and Social Creativity," *Kommunist*, November 1989. JPRS-UKO-90-002.

5. *Pravda*, May 11, 1988.

1

THE PAST AS PROLOGUE: THE HOUSE THAT STALIN BUILT

We the leaders are responsible for everything. Therefore, we must understand everything, recognizing right from wrong, and good from evil, supporting the right way and vanquishing the wrong way.
—Khrushchev to agricultural workers in 1957

AVOIDING MIRROR-IMAGING

Quite unlike most systems elsewhere in the world, especially those of the Western nations, the Soviet Union was a command system—not only a command economy but also a command polity and a command society. Thus, as expressed by Nikita Khrushchev, the leaders claimed responsibility for *everything*.

Gorbachev, too, shared Khrushchev's attitude about the responsibility of the country's key leader. In a 1989 speech to the Soviet Congress, Gorbachev attempted to dispel the illusion that he was not aware of the mood of the people by saying: "I even know about the following instance: Veterans riding the last bus in Moscow carried with them some 'visual aids'—Brezhnev's portrait covered with medals and Gorbachev's portrait covered with ration coupons. *I know everything*" (emphasis added).[1]

The world over, people put on their trousers one leg at a time. All human beings hurt and bleed when cut. Yet momentous differences do exist among societies.

Human beings everywhere tend to view the world and other societies through the familiar lenses of their own experiences. Such mirror-imaging is natural, but it is responsible for much of the misunderstanding that exists in the world, including Western misconceptions about the former Soviet system and, now, the successor independent states. Understanding the Soviet phenomenon and the newly independent republics that have succeeded it requires setting aside preconceptions based on one's experiences and knowledge about his or her own system.

For example, elections as practiced in the Soviet Union were not the same as Western elections. Until the 1987 election, voting did not serve to select leaders. Only one name appeared for each office on the ballots. Yet election days were important. They were national celebrations, legitimizing devices; thus, going to the polls was the proper thing to do. Consistently, nearly 99 percent of the eligible citizens voted.

Soviet labor unions played a significantly different role than do unions in most nations. Strikes were illegal. The party tightly controlled the unions. The unions, however, controlled housing (always scarce), access to vacation resorts, and other amenities. Also, belonging to them was the thing to do, and virtually all eligible workers were union members. Much else that is familiar in the West was different in the USSR. Indeed, "truth" as seen through Soviet eyes, especially as it was officially defined until the advent of glasnost, was also quite different.

What was true in the USSR, as repeatedly stated by Soviet philosophers, was rooted in the Marxist-Leninist science of society, which was said to provide the base for all correct attitudes and behavior. Therefore, individual and collective success and progress could come only from activities determined by the perception of necessity. That is to say, the only correct Soviet way was to know and practice the "laws" discovered by Marx and Lenin, especially as interpreted by the incumbent party leadership.

A COMMAND SYSTEM

The past is prologue for nations as well as people. Thus, the Soviet system that existed until the end of 1991, even the newly independent republics that exist at this time of revolutionary upheaval, cannot be understood without a knowledge of the house that Stalin built.

Although important changes were made in the USSR between the death of Stalin in the spring of 1953 and the beginning of the Gorbachev era in 1985, the Stalinist system remained largely intact until the end of the 1980s. Interestingly, although the use of the word *totalitarianism* to describe the system was largely abandoned by Western Sovietologists in the 1960s, after the advent of glasnost, many Soviet commentators employed the word to describe the system inherited from Brezhnev and his immediate successors.

For example, in 1988 the Soviet historian and academician A. Migranyan observed:

There has been no example in history of a totalitarian political system peacefully developing into a democratic system. . . . I think that our country is now going through a period of transition from totalitarianism to authoritarianism. . . . But the road to this [a democratic society] won't be easy and we are just at its beginning.[2]

This is not the place to describe in detail the pre-Gorbachev system. A brief exploration of essential aspects of the system that Gorbachev inherited will help, however, to put into context the reforms called for since the advent of perestroika. In a few words, what existed, totalitarian or not, was an extreme authoritarian system, legitimized by the so-called Marxist-Leninist science of society that, it has been asserted, provided the "laws" that must be obeyed in building the nirvana of Communism.

With the caveat that, although for the purpose of syntax, the past tense has been employed in the following catalog of key characteristics of the institutions and practices inherited from Brezhnev, many still persist during this period of transition into an uncertain future, but virtually all have been challenged.

For example, although the final months of the Gorbachev era witnessed much discussion about adopting a market system, a law was passed in 1991 making it a crime (punishable by up to ten years of incarceration) for anyone to sell goods at prices higher than the established retail prices. Will the people of Russia, Ukraine, and the other newly independent republics really tolerate market-determined prices across the board—for example, for essential foods—or will the cries to throw the new leaders out accelerate?

Until the end of the USSR, key characteristics of the system were as follows:

1. All of the land was owned by the state.

2. Virtually all economic enterprise was owned and directed by the state. With the exception of private plot produce sold in the collective farm (kolkhoz) markets and a few private craft and service activities, there were virtually no legal private enterprises, no markets, and no prices that fluctuated according to supply and demand. Detailed central planning prevailed. The Soviet Union was a command economy.

3. With the exception of the children and the elderly, virtually every able-bodied adult worked for the USSR, Inc.

4. There was no legal private press in the sense that all publishing and broadcasting were monopolized by party and state institutions. Only information sanctioned by party and state officials was fit to print or broadcast. Orwellian thought control prevailed.

5. The party jealously guarded its "right" to have a sole monopoly over leadership and decision making on all matters that it deemed important—that is, the right to control (*Pravo kontrolia*). That right was guaranteed by Article 6 in the constitution. There was no concept akin to the notion of rule-of-law. The Soviet Union was a command polity.

6. The ultimate measure of the rightness or justice of any activity was the so-called science of society (i.e., Marxism-Leninism), which was said to govern all human activity.

7. The ultimate directorate of all human activity, including the final interpretation of the

laws of the science of society, was the party, with the politburo having the final say
in all matters. The Soviet Union was a command society.

8. The collective was stressed, and individualism was discouraged.

In sum, the USSR was the world's most controlled system. At least on paper,
all of that is to change in the new republics in the name of reform. Major
questions, however, remain: How much will change? What are the major points
of resistance to change and how strong are they?

Several major changes have been made that are probably irreversible without
the reimposition of extreme authoritarian rule backed by force. Most important
has been the breakup of the old internal empire. Of great importance has been
the unleashing of previously withheld information in the name of glasnost. Also,
the Communist party has been decimated. In the newly independent states, there
is no Article 6, as was the case in the Soviet constitution. The lead sentence of
Article 6 in the former constitution reads as follows: "The leading and guiding
force of Soviet society and the nucleus of its political system, of all state organizations and public organizations, is the Communist Party of the Soviet
Union."

Now the party has been shorn of its monopoly over state leadership, and overt
opposition parties and groups have appeared. Beyond that, there has been an
attempt to curtail the command system, especially in the economic realm, wherein
orders from the center are increasingly ignored. There is great confusion over
what the new rules of the game might be, indeed what they ought to be, however.
Thus, by way of important example, the introduction of a viable market system
is far from being realized.

POLITICAL SOCIALIZATION AND POLITICAL CULTURE:
SHARED VALUES AND BELIEFS

Four major components of any viable socioeconomic-political system are (1)
shared values and beliefs, largely the stuff of nationalism, (2) political institutions
and practices, (3) economic institutions and practices, and (4) society and its
social and political culture. The particular nature of any system is largely a
reflection of the interaction of these components.

As described by political scientists, political culture is the collection of political
attitudes, beliefs, and values shared by most citizens. Political socialization is
the process by which the citizens in a society, from childhood on, arrive at their
shared attitudes, beliefs, and values. As discussed in the "Introduction," Robert
M. MacIver observed in his classic work, *The Web of Government*, that a crucial
base of any society is its myth-system. It is the stuff of nationalism and social
cohesion, the essential glue that holds together every viable society, most especially the political system. Even violent revolutions cannot wholly destroy
overnight, nor even over several years, all of the ways of people. Thus, a political

culture nurtured under a thousand years of unbroken authoritarian rule provided fertile ground for the Marxist-Leninist-Stalinist dictatorship.

The inhabitants of both the old (Russian) and the new (Soviet) empire found security in having a firm hand at the helm. Studies of the values and attitudes of emigrants from the former Soviet Union revealed important beliefs that fit more with authoritarian than democratic political culture. For example, large numbers of emigres from the USSR expressed fright on learning that in market societies an individual must find his or her own job. They expect the state to provide employment for its citizens.

Now, with the advent of glasnost, numerous public polls provide new evidence that many of the attitudes associated with the pre-perestroika, authoritarian system are still deeply embedded in the peoples' minds. Thus, for example, early in 1991 the Komsomol (Young Communist organization) went on record proclaiming that it is the state's duty to provide employment for the nation's youth. Also, although there seems to be a widespread agreement on the need to introduce a market economy, national public opinion polls reveal a strong resistance to the introduction of free-floating (i.e., market-determined) prices for consumer goods.

Just as the peculiar myth-complex of a nation evolves over many generations, so important changes in a political culture cannot occur in a brief span of time. Thus, any probe into the current state of affairs, as well as possible future change, must take into account the beliefs and values that have been propagated in the past. For example, most of today's teachers in the republics of the former Soviet Union have been in their posts for years. The syllabuses and the texts may change in a short period of time, but not the values of the teachers. Moreover, most of them, especially those in the most influential positions, have been members of either the Komsomol or the party.

The values and behavioral patterns shaped by the institutions and practices that dominated every phase of Soviet life for seven decades cannot simply be legislated out of existence in the minds of the people overnight. In 1991 Boris Yeltsin succeeded in obtaining legislation officially banning party units in the Russian republic's governmental organs and enterprises. Yet the vast majority of the most important positions in the government, the military, the industrial, and the service sectors are still held by party or former party members. Indeed, as far as the Russian Federation is concerned, estimates are that the former "party-state nomenklatura [i.e., party-appointed leaders to key posts at all levels] constitute up to 70–80 percent, and in some regions, even more" of the new power structure, both at the center and in the hinterland.[3]

What, then, was the state of mind of the Soviet people prior to the introduction of perestroika and glasnost? The myth that a selfless, society-oriented "new Soviet man" had evolved was false. Overtly, many of the values of that person were expressed, but there is ample evidence that privately the average Soviet was quite different. Dissent existed and sometimes surfaced in such forms as occasional, usually small, demonstrations and the publication of *samizdat*—illegal, self-published tracts. Still, there was (and is) a Homo-Sovieticus with values, beliefs, and behavior quite different from that of the English, French, Americans, or members of any other noncommand system not infected with Marxism-Leninist values.

No society, not even one that is subject to totalitarian rule, can be held together totally by force. In Stalin's time, a conventional wisdom, shared by many outside observers, was that without mass terror, the Soviet Union would disintegrate. Terror was said to be the linchpin of Soviet rule.[4] Yet Khrushchev presided over the removal of the Gulag Archipelago, and the Soviet Union remained relatively tranquil for more than three decades. Central Asians, Ukrainians, and so on, retained many of their cultural traits, but for most people in the USSR there also was an overlay of Soviet behavior and values.

A combination of such disparate factors as the repeated promises of an eventual Communist utopia, a continual drumbeat reminder of the enormous shared sacrifices the people made during the Great Patriotic War, and a socioeconomic system that guaranteed employment and at least survival incomes produced a kind a Soviet sociopolitical culture shared by most of the masses that kept domestic strife to a minimum and the system operating, however inefficiently.

Attempting to control everything, the party used both the carrot and the stick to manipulate public behavior. Although Khrushchev tightened the reins somewhat on the secret police, the KGB did not disappear. To repeat the point, however, negative forces were not the only factors that held the system together.

A belief that criticism of the Soviet state was traitorous was widely held until the latter 1980s. With the advent of glasnost, both the party and the government were subjected to considerable criticism. Yet, public opinion polls revealed an attitude that there should be some restrictions on criticism of the government in areas in which such criticism is freely tolerated in democratic, pluralistic systems.

Marxism-Leninism, especially the doctrines of Lenin, infiltrated by lingering strains of traditional Russian nationalism, not only became the lingua franca of Soviet political discourse but also provided legitimization for the policies and deeds of Party leaders. Stalin deified Lenin, claiming that the corpus of his writings provided a science of society. Subsequently, until the final years of the USSR, every party leader in virtually every major speech pointed to the discoveries of Lenin as the unchallengeable justification for his actions and proposals.

In 1936 Stalin found appropriate passages in Lenin's writings to bolster his claim that under his leadership, socialism in one country was being constructed. In his 1956 de-Stalinization speech, Khrushchev invoked Lenin's observations to support his condemnation of Stalin's abuse of power. Brezhnev proclaimed that by following the path charted by Lenin, the USSR had reached the advanced stage of developed socialism.

Clearly, Leninism has been downgraded. Yet at the beginning of the 1990s, his mausoleum remained intact and continued to be Moscow's major shrine. Unlike his predecessors, Gorbachev did not adorn every speech with Lenin's verities. Nevertheless, he justified his call for restructuring as a need to return to the true Leninist model.

Since the fall of 1991, there has been a movement to bury Lenin's body (according to his wishes) in St. Petersburg (until 1991, Leningrad). A poll of Muscovites indicates, however, that a solid two-thirds majority of the respondents want to preserve the mausoleum.[5] Can needed reform really succeed unless the mausoleum (i.e., what it stands for) is dismantled, even if Lenin is given a decent burial in St. Petersburg?

Prior to the changes introduced at the end of the 1980s, the Soviet Union was a dictatorship led by an oligarchy centered on the politburo. Following the failed coup of August 1991, President Gorbachev resigned his position as general secretary of the CPSU, bringing an end to party rule. Crucial to the working of the old system was the Leninist doctrine of democratic centralism. Assertedly, the party and the public freely discussed and deliberated all issues until a decision was made. Once it was made, however, it became law and no further discussion was tolerated. Since the party, dominated by the politburo and led by the general secretary, always insisted on setting the agenda, however, central control was the ruling principle, not grass roots democracy.

Certainly there was dissent, particularly among the ethnic and religious minorities. Yet even with their private doubts, most of the Soviet people seemed to regard themselves as good citizens. Even beyond the relative calm that pervaded the society, perhaps the most important single piece of evidence that most of the citizenry accepted the basic system can be found in the realm of political dissent. First, the expression of public political dissent was far less common that religious and national dissent. Second, when political dissent surfaced prior to the end of the 1980s, it was overwhelmingly communist in content. Thus, the call was less to change the system that it was a cry that the leaders were not acting as proper Marxist-Leninists.

The tsarist experience that incorporated a state bureaucracy, the nobles, and the church taught that there was security in strong leaders who provided the right answers to the problems of life. Although claiming a different philosophical base, the Soviet system provided a new set of strong leaders who claimed that their Communist orthodoxy offered the true guidelines for all human affairs. Now their claim to possessing the science of society as the base for correct human behavior in all areas of life has been swept aside. What will take its place?

Under tsardom there was a strong sense of messianism, especially among the majority who adhered to the Russian Orthodox faith. Surely that conviction helped pave the way for the acceptance of a new faith that, led by Moscow, the world would achieve the nirvana of communism. A thousand-year-old Russian messianic aspiration will not die easily. Even if all of the other fourteen republics maintain their independence, will the new Russia refrain from attempting to dominate its neighbors? Will the people in the new Russian federation lay aside old dreams and aspirations of world leadership? Specifically, will Russia abandon any claim to superpower status, including willingly giving up its claim to being the successor to the USSR as one of the permanent members of the United Nations Security Council?

The vast majority of the population in 1917 was peasant, and their experience in the council (*mir*) and the village commune was not that of free individualistic farmers. Private farming, indeed individual entrepreneurship in agriculture and elsewhere, had weak roots in tsarist society.

Serfdom ended in 1861, but the village commune (i.e., the closely knit village society) and the mir remained strong. Led by the *starosta* (village elder), each *dvor* (male head of a household) sat on a council that dominated village life. No aspect of life was immune from the council's hand, for it could and did undertake periodic redistribution of the land, determine times for sowing and harvesting, and even resolve problems that arose between husbands and wives.

Even though there was widespread peasant resistance to Stalin's revolution from above that forced the rural population into the collective and state farms in the 1930s, much about the new farms was familiar to Russian historical experience. Indeed, the base for the original *kolkhozy* (collective farms) was the old villages.

Important to understanding the Soviet past and the possible future of the independent republics (especially since the provision of food is the most serious economic problem) is the knowledge that the kolkhozy and the *sovkhozy* (state farms) imposed a new kind of authoritarian control, state-serfdom, on the peasantry. Many of the attitudes, values, and behavioral patterns of the peasants— for example, guaranteed housing and minimal incomes—have been shaped by a socialist way of life that is not easy to abandon. Yet many argue that a change to private farming, involving the inherent risks of such enterprises, is essential if the food problem is to be resolved.

One of the most important aspects of Soviet society is rooted in the hard-to-translate concept of the *obshchina* (roughly, the collective). As noted, in predominantly peasant tsarist Russia, the village commune and the *mir* fostered collective activity and responsibility while downplaying the individual. The attitudes engendered by that experience fit nicely with the doctrines of Marxism-Leninism and the goal of creating the new Soviet person. According to the ideal, such a person would be totally unselfish, marked by a Marxist-Leninist social consciousness, and thus totally devoted to the collective.

At the local level, every individual in schools, economic enterprises, farms, and so on was identified as a member of a collective. Nationwide, all citizens were said to be part of a larger Soviet collective. Collective identification was not passive; it was actively fostered. For example, in the primary schools, the children in a class were divided into *zvenya* (small links or teams). Rewards and punishments were directed largely at the links rather than at the individual. Similarly, activity was organized in the factories and on the farms, and collective competitions were instituted among such groups.

In the party, union, and farm meetings, *kritika i samokritika* (criticism and self-criticism) were important tools of political socialization. For example, worker who was late, drunk on the job, or whatever was expected to stand up before a meeting of his or her peers, confess his or her sins, and promise to do better. Moreover, he or she was expected to report on similar transgressions committed by colleagues.

Are all such practices and behavioral patterns destined to be eradicated? There is evidence that finding security in the collective is far from dead. With such a dependence, how long will a new sense of individualism take to evolve?

Something very important and often missed in appraising the attempts to create communism is that central to Marxist-Leninist doctrine was the gospel that the ills of society and the world were someone else's fault. The capitalists had exploited the helpless proletariat. Individually, the workers were powerless; only collectively could they cast off their chains. Among all human beings, there is a strong tendency to blame someone else rather than oneself for faults and errors. What child has not told his or her parents, "It is not my fault. The other kids [the teacher or someone else] made me do it"? Again, there was nothing akin to a Protestant work ethic in the house that Stalin built. Self-reliance and individual initiative were discouraged.

The party-state monopoly over the press and broadcast media was a powerful tool for shaping public attitudes and beliefs. Former Soviet journalists who emigrated from the USSR reported that although censors existed, their need to delete material was relatively rare. Such institutions as the writer's union trained Soviet journalists to be their own censors. Writers and broadcasters held privileged positions, and membership in the unions was essential to the pursuit of their careers. Expulsion from the union was a major punishment used against those who broke the rules.

Some Soviet citizens listened to foreign broadcasts beamed to the USSR when they were not being jammed. Listening was not illegal, but spreading the falsehoods heard was a crime that often resulted in serious punishment, especially if the material was critical of the USSR.

Dissenters with a literary bent produced illegal samizdat (literally, self-edited) tracts, which were often copied by their sympathizers. Those who produced such material that was judged to be seriously threatening to the system were often caught and punished, sometimes by long imprisonment.

While dissent existed, Soviet society was marked by correct overt public behavior. Anyone who traveled on the Moscow subway knew that it was freer of litter and graffiti than most U.S. university buildings. Moreover, if some wayward individual did drop a cigarette butt on the subway floor, there was considerable likelihood that a *babushka* (grandmother or old woman), rather than a uniformed guard, would accost the sinner and lecture him or her for the errant behavior.

In the past, virtually every eligible worker belonged to the centrally directed labor unions. As noted, strikes were illegal and the unions did not negotiate for higher wages, but everyone belonged because the unions did play an important role in matters such as managing pensions and obtaining scarce housing and because joining was the thing to do.

From Lenin onward, the leadership continually referred to the collective farms and unions as "schools of communism." One of the primary functions of these schools was to promote correct collective behavior. Union and farm meetings included lectures by party propagandists explaining the latest line from Moscow—for example, under Gorbachev, the importance of openness and restructuring to improving the economy. The most important local union committee was the production committee in which the workers were encouraged to contribute ideas that would enhance achieving plan targets.

Most people in most most societies do not judge their position by external standards. What is important to them is how they fare in comparison to their grandparents, parents, and peers. For most Americans, Soviet life would have been drab, unrewarding, and restricting. For most Soviet citizens from Stalin's time on, life improved, until the onset of the crises under Gorbachev's watch, and the vast majority were as well off as their neighbors. This had an important positive impact on their view of the system.

In our view, the creation of the ideal "new Soviet man" does not square with human nature. Nevertheless, for reasons suggested here, political socialization as practiced in the USSR went a long way toward shaping overt public behavior in ways desired by the leaders. The evidence that has surfaced with the unleashing of glasnost does reveal, however, that, although far from the the ideal "new Soviet man," a Homo-Sovieticus, did evolve, as discussed in chapter 5, and that is the clay from which the future will be molded.

NOTES

1. May 25, 1989, speech to the Soviet Congress of Deputies, *Pravda*, May 26, 1989.

2. A. Migranyan, "Is It Easy to Become Europe?" *Century and Peace*, no. 12, December 1988. JPRS-UPA-89–015.

3. Robert Minasov, "The Nomenklatura Prepares to Take Revenge," *Rossiyskaya gazeta*, March 4, 1992. FBIS-SOV-92–048, March 11, 1992.

4. See the first edition of Merle Fainsod's *How Russia Is Ruled* (Cambridge: Harvard University Press, 1952).

5. *Moscow News*, September 29–October 6, 1991.

2

PROBLEMS OF COMMUNISM

A COLLAPSED SOVIET STAR

Soviet commentators frequently employed the words *anarchy*, *chaos*, and *crisis* to describe the state of affairs in the USSR during its final years. The economy was said to be in the state of deep depression. As a result, the Union fell apart. At this time of great flux, this student of Soviet (and now post-Soviet) affairs for nearly forty years, cannot predict with great confidence what the coming decades may bring. Clearly, however, this modern time of troubles is destined to persist for many years to come.

Inflation has skyrocketed (some 300 percent between early 1991 and early 1992). Massive unemployment is forecast. Consumer shortages, especially of food, are serious and promise to worsen. Rationing is widespread. There are increasing shortages of energy, especially fuel during the winters. According to *Izvestia*, the "country's entire transport system is 'on the verge of a heart attack.' "[1]

There has been a disturbing increase in the crime rate. In many parts of the country, pollution of the land, the water, and the air has reached life-threatening levels. Ethnic tensions are at fever pitch, lives have been lost, and in some republics local bloodletting threatens to escalate into major civil war.

The multiple economic crises that destroyed the Union and constitute the heritage of the newly independent republics are discussed in more detail in the section, From Economic Stagnation to Catastrophe, in chapter 3.

The icon of Marxism-Leninism that legitimized the old system has been seriously savaged, and there is no new agreed-upon set of beliefs to take its place. Although the purpose of this book is not to delve into institutional changes or the revelations of glasnost as related to political history—for example, the crimes of Lenin and Stalin—before we proceed with an analysis of current forces at work, one hideous example of what has been unearthed from the past is in order.

A *Komsomolskaya pravda* commentator and press secretary to Russian Federation President Boris Yeltsin gained entry to the top secret documents in the offices of the former CPSU Central Committee. Citing from the documents, he recorded the following:

[I]t was he [Lenin] who conceived the following idea (and I quote from genuine archive sources): "to try to punish Latvia and Estland militarily (for example, on the shoulders of Balkhovich move the border somewhere by a verst, say, and hang 100–1,000 of their officials and rich men). . . .

"In the guise of greens (we will blame it all on them later) go in 10–20 versts and hang some kulaks, priests, and landowners. The prize: 100,000 rubles for each hanged man."[2]

In the search for a new source of legitimization, most of the new contenders for leadership mouth the word *demokratsia*, but there are serious differences in opinion as to what democracy should mean in practice. In sum, what was written in a *Pravda* editorial (February 7, 1990) applies as much to the independent republics in 1992 as it did to the old Union in its final years:

[R]estructuring . . . in less than five years has plunged the country into the abyss of a crisis and has brought it to a point at which we have come face to face with a rampage of anarchy, the degradation of the economy, the grimace of general ruin and a decline in morals. In this situation, to claim that the people are "for" all this, that it pleases them is politically indecent, to say the least. The people are against this, and they are saying so more and more loudly.[3]

In virtually all of the republics, rule by presidential decree has been instituted.

No one knows what is going to unfold in the future. We can merely speculate. But as we speculate and examine the astounding revelations of glasnost, a number of possibilities come to mind that, in themselves, reveal the vast complexity of the problem.

The death of the Soviet Union can be compared to that of a collapsed star, a polity that has become a black hole in the political universe of nations. The former fragments of the Soviet empire have been cast into their own uncertain orbits, but as entirely different entities—that is, independent states constituted along ethnic lines. If the attempt to create a viable Commonwealth of Independent States is successful, most likely before the last decade of the twentieth century has ended, a new Russia will emerge confined largely to the people residing in the territory of the former Russian republic plus a loose alignment with most of the former republics but excluding the Baltic republics. At this juncture, the possible future course of Georgia is hidden in the cloud of internal strife in that republic.

Unfortunately, given the lack of any democratic experience (for a brief period in history, the Baltic states were an exception) and the almost total absence of a sense of civic culture among the peoples, the bulk of the new regimes will surely be held together by one form or another of authoritarian rule, at least for many years to come.

The lack of a civic society and what that portends for the attempt to build a democratic system was the concern of many thoughtful Soviet citizens, including deputies to the Soviet Congress during the 1989–1990 period, who were charged with charting such a course.

If I acknowledge the need to build up the leader's power during the transition from totalitarianism to democracy, that doesn't mean I like authoritarian rule. And yet I'm sure that a transition to democracy must go through such a stage. . . . [Today], the People's Congress cannot take all power. . . . It cannot take power in principle because we don't have a civic society, that is to say a society separate from the state. As a result, we don't even have a real state. . . .

Actually, the first Congress would have made sense only on one condition: if it had acknowledged that our country is in crisis, the economy in disarray, social conditions a disaster, and inter-ethnic relations in deadlock.[4]

Ethnocentric forces, with an attendant drive to national self-determination, had a virulent rebirth in the Soviet Union. Ethnic nationalism was a major force in the death of the Union. In the collapse of the Soviet Union, however, aspirations for self-determination were less a cause and more a symptom, an outgrowth, of the malaise that gripped the people of the USSR.

It is true, that many, perhaps most, of the non-Russian inhabitants of the old internal Soviet empire long yearned for greater freedom from the Russian-dominated communist yoke. After all, the Baltic states were incorporated into the union by force during World War II. Earlier, during the Civil War (1918–21), the Red Army denied the attempt by Georgia and Ukraine to become independent nations. Again, however, the revival of national aspirations was not the primary cause for the breakup of the Union. Indeed, and ironically, although a major platform of Boris Yeltsin in winning the presidency of the Russian Federation was the independence of Russia from the Union, that claim was inexorably linked with his promise to reverse the sharp decline in standards of living.

By the end of the 1980s, the drive for change heard in all quarters of the empire was rooted primarily in the no longer deniable fact that the experiment in building communism, with its promise to create a welfare utopia, had failed totally. Instead of fulfilling the Marxist promise of eliminating the increasing circle of misery among the masses, the level of misery precipitously deepened starting in the early 1980s.

The failure of communism was summed up by one Moscow housewife who said, "[T]his place would really have been paradise . . . if only the Bolsheviks had managed to create people who don't need to eat."[5]

Much that was once hidden behind the claimed omnipotence of the Communist party through censorship and the enforcement of the doctrine of socialist realism has now been brought out into the open in the name of glasnost.

The question remains. Economic stagnation was recognized as having started under Brezhnev. Gorbachev admitted in the mid-1980s that the stagnation had evolved into a crisis. Why, then, did serious moves to national separation as the solution to the problems faced not surface until the beginning of the 1990s? What was behind the revolutionary groundswell that arose after the failed coup of August 1991 and destroyed the Soviet Union within a few short months?

Again, the aspirations for self-determination, especially among the minority ethnic peoples, were always there. The evidence is now overwhelming, however, that a combination of the deterioration of the political environment (i.e., the mounting corruption under Brezhnev) and especially economic crises brought the Soviet Union to the brink of chaos. Clearly, the depth of the crises could no longer be denied by the mid-1980s. That reality paved the way for the birth of the Gorbachev era and the call for perestroika.

WHY 1990–91?   THE CONTRADICTIONS OF SOVIET SOCIALISM

Surely the primary forces that fanned the winds of change into a revolutionary velocity at the start of the 1990s were the ever-deepening social, political, and economic crises that brought a new kind of terror to the Union, especially a deeply rooted fear of the future. The trauma that pervaded the Soviet Union was demonstrated in both the rhetoric of opinion makers and the opinions of the people. Beyond the deepening crisis, other forces served to bring events to a revolutionary climax.

Was Thomas Jefferson right when he declared that the "laws of nature and of nature's God" contain universal, "self-evident" truths for all of mankind? If he was, the people of the former Soviet Union, and all other nations where oppression has dominated, have hope for a future in which they can enjoy the right to "life, liberty, and the pursuit of happiness." In contrast, however, there is the grim reality for most of the people in the world described by Thomas Hobbes, that life is "solitary, poor, nasty, brutish and short." Thus, Hobbes concluded that to minimize chaos within nations, a strong dictatorial hand was required, a kind of system that was imposed on the Soviet people, providing a surface tranquility in society after the carnage of forced collectivization and the purges of the 1930s had eliminated any viable opposition to the dictatorship— à la Plato, they were self-appointed philosopher kings.

To my knowledge, prior to the events that came to a head at the end of the 1980s, no serious student of Soviet affairs foresaw the collapse of the Stalinist-Brezhnev system. Among other things, we did not heed Abraham Lincoln's wisdom: "It is true that you may fool all of the people some of the time; you can even fool some of the people all the time; but you can't fool all of the people all the time." Obviously, time finally ran out for those rulers in the Kremlin whose minds were held in the vice grip of conventional Marxist-Leninist doctrine. Surely the events that culminated in the demise of the USSR are proof of the old saw that an idea, rooted in truth, will have its day when the time is ripe. Ironically, the thinking of Marx and Engels helps to illustrate the point.

The most famous section of the 1848 *Communist Manifesto* is: "[t]he proletarians have nothing to lose but their chains. They have a world to win. Workers of the world, unite!" Yet Marx and Engels did not believe in 1848 that the time was yet ripe for the revolution they believed to be inevitable. They argued that over time, the increasing misery of the exploited workers under capitalism at the height of the industrial revolution would create what they called a growing class consciousness, a togetherness that would cause them to rise spontaneously and seize power.

Why did no one foresee the momentous events that overtook the Soviet empire? Most outside observers of the Soviet scene were blinded by the seeming strengths of the house that Stalin built. We, this analyst included, were overawed by the discipline that the leaders imposed on the Soviet populace. Also, although we knew that living standards were well below those of the prosperous developed nations, until the recent revelations of what was formerly hidden by the Soviet propaganda machine, we failed to appreciate the full depth of economic and welfare depravity faced by most Soviet citizens. Moreover, we failed to read the signal of the Brezhnev stagnation that the lot of the people was destined to worsen. After all, as compared to people in the poorest nations of the world, virtually all Soviet citizens had a roof over their heads. Hunger did not seem to be a problem. Health care was "free." Surely, given the vast natural resources of the USSR, the nation that was first in space and one of the world's two superpowers would eventually solve its domestic consumer problems.

Certainly, all the Soviet leaders until Gorbachev, and even he,—at least until 1991—reflected a deeply held conviction that the Soviet system was fundamentally sound. That, of course is why he called for restructuring the system, not fundamental reform.

A key point that needs to be made in answer to why this happened at the end of the 1980s is that, in spite of the Orwellian rhetoric of good times ahead, not only did the Soviet citizenry know from their own life experiences how depressing their existence had become by the beginning of the 1980s but also they experienced a further, accelerating decline in their living standards due to the economic stagnation under Brezhnev that evolved into catastrophe under Gorbachev. All of that needs to be put into the perspective that from 1917 onward, the whole rationale of the system was built on the premise of building a better life for the citizenry, indeed, a way of life that would be superior to that found anywhere else in the world.

The relative blindness of outsiders to the failure to fulfill even the minimum material aspirations of the Soviet people was compounded by the Marxist-Leninist propaganda, echoed by their "fellow travelers" (a label invented by Soviet Leninists, not Western McCarthyites), espousing the belief that political and economic freedom are fundamentally separable. Such thinking, which is still widespread, especially in Western universities, includes the claim that the economic egalitarianism imposed in the USSR is a self-evident, democratic-humanitarian truth that should receive top priority in ordering an economy. Ironically, therefore, one of the most revolutionary changes in the rhetoric introduced by Gorbachev was the pronouncement that wage leveling must be abandoned if the creative initiative of the workers is to be unleashed.

Given the advantage of hindsight, one can see that, beyond the mounting socioeconomic crises, two other forces that must have contributed mightily to the ethnic revolutionary upheaval that destroyed the Soviet Union were at work.

First, nearly half a century of peace in Europe, undergirded by an increasing conviction that nuclear war is unthinkable, destroyed the argument stressed by Gorbachev's predecessors that extreme secrecy, strict discipline, and economic sacrifices on the part of the population were demanded to strengthen the military in the name of security.

The arguments for a siege mentality, which the pre-Gorbachev leadership relied on so heavily, as an unchallengable legitimization for the extreme Soviet authoritarian system, became untenable. The August 1991 coup failed, but the possibility still remains—we hope slight—that still another attempt by Soviet-style reactionaries to seize power in the Central Eurasian states might succeed. If such a tragedy occurs, surely one of the major claims to legitimacy will be the asserted need to protect the remnants of the Soviet empire from external enemies.

Second, there was the increasing penetration of the iron curtain by formerly forbidden information. Particularly important was the introduction into the USSR of the ideals expressed in the Universal Declaration of Human Rights and a heightened knowledge of the standards of living enjoyed in the developed market economies, standards of living that were undreamed of by the Soviet masses. For example, thanks to glasnost, in August 1989 the Soviet reader learned from a study by a Soviet economist that "in the developed countries the percentage of average income of families is about six times higher than here, while in the GDR, Czechoslovakia and Hungary, it is about four times higher."[6]

Part of the new dialogue that has been generated has been the argument that political and economic freedom are, indeed, inseparable—especially the right to the fruits of one's labor. In that regard, the modern communications media, particularly the broadcast media, served as a major catalyst for the events of the final years of the Soviet empire.

To paraphrase Marx, the Soviet people, long enslaved under the state-serfdom of Marxism-Leninism-Stalinism, now had an opportunity to evolve a new level of shared international consciousness, not of class but of the rights of man. One can hope that over the course of the coming years (but the period will be long and the process painful), a critical mass of new thinking will become reality, and the people in the post-Soviet states will demand a level of political, social, and economic humanity that is enjoyed in the open societies of the world. It is ironic that the workers may at last cast off their chains, led in the beginning by Mikhail Gorbachev, a man who professed the Marxist-Leninist ideology.

With the unleashing of glasnost, a political crisis was inevitably added to the social and economic crises. Gorbachev was absolutely right in his repeated assertion that more than anything else, a prosperous society could be achieved only if new thinking could be realized. Unfortunately, such a profound change in the values of a nation's people within the space of a few years is probably impossible without major suffering, and is certainly unprecedented. Post–World War II Germany and Japan are hardly evidence to the contrary. The democratization in those nations took many years. Moreover, the flowering of political freedom in those nations came only after devastating defeat in war and a long period of foreign occupation and oversight. Also, the German and Japanese authoritarian regimes had not been bound in the fetters of a command economic system.

Although the forces shaping the future of countries and peoples are never fully understood, the lessons of history and the fruits of scholarly analysis can provide some insight into the unfolding of revolutionary change in the affairs of nations. In this regard, the seminal work of Charles Tilly, *From Mobilization to Revolution*, provides much food for thought about both the demise of the Soviet Union and the situation in the newly independent republics.

Tilly's discourse on the "proximate causes of revolutionary situations" provides a remarkable description of the state of political affairs in the USSR and in the new regimes at this juncture in history. As he wrote, the key to "the definition of a revolutionary situation" is "multiple sovereignty."

Especially during 1990 and 1991, the Soviet political dialogue increasingly became dominated by separatist claims of sovereignty by the new leaders of the individual republics, including Russian President Boris Yeltsin's mounting proclamations of the Russian republic's independence from Soviet control. For Tilly, "there are three proximate causes of multiple sovereignty":

[1.] The appearance of contenders, or coalitions of contenders, advancing exclusive alternative claims to the control over the government which is currently exerted by the members of the polity.[7]

In the USSR, new, strange political bedfellows developed, such as the leaders in the Russian and the Baltic republics who established alliances. One by one, the union republics declared their independence from the Union.

[2.] Commitment to those claims by a significant segment of the subject population (especially when those commitments are not simply acknowledged in principle, but activated in the face of prohibitions or contrary directives from the government).[8]

The evidence is that within the republics the new leaders who called for separation were far more popular than the central figures, including Gorbachev.

[3.] Incapacity or unwillingness of the agents of the government to suppress the alternative coalition and/or the commitments to its claims.[9]

Increasingly, the new leaders in the republics made statements and took actions that a few years earlier would have meant instant incarceration or worse. All now talk about creating their own defense forces and their own currencies.

Further, Tilly states that the "critical signs" of a proximate revolution "are signs of the emergence of an alternative policy." New parties, formerly outlawed by Article 6 (now abandoned) of the constitution that gave the Communist party a monopoly over political affairs, sprang up like weeds on uncultivated ground. Further, Tilly states that such signs may well be related to the "conditions other analysts have proposed as precipitants of revolution: rising discontent, value conflict, frustration, or relative deprivation."[10]

Finally, although it is far from all that Tilly has to offer on the the matter, he cites the "four preconditions for major revolutions" made by Barrington Moore in 1969:

[1.] elite's loss of unified control over [the] army, policy, and other instruments of violence;

[2.] the emergence of acute conflicts of interest;

[3.] the development of widespread challenges to prevailing modes of thought and to the predominant explanations of justifications of human suffering;

[4.] the mobilization of a revolutionary mass, most probably through some sudden disruption of everyday life coupled with increase of misery.[11]

Moscow's monopoly over the instruments of state violence disappeared. What is left of the party has split into fragments. Even the cult of Lenin has been seriously challenged. Ample signs of increasing misery—worsening health problems, fuel shortages, increasing crime rates, and so on—go beyond shortages of food and many other consumer necessities.

Without exception, all of the preceding negative forces have been inherited by the new republics.

Gorbachev admitted that perestroika was a revolution from above.[12] Glasnost, he wrote, is the "powerful lever" of perestroika, which, by pointing out what needs to be altered, would allow "a drastic change . . . in social and political thought."[13] The goal was to unleash "the initiative and creativity of the masses." In sum, as recorded several pages later, "everything depends upon the people." Clearly, what he called for was changes that would create a mass attitude akin to, as noted here previously, what has been known in the West as the Protestant work ethic, *but Soviet socialist style*. That, of course, is where glasnost and democratization came in. In Gorbachev's words, early on in the campaign:

Lenin regarded democracy, the creative initiative of working people, as the principal force behind the development of the new system. . . . [Today] the Party is taking . . . steps to invigorate the Soviets, the trade unions, the Komsomol, the work collectives and the people's control bodies, and to promote publicity. . . . Our Party Program aims at the most effective exercise of all forms of *direct democracy*, of direct participation by the popular masses in the elaboration, adoption and execution of governmental and other decisions. . . . [W]e must look for modern forms of combining centralism and democracy, . . . *To promote society's level of maturity and build communism means steadfastly to enhance the maturity of the individual's consciousness and enrich his intellectual world.*[14]

A reading of Gorbachev's speeches and writings after his elevation to the post of general secretary of the Central Committee of the Communist party in 1985, including his 1987 book, *Perestroika: New Thinking for Our Country and the World*, reveals that in his mind, glasnost was not something akin to the First Amendment of the U.S. Constitution's guarantee of free speech. Indeed, his definition of democracy was quite different from that held in the West. For him, the stress was on mass mobilization, enlisting the population to the cause of perestroika. Further reading shows that from 1985 to his resignation from the presidency at the end of 1991, Gorbachev had no well-thought-out, coherent plan for restructuring the Soviet system.

What is left of the former Communist party in the USSR is very sick. Shortly after the failed August 1991 coup, Gorbachev resigned his position as general secretary, and other key leaders including Boris Yeltsin turned in their party cards. After assuming the presidency of the Russian Federation, Yeltsin decreed that party units could not be active in Russian governmental bodies. As crippled as the party is, the CPSU remains potentially the most powerful political force in the USSR, unlike the situation in most of the reborn Eastern European states. As of March 1992, 70–80 percent of the key posts at all levels in the Russian Federation were estimated to be held by former party nomenklatura. Moreover, one analyst asserts that "in Moscow, St. Petersburg, and Yekaterinburg, actual party bosses hold up to 30 percent of power, and if we are talking about the [former] party nomenklatura—a figure of 80 percent again."[15]

One of the key dogmas of Marxism-Leninism supporting the tenet that capitalism is doomed and communism is inevitable is the claim that capitalism (i.e., any system that relies primarily on free enterprise with private ownership of the means of production) has built-in, inescapable, contradictions that doomed it to destruction. To say the least, history has not borne out the Marxist-Leninist prophecy. Ironically, however, Marxist-Leninist dogmatists have insisted that there were no contradictions in Soviet-style socialist systems because the "right" relationships to the means of production had been created in the USSR and other centrally planned states.

As recently as the mid-1980s, persons in the USSR bold enough to challenge the rightness of Soviet socialism paid dearly for such views. They were incarcerated, committed to mental hospitals, forced to emigrate, or worse. After the unleashing of glasnost, however, hardly a day went by without some new public outcry indicating that the Soviet system was fatally flawed and devastated by contradictions.

The contradiction that the Soviet system destroyed individual initiative, although initiative by the masses was, and is, essential if the ills inherent in the former Soviet Union are to be cured, still lingers. As Soviet essayist Yu. Bogomolov stated, collectivism is not going away; it is just being transformed into a new tyranny of nationalism. That observation emphatically applies to the new ethnic regimes. In his words:

Individualism, which by the very recent standard of our society was a curse, a danger and a disease, has suddenly become an unbearable cross. . . .

As far as I know, one of the main problems in creating a law-based state is equalizing state and individual rights. . . .

For me personally, perestroika is an attempt to become free of the dictatorship of the collective. . . . free. . . . of the tyranny of collectivism. . . .

Let me remind you that it was Stalinist mythology that deified such collectivist concepts as class, party, state and revolutionary legality. . . .

The drama of perestroika processes stems primarily from the need to attain spiritual autonomy.

Such autonomy attracts and frightens at the same time. I remember the time when I was discharged from the army. It was the moment of happiness and horror. I was happy because I no longer had to march in a file and terrified because I would have to choose my own path in life and be responsible for every step I would take.

It was a fear of civilian life. I had a shameful desire (which I was unwilling to admit even to myself), to sign up for an extra tour of duty.

The dismay and troubles we now see and feel with our skin stem from the desire for, and fear of, general de-collectivization and doubt whether or not we could become individuals.

It is understandable that many want to sign up for an extra tour, especially those who cannot do anything except issue or obey orders.

Nationalism both of a street and an office variety, crude as well as intellectual, is a form of extra tour of duty at the Administrative Command System.[16]

Numerous other Soviet leaders and writers echoed observations similar to those that the greatest contradiction (impediment) to building a better future lies in the mind block of the people. According to one writer, they "believe in a state society, not a civil society, and it is so difficult to change these views."[17]

Another observer stated: "[T]he state . . . , we have been told from infancy, provides clothing, shoes, education, employment, food and housing. . . . Lack of money was sanctified and the cult of equalization and asceticism promoted for many generations. People have lost their ability to do something about their own plight."[18]

In an interview, Leonid Abalkin, vice chairman of the former Council of Ministers of the USSR, said, in regard to successful change to a market economy, "We have to overcome the ossified stereotypes of whole generations! Shaping a new mentality, getting rid of dogmas—these are the all-important and most difficult aims."[19]

According to a doctor of philosophy and leading scientific associate of the

Academy of Sciences, "[M]any people . . . who, in their youth, were not affected by the Stalinist repressive machinery, have found themselves alienated from the past, having grown up in an atmosphere of thoughtless placidity and blind reliance on the infallibility of the leaders." He observed further:

[Because of the command system] the working people became alienated also from the means of production and the distribution of the products of their labor as well as real power in their own enterprises. . . .

[W]e have actually not become accustomed to and still cannot live under conditions governed by broad democracy and glasnost. We have no experience in true democratic management.[20]

A Soviet historian stated:

The social ideal of Marxism, which was utopian but attractive to the lumpenized masses, and what seemed to be amazingly simple methods for realizing that ideal by means of the forcible redistribution of power and wealth according to the well-known formula "he who has nothing will become everything" fell upon exceptionally fertile Russian soil. The expectation of a miracle is a feature of our national character. . . .

Unfortunately, it must be said that dead dogmas still have us by the throat.[21]

According to another Soviet historian, "Stalinism created a mentality of slavishness among the Soviet people, and deeply rooted beliefs in conservatism and authoritarianism, an intolerance of pluralism, and compromise persist. Thus, the Soviet Union is 'Europe's sick man.' "[22]

In July 1991, Alexandr Yakovlev, former politburo member and sometimes close adviser to Gorbachev, said that "the ideology that has ruled in our country has taught us to mistrust each other, to suspect each other, and, on occasions to inform on each other."[23] To live in a truly lawful, democratic society, people must adopt an entirely different morality, he added.

In the past, one of the greatest flaws in the system rested in the existence of the nomenklatura. The collective masses, via the Soviets, were supposed to rule, but, in fact, the privileged few monopolized power. As for the present and the future, there is the contradiction that the system cannot go forward without the participation of the former nomenklatura.

A striking parallel exists between the position of the nomenklatura today and that of the kulaks in the later 1920s. The kulaks, the best farmers in the Soviet Union, produced the great bulk of the food. Oblivious to the fact that ample food production and procurement rested on the shoulders of the kulaks, however Stalin decreed their destruction, a tragedy from which the USSR never recovered and that is a major reason for pessimism over the possibility of solving the ongoing food crisis. Many observers, including Gorbachev, have stated that the food problem cannot be solved until the peasants feel that they are really masters of the land. The evidence is overwhelming, however, that the farmers who survived dekulakization and their descendants to not know how to be, indeed do not want to be, rural entrepreneurs willing to make the effort and take the risks necessary to increase food production.

Who in the former Soviet system except farmers are the individuals most endowed with the psychological traits and work experiences necessary for making the decisions and providing the leadership needed to shift to a market economy? The answer, of course, is the former nomenklatura at all levels. Herein lies a great contradiction.

The nomenklatura constituted the backbone of what Milovan Djilas described as a new class, which needs to be broken if needed reforms are to be achieved. Like the kulaks, who stood in the way of collectivized agriculture, the no-menklatura stand in the way of a transition to a market system. Thus, by one logic they must be destroyed. Yet, most ironically, they have a near monopoly on the very talents essential if an efficient, productive entrepreneurial system is to be fashioned.

NOTES

1. "Nowhere to Go, No Way to Get There," *Izvestia*, June 21, 1990. CDSP, vol. 42, no. 25 1990.

2. Pavel Voshchatov, "Land of Commandments: CPSU Short Course in Top-Secret Documents," *Komsomolskaya pravda*, October 2, 1991. FBIS-SOV-91–195, October 8, 1991.

3. *Pravda*, February 7, 1990. CDSP, vol. 42, no. 16, 1990.

4. "Interview with Igor Kliamkin, Ph.D. and Andranik Migranian, Historian," *The Literary Gazette International*, February 1990.

5. Peter Gumbel, "Soviet Ingenuity Is Filling the Food Gap," *The Wall Street Journal*, December 7, 1990.

6. M. Berger, "Who Owes Whom, or the Banker's View of Personal Savings," *Izvestia*, August 23, 1989. JPRS-UEA-89–031. September 15, 1989.

7. Charles Tilly, *From Mobilization to Revolution* (Reading Mass.: Addison-Wesley, 1978), pp. 200–201.

8. Ibid.

9. Ibid.

10. Ibid.

11. Ibid.

12. Mikhail Gorbachev, *Perestroika: New Thinking for Our Country and the World* (New York: Harper and Row, 1987), pp. 55–59.

13. Ibid., pp. 44, 48, 76.

14. Mikhail Gorbachev, "Report to the 27th Party Congress," *Pravda*, February 26, 1986.

15. Robert Minasov, "The Nomenklatura Prepares to Take Revenge," *Rossiyskaya gazeta*, March 4, 1992. FBIS-SOV-92–048, March 11, 1992.

16. Yu. Bogomolov, "A Film for Every Day," *Literaturnaya gazeta*, June 14, 1989, p. 11. JPRS-UPA-89–047, July 27, 1989.

17. Fyodor Buriatsky, chairman of the Subcommittee on Humanitarian, Scientific and

Cultural Cooperation of the Supreme Soviet Committee on International Affairs, *Meeting Report Kennan Institute for Advanced Russian Studies*, January 1990.

18. A. Manilova, "Social Accounting: Does Everyone Poor Mean Everyone Equal?" *Leningradskaya pravda*, January 23, 1990. JPRS-UEA-90–013, April 12, 1990.

19. "What Hinders Reform?" *The Literary Gazette International*, April 1990.

20. V. Leybin, "The Problem of Alienation through the Lens of Perestroika," *Kommunist*, April 1990. JPRS-UKO-90–009, June 19, 1990.

21. Aleksei Kiva, doctor of history, "October in the Mirror of Utopias and Anti-Utopias," *Izvestia*, November 5, 1990. CDSP, vol. 42, no. 44, 1990.

22. Andrei Giachev, "Will the West Save Us from Ourselves," *Moscow News*, December 1990.

23. Alexandr Yakovlev, *Central Television and "TSN,"* July 27, 1991. *Report on the USSR*, August 9, 1991.

3

GORBACHEV AND A NEW ERA, 1985–1991

"I don't see much sense in that," said Rabbit. "No," said Pooh humbly, "There isn't. But there was going to be when I began it. It's just that something happened to it on the way."
—A. A. Milne, *The House at Pooh Corner*

Some future scholars may place Mikhail Gorbachev alongside the great revolutionary figures in human history. They will be wrong. Certainly, he presided over the demise of the USSR. Like Nero, however, he fiddled during the downfall. Gorbachev had no intent to destroy Soviet socialism. For him, perestroika meant restructuring the party-state system, not fundamental reform. Unfortunately for Gorbachev as for Pooh Bear, "something happened" to perestroika on the way. Admitting that this analyst now has the advantage of a Monday morning quarterback, he finds that the "something" that happened was that the house that Lenin, Stalin, Khrushchev, and Brezhnev had built proved to be beyond repair if a healthy economy and a humane, pluralistc society are the primary measures of a successful modern nation state.

Without questioning Gorbachev's moral character as a leader (surely he was a far more humane general secretary than any of his predecessors), he was and is a great tragic figure. He did not have the vision of the great revolutionaries who recognized the need to make a total break with the past.

Whatever the apprehensions about shortcomings in the system prior to the mid-1980s, the population, not just the bureaucrats and the party apparatchiki in charge, seemed to share a belief that the future belonged to socialism, Soviet style. Prior to 1985, no one in authority, and certainly not the official press, publicly questioned the command-management system, the role of central planning, or the monopoly over political and economic power by the Communist party. In true Orwellian fashion, all leaders in responsible positions publicly proclaimed that great strides forward had been made and that such advances would continue into the indefinite future.

GLASNOST

From the beginning of the Khrushchev era in 1953 until the latter part of Brezhnev's rule in the beginning of the 1980s, the official line was the significant progress had been achieved in the post-Stalin era. Not only had the USSR emerged to challenge the United States as a super power but also, according to the Soviet lexicon, the USSR was the most democratic system in the world. The people were said to be well off and prosperity was just around the corner.[1]

Certainly by Soviet standards, shortages of consumer goods, especially food, were not critical. By the end of the 1970s, however, the era of stagnation had set in, although it was not publicly recognized. The growth of the Soviet economy had come nearly to a standstill, and, subsequently, satisfaction of consumer demand declined. Such grim realities were increasingly difficult to hide.

The short-lived Andropov-Chernenko interregnum offered no effective solutions to the mounting crises, which were yet to be publicly admitted. Privately, however, the leaders in the Kremlin must have been increasingly concerned over the deteriorating state of affairs, so worried that they turned in 1985 to the relatively youthful Gorbachev, with his ideas for perestroika, especially in agriculture, as a solution to the most serious of all problems, mounting food shortages. In 1972, the Soviet Union had become the world's leading grain importer, an unenviable position that continues into the post-Soviet era.

For more than a decade, the mounting deterioration of the economy was publicly ignored. Then the tragic accident at Chernobyl in 1986 literally blew to pieces the public mood of complacency and undermined confidence in the future.

It is true that Gorbachev had been elevated to the post of supreme power the year prior to Chernobyl. Perhaps he would have proceeded anyway with whatever plans he had at the time for perestroika. His administration's first reaction to the tragic nuclear accident was to try to cover it up, however, by downplaying the magnitude of the tragedy and ignoring the fact that the response to it laid bare major faults in the Soviet system. The cover-up proved impossible, however, as the clouds of radiation crossed international borders. As a result, Chernobyl must be credited with making glasnost imperative if the Soviet Union were to have any chance to put its house in order.

Prior to Gorbachev, a major principle of Soviet governance was akin to the need to know principle that guides foreign intelligence–gathering agencies, armies, and even democratic governments during wartime. Subordinates in the Soviet hierarchy and, of course, the members of society at large were told only what those in charge believed was necessary to achieve centrally directed goals.

In the economic, environmental, and public welfare realms, that approach is now as dead as the Chernobyl reactor. That is not to say, however, that the new republic governments are paragons of support for freedom of information.

As Gorbachev repeatedly stated, glasnost was necessary because, if the economic crisis were to be ended, the values and attitudes of not just the party apparatchiki and the bureaucrats but also the masses had to be changed. The population at all levels must know what is at fault if they are to participate in fixing it. Perestroika without a strong dose of glasnost would be impossible.

As Will Rogers, the great American humorist of the 1930s, once said: "I only know what I read in the newspapers." If we now include the broadcast media, there is still fundamental truth in Rogers' remark. The nature and content of information available to the people changed profoundly; in the final years, the Soviets stopped jamming VOA and Radio Liberty transmissions. Surely, Rogers was right and Gorbachev was right that people's beliefs and actions are shaped largely by what they know. If that is true, their values and aspirations can be changed over time by new knowledge—but as explored here, the length of time required for a major change in public behavior is uncertain.

"Sticks and stones may break my bones, but words can never harm me," may be the most wrong-headed, misleading of the old nursery rhyme shibboleths. Often ignored and surely underrated is the fact that the upheavals that have occurred in Eastern Europe and the former Soviet Union were spawned by words and facts that first surfaced in the USSR in the name of glasnost.

The information revolution has been the most profound change to date in the former USSR. Without it, the system would not have collapsed. The upheavals of strikes, increased dissent, and national minority uprisings and declaration of independence that doomed the Soviet Union cannot be divorced from the people's increased exposure to a combination of new knowledge generated by, and the increased availability of, foreign publications and broadcasts. For example, as other observers have noted, the vast majority of East Germans could, and did, watch West German television. Surely that fact alone was a major contributor to the ultimate destruction of the Berlin Wall, followed by the reunification of Germany. When, in November 1989, Lech Walesa was asked in an interview what impact Radio Free Europe and Radio Liberty had had on the domestic activity of Solidarity during its growth in Poland, he most eloquently answered, "[T]he degree cannot even be described. Would there be earth without the sun?"

Under glasnost, Soviet citizens were inundated for the first time with a plethora of formerly forbidden knowledge, most (but not all) of which initially was generated by the Soviet official media in the name of perestroika. Ironically, when the Soviet Pandora's box was opened in the name of glasnost, all sorts of other demons of knowledge escaped as well. That fundamental change in the Soviet rhetoric needs to be seen in historical perspective of the need-to-know system that existed prior to the Gorbachev era.

Under Stalin, no systematic statistical series concerning the health of the economy and the welfare of society was published. With rare exception, reporting on such matters was limited to an occasional reference in the press to some change, invariably with the assertion that progress had been made—for example, an article in *Pravda* containing a statement that the grain harvest that year was 10 percent above the previous year's achievement.

In 1956, three years into the Khrushchev era, he made his "secret" de-Stalinization speech. He also introduced a new level of openness by permitting publication of a slim volume, *Narodnoye khozyaistvo SSSR v. 1956 (The National Economy of the USSR in 1956)*. Subsequently, annual volumes of that statistical handbook grew to a few hundred pages. Also, a trade handbook was published and, after particularly favorable crop years, several Soviet agricultural statistical handbooks were published. Those volumes, minuscule in coverage compared to Western statistical publications, constituted virtually all of the systematically assembled statistical measures (i.e., especially time series) of Soviet affairs available to the Soviet reader. Although many restrictions on the availability of knowledge remained, Khrushchev had introduced a limited version of glasnost.

Until the advent of Gorbachev's glasnost, the post-1956 statistical series that were published were a major advance over what had been available previously, although all such revelations were characterized by the inclusion of data that put the USSR in the best possible light and by the exclusion of unfavorable measures of Soviet affairs—for example, statistics on crime rates. Moreover when continued publication of a particular statistical series showed the Soviet Union in poor light, the series was often discontinued. For example, when grain production advances came to a near halt in the early 1980s, no official grain production data were published for several years.

Every editor, radio and TV director, and so on, possessed a copy of the *Index of Information: Not to Be Published in the Open Press*, itself a top secret document. According to one former Soviet journalist, that was the official guide to all the news that was not fit to print in the USSR.

[Listed were all] the types of news matter not for publication without special authorization in every individual case, including information about earthquakes, avalanches and other natural disasters within the territory of the USSR: news about fires, explosions, train or plane crashes, naval and mine disasters: any comparison of the budgets of Soviet citizens or the retail price of goods; any reports on increasing living standards anywhere outside the socialist countries; any average statistical information about the USSR as a whole, not taken from official reports of the TsSU (Central Statistical Administration); data on the salary or earnings of Party and government workers: reports on food shortages in the USSR; the names of any members of the KGB apart from that of the Chairman, and any references whatsoever to the censorship organs or to the jamming of foreign radio broadcasts.[2]

During the Gorbachev era, especially at the end of the 1980s, there were almost daily new, astounding revelations of shortcomings relating to the health of the economy and the welfare of the citizenry; these continue today in the post-Soviet republics. Not only has there been a reinstitution of publishing official grain figures (in spite of dismal output most years) but also all sorts of other previously forbidden information have surfaced.

Under Gorbachev, however, glasnost was not meant to guarantee the freedom of the press and discourse enjoyed in the open societies of the West. Glasnost was designed to strengthen Soviet socialism. Thus, Gorbachev said in a 1987 speech:

As I have said several times, openness and democracy—and I think this is our common viewpoint—do not mean that everything is permitted. Openness is called upon to strengthen socialism and the spirit of our people, to strengthen morality and a moral atmosphere in society. Openness also means criticism of shortcomings. But it does not mean the undermining of our socialist values.[3]

FROM ECONOMIC STAGNATION TO CATASTROPHE

What are the tangible measures of the public welfare and the health of the economy that glasnost has unveiled? What are the people now reading in their newspapers?

The Gorbachev era lasted six years. Yet the half-hearted attempts at perestroika failed. By the beginning of the 1990s, by almost any measure, the economic crisis had worsened. As a result, most of the leaders and the people fell into a pit of despair. Although the republics have achieved their independence, morale is far worse than at any time since Hitler's 1940 invasion. For example, one economist produced several pages of grim statistical comparisons of living standards in the USSR and the United States, as well as other countries—something absolutely forbidden by the old index.

Included among the revelations of glasnost have been indicators of the people's major concerns. Thus, in 1990 we learned that "[a]ccording to . . . data collected by [Soviet] sociologists people place the issue of the growing shortage of food first among their concerns. Second, among their concerns, are the inter-nationality conflicts, third is the struggle against crime, and fourth are the privileges of the nomenklatura."[4]

Externally, the East European satellite nations have been lost. Internally, the old Union has been destroyed. The economies of the newly independent states are on the verge of collapse. Many consumer goods have disappeared from the shelves in the stores. Per capita production of some key food items, often previously in short supply, has actually declined. Rationing is widespread. Both production and distribution of many essential commodities are in chaos. These facts are now widely discussed by the public news media.

As documented in chapter 5, the grim revelations of glasnost have fueled the declining morale of the people. Glasnost has brought into the open the dismal plight of the average consumer (e.g., most of the population believes that their diet is inadequate) and unleashed a rising crescendo of name calling, fault finding, and expressions of discontent at all levels of society.

The use of the word crisis to describe the unfolding scene became passe in the final years of the USSR, and such words as *catastrophe* and *depression* were increasingly employed. For example, a transcript of July 21, 1991, Moscow television newscast reads, in part, as follows: "The GNP for the first six months [of 1991] has decreased by 10 percent in comparison with the corresponding period last year. According to Western economists' assessments, this puts us somewhere between deep depression and a total disintegration of the economy."[5]

From the very beginning of glasnost, a major theme of discourse was that the Brezhnev era had produced a stagnation of an already seriously faulted economy. For example, in mid-1988, the following dismal picture of the economy was presented in the pages of the journal *Agrumenty i fakty*:

Among the 102 nations for which such data was available on Per-Capita Gross Domestic Product in 1985 the USSR ranked 68th, just below Yugoslavia and slightly superior to Poland. According to the measure the US Per-Capita Gross Domestic Product that year was $12,623 and that of the USSR was $4,996, or only 39.9 percent of that of the United States.[6]

Expenditures on arms resulted in a major drain on the economy. Western estimates of the annual cost have varied considerably. Whatever the ultimate truth, the following is an estimate that *Izvestia* published at the end of 1989: "Not one developed state in the world today lays out, as we do, more than 9 percent of its gross national product for military spending. The figure for the United States is 5 percent, for the FRG 3 percent, and for Japan 1 percent."[7]

Although the people could not read about Soviet problems in their periodicals prior to glasnost, they could not escape knowing from real-life experience that their living standard was abysmal. From 1917 until the end of the Union, shortages of necessities and shoddy quality of what was available were the norm. Except for the pampered nomenklatura with special stores and other privileges, life was grim for Soviet citizens. The people did not need the newspapers to tell them that there was a severe housing shortage and that health care was poor. All but those who had access to the special party stores daily faced the reality that some necessities (e.g., foods and items of clothing) often were not available in the shops.

Since the demons of knowledge have been turned loose, the press daily has documented the worsening severity of the situation. Articles by journalists, scholars and, sometimes, public officials have revealed such formerly forbidden information as the following: "[I]t turns out that the country was fed better in 1926 [at the height of the NEP (New Economic Policy) recovery] than is the case at the present time, notwithstanding today's modern technologies, colossal technical pool and so forth."[8] That finding was published in 1989, before things were to become much worse.

According to the calculations of Russian economists, "By the end of 1991

Table 3.1
Standard of Living Index: 1913, 1990 and 1991

	1913	1990	Dec. 1991
Standard of living index*	1	1.83	0.41
Cost of daily food basket (rbls)**	0.70	2.88	18.60

*The ratio between the wages index and the prices index.
**A conventional food basket, family of two parents, three children.

Source: Andrei Tkachenko, "Wages and Prices: Living as We Did 45 Years Ago, if not Worse," <u>Independent Newspaper</u>, March 20-21, 1992.

the standard of living . . . was flung back to the level of 1946—a time when almost all of the people went hungry." According to their analysis (Table 3.1), the major decline in consumer welfare occurred between 1990 and 1991. The base year for the calculations was 1913.

The average citizen would surely agree with Mikhail Gorbachev's statement on July 10, 1990 to a CBS news commentator that 80 percent of the problems are related to food shortages, which have worsened in recent years, resulting in widespread rationing. Prices of what is available (especially in the collective farm market) have increased significantly. Numerous polls reveal that a majority of the population spends half or more of its income on food.

The availability of nonfood necessities, including clothing, also has declined. Consumers knew earlier that sometimes they could not find necessary items of clothing, but in 1990 they were told something else: "At the current rate of light-industry development, the public demand in our country for knitwear would be fully satisfied in the year 2001, for hosiery—2020, for sewn garments—2033 and for leather footwear—2059."[9]

Until the revelations of glasnost, to my knowledge, no one challenged the oft-repeated myth that by world standards, housing was very cheap for Soviet workers. In 1988, however, the Soviet reader learned that "the average worker (in a city) in the USSR has to work 1.23 hours to pay for each square meter of actual living space for a month, with the state subsidizing part of the cost, but this costs the worker in the United States only 0.87 hours (and only out of his own pocket)."[10]

From personal experience, Soviet citizens have long been acutely aware of serious housing shortages. Now they know the dimensions of the problem. According to an analysis published early in 1990, "[T]he number of city families and single people in need of improved housing . . . was more than 14 million or 23 percent of the overall number of city families and single residents."[11]

Given the former USSR's vast mineral, coal, petroleum, and natural gas deposits, one might wonder why the Soviet leadership started bringing in outside help to increase fuel production prior to the revelations of glasnost. As reported

Table 3.2
The Rich versus the Poor: USSR versus United States (percentages)

	USSR	USA
Rich	2.3	3
Well-off	--	17
Middle class	11.2	60
Poor	86.5	20

Source: A. Zaichenko, "Inequality of Wealth," _Argumenty_ _i_ _fakty_,
July 8-14, 1989, pp. 5-6. JPRS-UEA-89-027.

in the Soviet press, in 1990 crude oil production was down 6 percent and coal was down 5 percent compared to that of 1989. Indeed, coal production was 9 percent lower than it had been two years earlier.[12] Obviously, drastic measures were required.

Until the final years of the former regime, poverty was said to have been eliminated in the USSR. Now the truth is out and the debate is not over whether there was poverty but how widespread it was. Writing in the often controversial journal _Argumenty i fakty_ in 1989, a Soviet analyst came up with the USSR–USA comparison shown in Table 3.2.

Since 1989 the situation has worsened. Thus, in early 1992, "according to Russian Goskomstat [State Statistics Committee] figures . . . , about 90 percent of the republic's population is living below the poverty line. The population's average monthly income is now 895 rubles. Goskomstat considers the minimum sufficient income to be 1,500 a month. Only 7 percent of the population receive this amount."[13] For most of the other republics the situation is even more grim. By 1992, in virtually all of the republics, the presidents ruled by decree, several under an officially declared state of emergency.

Serious inflation, approaching hyperinflation levels—well over 100 percent annually and climbing—exists. According to estimates by Soviet statisticians, "The [inflation] index of average retail prices for the [1986–88] period was 107 percent, including 111.6 percent for foodstuffs and 102.8 percent for durable goods."[14] During the period, "[m]eat and poultry increased by 4 percent, bakery goods by 22.3 percent; potatoes, 21.8 percent; vegetables, 18 percent; clothing and underwear, 13.8 percent; porcelain and chinaware, 4 percent; refrigerators, 10 percent and television sets 27.1 percent." In retrospect, those increases were relatively modest compared with the estimates of an overall increase in 1990 of 24 percent, and of 23 percent just during the first three months of 1991,[15] and by the end of the year a "four-fold" increase.[16] Then most prices were freed up in January 1992.

According to Russian Federation Goskomstat figures, "The consumer price index for Russia as a whole in the first quarter of 1992 stood at 619 percent compared with December 1991."[17] Although the minimum per capita income should be 1,500 rubles per month, according to Goskomstat, "more than 50 million people—one third of Russia's population—had incomes of less than R900 a month.''

According to the economist Pavel Bunich, as of May 1992, ''Monthly inflation [in the Russian Federation] is 30–40 percent. If the bank pays 80 percent a year, bank deposits will depreciate by 700 percent a year.''[18]

Wages, too, were significantly increased, but they in no way kept up with the cost of necessities. For example, due to the loss of purchasing power born of inflation, in Ukraine at the beginning of 1992, ''[p]er capita sales of food and other consumer goods . . . is half as much as in February 1991.''[19]

Some of the new leaders optimistically have stated that the economic decline would bottom out in 1992, but other observers are less sanguine about the future. For example, in an interview, Ye. G. Yasin, general director of the Russian Federation's Union of Science and Industry's Committee on Economic Reform observed that ''the optimistic statements by Boris Yeltsin and the Russian government to the effect that the low point will be reached in the autumn of 1992 are too optimistic. I think that 1993 will be the most difficult year.''[20]

In addition to this limited sample of the overwhelmingly negative litany of information now available to the man and woman on the street, there have been reports on the alarming increase in the crime rate, data that were totally hidden from the public until the end of the 1980s.

When this analyst first visited the USSR in 1960, he felt far safer in body and possessions in Moscow than in most major U.S. cities. For example, one could leave luggage temporarily unattended in a transport terminal without danger of thievery. In 1976, however, one member of a group I was traveling with was attacked on the street. Virtually everyone on our tour had something stolen from his or her hotel room. Now the 1970s must seem like the good old days.

Removing the lid from publishing crime statistics has provided such information as the following: ''Internal affairs agencies and agencies of the prosecutor's office recorded 2,461,692 crimes in 1989; that is 31.8 percent more than in 1988.''[21] In an interview, Boris Karlovich Pugo, then the minister of interior, stated that ''in 1990 [the crime rate was] 13.2 percent higher than the previous year. . . . [T]he number of violent personal assaults has grown by 11 percent, while crimes involving use of firearms has increased by a third.''[22]

The birth of the independent republics was accompanied by a further sharp increase in crime. For example, permission to acquire smooth-barreled firearms was given to some private farmers in the Russian Federation Jewish Autonomous Oblast. Why? ''They are being forced to arm themselves by the need to defend their property from thieves and robbers.''[23] Indeed, according to data from the Russian Ministry of Internal Affairs, throughout the federation ''crime increased by 36 percent in the first half of 1992.''[24]

Not surprisingly, the founding conference of the Nongovernmental Council came to ''the conclusion that honest business in Russia today is impossible.''[25]

Surely one of the most astounding revelations of all, given past claims for the superiority of Soviet socialism, was provided by a Soviet economic analyst who calculated that in the expenditure of "public consumption funds (PCF) [e.g., for education, medical expenses, and other services], . . . for the general public the United States passed us up in terms of proportional government-financed PCF . . . in the middle 1970s." In sum, according to his measure, the United States was more socialist in the state welfare realm than the USSR.

The deluge of once forbidden fruits of knowledge that now bombards the public has had an enormous impact. Public opinion polls are in, including surveys that reveal an enormous apathy about the reforms; indeed, surveys indicate that two-thirds of the public believe that the "worst times are ahead."[26]

Perhaps things will take a turn for the better for the newly independent republics as the 1990s unfold. The evidence offered by internal reporting points, however, to the conclusion that for any foreseeable future, the situation can only continue to deteriorate. Many of the more crucial problems can only be magnified by the change to independence. For example, the chronic difficulty with distribution of goods and raw materials escalated into a major problem during the final months of the old regime. In 1992 with the achievement of independence by the republics, the problem reached catastrophic levels.

The distribution system for many essential commodities has disintegrated. Thus, not only has food production fallen but also its distribution, especially to many of the major cities, has declined significantly. The distribution of other essentials, especially fuel, has been seriously disrupted. For example:

Today, 17 December 1991, Aeroflot has cancelled seventy-five flights. Passengers can neither travel to nor from eighty-seven of the country's airports. There is only one reason— there is no fuel. There is no fuel in Simferopol, Sochi, Tashkent, Mineralnyye Vody, or in many other cities. Even in Moscow, there is only sufficient aviation fuel for ten days.[27]

According to another report,

Our country's impoverished stores will soon become even more destitute. The fisherman of the Far East stopped fishing and distributing their products.

Such a spectacle may be observed in all the ports and bays of the Atlantic Ocean shore. Floating fish canning factories and fish processing ships are laid out; hundreds of trawlers did not put out to sea, and for one reason only—the lack of fuel and diesel oil.[28]

At the end of 1991, the Lisichansk Oil Refinery, the largest in Ukraine, was "working at only 50 percent of its capacity because of the shortage of raw materials."[29]

Jealously exercising their sovereign independence, desperately trying to cut the best deals possible for their own republics, the new leaders have, in effect, placed embargoes on the trade of commodities that formerly flowed easily throughout the USSR. For example, even before the total collapse of the USSR, there was the following report: "Coal production at many of the mines in the [Ukrainian] Donbass coalfields has come to a standstill or been drastically cut back. According to Mr. Valentin Pudak, technical director of Donetskugol, this has happened because [embargoes have caused] the Donbass [to get] only a quarter of the prop timber it requires from Russia.''[30]

Since the demise of the USSR, the imposition of such embargoes has multiplied. For example:

The Belarussian Council of Ministers ordered Wednesday [March 11, 1992] to cut meat supplies to Russia by almost 10,000 tonnes [as received]. As IF [*Interfax*] learned from sources in the republican government, the decision is a response measure to Russia's sudden refusal to supply 22,000 tons of fish flour for the production of combiforage [animal feed] in Belarus.[31]

Such actions have been a primary contributor to the increasingly catastrophic state of the economies of the independent republics. The following describes the situation.

In January this year [1992] national income within the states of the Commonwealth fell by 17 percent. The drop in industrial production came to more than 17 percent. Coal output went down by 10 percent and oil by 12 percent. Production of freight wagons and cars was down by 20 percent. Production of tractors—and this on the eve of spring sowing—fell by 40 percent.[32]

In January 1992, a *Pravda* journalist wrote, "I do not think that during the whole postwar period the country has ever gone into winter so unprepared as it was this year.''[33] By way of example, he noted that in Siberia alone there has been a "reduction in oil output . . . over the past three years by almost 100 million tons.''

On balance, the situation grows worse by the day. In an interview, academician Abel Aganbegyan observed, "We won't get the economy on its feet in 1992. I don't think we will get it on its feet in 1993, either. . . . The falloff of production was 13 percent in 1990, and in 1991 it was 15 percent. This is by no means the limit. . . . I think the falloff in production will reach 25 percent to 30 percent.''[34] One of the greatest tragedies in human history may be unfolding.

INCREASING MORTALITY AND MOUNTING ECOLOGICAL DISASTER

In addition to the false myth about cheap housing was the claim that health care was good and was free. Health standards in the Soviet Union were described as being among the highest in the world.

Of course, the ordinary Soviet citizen, who did not have access to the special party hospitals, knew from experience that most of the hospitals were in deplorable shape. For example, several years ago, a University of Kansas doctoral candidate spent a year in Leningrad supervising American exchange students. One of his charges broke her leg. When he took her to a nearby metropolitan hospital, he had to carry her up the stairs to the treatment room because there was no elevator.

Now the health problem in the former USSR has been revealed by glasnost, and it is growing worse. Long before glasnost, Soviet citizens knew that receiving the best medical care available required extra, under-the-counter payments to health care providers. Now those who cannot afford such payments often go without any care at all.

Infant mortality is associated worldwide with malnutrition. According to a 1987 study by the state statistical commission, "Soviet infant mortality was 2.5 to 5 times higher than in France, the USA, Great Britain and the Federal Republic of Germany."[35] As reported in 1990 in *Moscow News*, "[T]he majority of Turkmenian children today do not get enough to eat."[36] In further elaboration on that tragedy, *Komsomolskaya pravda* stated that starvation among children in Turkmenia was largely because malnourished infants were born to mothers with inadequate diets.[37]

For most Soviet citizens, medical care was shockingly inadequate. The following is an example:

Every year on the nation's highways, about 40,000 people are killed and 260,000 are maimed, as the result of which half of those suffering become invalids or die prematurely. . . . For every one hundred people who have suffered on our highways, thirteen have died. In the GDR and the ChSSR—3–4 persons, in the FRG—2 and in the United States— 1.3 persons. . . . In other words, the severity of the results . . . in the United States is tenfold lower than in our country.[38]

According to Aleksey Vladimirovich Yablokov, state counselor of the Russian Federation for Ecology and Health,

[T]he average life expectancy in Russia reached its maximum in the mid-60s when it amounted to 70.4 years and then it fell to 67.6. In the United States, the average life expectancy is now six years more than ours, and in Japan it is eight years more. Forty percent of the men who died in Russia in 1990 were of working age.[39]

Other evidence that the physical and mental health of the people is deplorable includes reports on the severity of the alcohol problem and the suicide rate. The latter is reported to be nearly four times greater than in the United States. "Every year some 60,000 persons commit suicide in our country." That is 30/100,000 compared to the U.S. rate of 12/100,000.[40]

Almost by any measure, the Soviet Union's record on environmental protection is the world's worst. Huge regions of despoiled land, numerous poisoned lakes, seas, and rivers, and many cities with polluted air and water are a grim inheritance of the newly independent states.

As noted, until the 1986 Chernobyl disaster blew a hole in the curtain of secrecy about anything that reflected negatively on the USSR, public mention of the mounting ecological ruin was forbidden. Now it has been admitted that untold thousands have either perished or are sentenced to early deaths because of the Chernobyl accident. Although the whole Chernobyl story is still unfolding, more and more of the truth has surfaced. In April 1992, *Pravda* revealed that land affected by radiation from the "Chernobyl catastrophe . . . makes up 1 percent of the total area in Russia and 4 percent in Ukraine, the figure is 24 percent in Belarus."[41] In sum, the land so contaminated is 94.5 thousand square miles, an area larger than the state of Kansas (82.3 thousand square miles).

Tragically, the region despoiled by Chernobyl is far from the only disaster area in what was the largest country in the world, and radiation is not the only cause of ecological ruin. According to Russian scientists, the huge Archangel region in the Russian north is seriously affected by both toxic radiation and "destructive emissions from local industrial enterprises,"[42] both of which also have polluted the White and Barents seas.

According to a report that surfaced in June 1992, in the years 1949 to 1967, "[P]lanned and accidental discharges from the Mayak [military] facility in the southern Urals dispersed 150 million curies of radiation into the environment." That was described as "higher than the quantities discharged in Hiroshima and Chernobyl." According to the report, a "half-million people were irradiated, 28,000 severely so, and 8,015 died over a thirty-two-year observation period as a result of the discharges."[43]

In 1989, the findings of a state committee summed up the situation in the Russian republic, stating that "[i]t is common knowledge that ecological ruin has befallen not only the atmosphere, but the soils, waters, and forests as well. . . . Five economic regions of the RSFSR, the Ural, the West Siberian, the East Siberian, the Central and the Northern, are on the brink of ecological disaster."[44] Two years later, according to an estimate published in *Moscow News* in November 1991, 300 regions in the Soviet Union were "unfavorable for human population, . . . 16 percent of the country's total area."[45] That is equivalent to 39 percent of the area in the 50 United States.

A summary of a 1989 report states the following:

Theoretically, it is impossible to live in every seventh city of the 273 RSFSR [Russian] cities which conduct observation of atmospheric air conditions. . . . [For example,] there is twenty times as much of nitrogen oxides as the norm in the air of Gorky, Smolensk, and Omsk; . . . and the benzopyrene content in Novokuznetsk's air is 598 times as much as the maximum possible norm![46]

The newspaper *Izvestia* reported a year ago that the "public health services of Latvia continue to prohibit—or at the very least to recommend against—swimming in the Baltic Sea. The reason is a concentration of bacillus coli so high that it exceeds the permissible norms more than 10-fold and in spots even 100-fold."[47]

Not surprisingly, the physical health of the people has deteriorated significantly. As noted, infant mortality has increased and life expectancy has declined by several years. Certainly, part of the cause has been increasingly serious shortages of medicines—for example, insulin for diabetics and antibiotics for viral diseases. The evidence strongly suggests, however, that the declining health of the people is due largely to the environmental degradation, a major price paid for the seventy-four-year experiment in building communism. For example, according to a 1990 report by the chairman of the Soviet State Committee for Environmental Protection, each year 100,000 "hereditary sick children are born" due to heavy metal poisoning of their mothers.[48]

According to a 1991 report by the medical authorities in the Ukrainian Academy of Sciences,

The increment in the birth rate in the republic (according to 1991 data) is zero. Many more of us are dying than are being born. . . . Already, ineluctable statistics indicate that in some regions only 20–30 percent of school-age children can be considered healthy. On the whole, the disease rate for Ukraine's population has increased by a factor of 2.2 for all classes of disease.[49]

As noted, the Archangel region is a major ecological disaster zone. A report aired on Radio Moscow in May 1992 stated that scientists of the Archangel Medical Institute have concluded "on the basis of twenty years research" that 95 percent of children in the region "are born in a weakened condition. That is four times more than in the first postwar year of 1946."[50] (In 1946 there were major shortages of both food and medicines.) Moreover, the reporter noted that "over the past three years, the number of instances of children falling ill with blood diseases and cancer has tripled." The scientists placed all the blame on environmental factors, especially toxic radiation.

Almost every week some new revelation surfaces. One of the latest came to light in June 1992 when in a Moscow Radio interview Aleksey Yablokov, ecology adviser to President Yeltsin, said that enormous amounts of radiation have been leaked from two Siberian nuclear reactors.

For hundreds of kilometers along the Yenisey [River] below Krasnoyarsk, the radiation contamination is in places higher than in the most dangerous regions of Chernobyl, up to 160 curries per square kilometer. That is incredible radiation. These are small patches, of course, perhaps 100 square metres, where there is no contamination, but this information [has been until now] kept secret from the people who live there.[51]

The catalog of life-threatening environmental factors offered here is far from complete. For example, for decades Western visitors to St. Petersburg (formerly Leningrad) have been warned not to drink the city's tap water; it is infested with *Giardia lamblia*, an intestinal parasite. That the situation worsens every passing day with no end in sight must be stressed. Preoccupied with other major problems that threaten immediate catastrophe, especially the economic crisis and ethnic quarrels that threaten war(s), the new leaders have paid almost no attention to the less tangible, but mounting, ecologic catastrophe. If the threats of civil war can be eliminated and the economy set on an even keel, there would still be the seemingly unsolvable problem of finding the many billions of dollars needed to set right the numerous huge ecological disasters that are the tragic heritage from the former Soviet Union.

Such is the legacy of the independent states born of the collapse of the Soviet Union. To gain a perspective on the unprecedented disaster faced by the nearly 300 million former Soviet citizens, let us imagine that the United States was faced with such a plight at the onset of the 1990s.

We would find ourselves in the deepest depression in the history of the country, far worse than the one that followed the 1929 stock market crash. Moreover, unlike in the depression of the 1930s, there would be skyrocketing inflation (e.g., in 1992 the price of food would be several times higher than it was the year before) accompanied by severe shortages of nearly all necessities, including livestock products, fresh vegetables, clothing, and even school children's papers and pencils.

Even with massive imports of grain, the demand for bread would not be met. In major cities isolated from agriculture, such as New York and Los Angeles, hording would be widespread. People would be drying bread, saving the hardened loaves in fear that food shortages would worsen in the future.

Manufacturing in such industrial cities as Pittsburgh and Detroit would be down precipitously. Many plants would be closed, or on short shifts, largely because of breakdowns in the distribution of raw materials and energy. Many homes would be cold because of fuel shortages. Moreover, gasoline for private cars often would be unavailable. Public transportation, including domestic air flights, would be sharply curtailed. For example, in Atlanta and Denver there would be, at best, only one flight to Washington, D.C., each day. Kansas and Missouri farmers would be informed that fuel would be rationed during the upcoming sowing season.

The crises would not be just economic. As a result of decades-long abuse of the environment, health officials would report that 16 percent of the country is unfavorable for human habitation—that is, an area larger than California and Texas combined.

The press (sharply curtailed by newsprint shortages and rising publication costs) would report an increase in death rates due to the lack of lifesaving medicines, for example insulin for diabetics. For such reasons, life expectancy would have declined by two years in the last two decades.

Americans would also learn that in the agricultural heartland, we had lost 20 percent of the cropland since 1940 due to abusive cultivation practices. The food problem would be the most alarming of all. There would have been a decline in production, serious disruptions in distribution, mounting postharvest waste, and spoilage of fresh produce—as much as 40 percent of fruits and vegetables would be lost. As a result, some agricultural authorities would be predicting the possibility of widespread famine before the next crop could be harvested.

Finally, although these are far from all of the catastrophes that the United

States would face under such circumstances, there would be the dissolution of the Union itself. There would be fifty sovereign states, each calling for the questionable fruits of independence, such as their own currencies and military forces. Several of them, including Missouri and Wyoming, would be armed with nuclear weapons. California and Washington would be quarreling over who owns the Pacific fleet. Furthermore, in some of the newly independent states with large minority populations, for example Texas and Alabama, pockets of civil war between ethnic groups would break out.

For the former citizens of the Soviet Union, these situations are not imaginary; they are stark reality. Moreover, as noted, the agricultural/food problem is most serious of all; thus, it deserves special attention.

NOTES

1. *Democracy*: "Socialist democracy is the only genuine democracy." In Marxist-Leninist theory, there is no democracy except under communism. The emphasis is on equality, especially economic equality as determined by all having the same relationship to the means of production. Although standards of living in the Soviet Union lagged far behind those of the developing nations of the West, the welfare of Soviet citizens was advancing. See Roy D. Laird and Betty A. Laird, *A Soviet Lexicon* (Lexington, Mass.: Lexington Books, 1988).

2. *RL 352/74* [Newsletter published by Radio Liberty], November 1, 1974.

3. Gorbachev speech to media representatives, *Pravda*, July 15, 1987.

4. Vladislav Starchevsky, "They Will Fight for Their Privileges," *Nedelya*, July 2–8, 1990. An interview with Ella A. Pamfilova, a member of the Supreme Soviet of the USSR, the secretary of the commission concerning privileges. JPRS-UPA-90–058, October 9, 1990.

5. A. Goryachev, "Television News Service," Moscow Central Television, July 21, 1991.

6. *Argumenty i fakty*, July 2–8, 1988. Per capita data calculated on the basis of officially estimated population levels.

7. Congress debates, *Izvestia*, December 18, 1989.

8. "Vladimir Tikhonov: Land for the Peasants," *Yunost*, October 1989. JPRS-UPA-90–001.

9. S. Pastukhov, "Looking toward a 'Revolt of the Naked,' " *Pravda*, October 2, 1990. CDSP, vol. 42, no. 40, 1990.

10. "Comparison of U.S.-Soviet Living Standards," *SSHA: Ekomomika, Politica, Ideologiya*, December 1988, pp. 12–22. JPRS-USA-89–007, April 14, 1989.

11. "The USSR Economy in 1990," *Ekonomika i zhizn*, January 1991. FBIS-SOV-91–023, February 4, 1991.

12. Ibid.

13. "Vesti," Moscow Russian Television, March 18, 1992. FBIS-SOV-92–054, March 19, 1992.

14. Interview with V. K. Senchagov, chairman of the USSR State Committee for Prices, and V. V. Gerashchenko, chairman of the board, USSR Gosbank, *Kommunist*, November 1989. JPRS-UKO-90–001.

15. Vasiliy Selyunin, "What Is Happening to Our Money?" *Rossiyskaya gazeta*, August 1, 1991. JPRS-UEA-91–034.

16. TASS, November 18, 1991. FBIS-SOV-91–223, November 19, 1991.

17. "Goskomstat Reports," *Rossiyskaya gazeta*, April 24. FBIS-SOV-92–080, April 24, 1992.

18. Vtacheslav Goncharov, "One Lot of Wages, Two Lots of Wages," *Kuranty*, May 22, 1992. FBIS-SOV–102, May 27, 1992.

19. "Domestic Market," *Postfactum*, March 18, 1992. FBIS-SOV-92–055, March 20, 1992.

20. *Birzheviye vedomosti*, January 1, 1992. CDSP, February 5, 1992.

21. Interview with the head of the USSR Ministry of Internal Affairs' Chief Information Center, *Izvestia*, January 10, 1990. CDSP, vol. 42, no. 2, 1990.

22. S. Ovsienko, "From a Position of Law," *Veteran*, February 1991. JPRS-UPA–91–021, April 18, 1991.

23. "Peasants Defend Themselves," *Izvestia*, April 15. FBIS-SOV-92–078, April 22, 1992.

24. Valery Ivanov, "25,000 People Are Missing," *Izvestia*, April 29, 1992. CDSP, May 27, 1992.

25. "Domestic Market," *Postfactum*, May 1, 1992. FBIS-SOV-92–086, May 4, 1992.

26. "Viewpoint," *Interfax*, October 21, 1991. FBIS-SOV-91–203, October 21, 1991.

27. V. Luskanov, "Television News Service," Moscow Central Television, December 17, 1991.

28. L. Savitskiy, "TV Inform," Moscow Central Television, December 17, 1991.

29. Nikolay Lisovaenko, "Direct Line: Donbass Cut Off from Groznyy Oil," *Izvestia*, December 20, 1991. FBIS-SOV–91–248, December 26, 1991.

30. "Soviet Business Report," *Interfax*, December 1, 1991. FBIS-SOV-91–233, December 4, 1991.

31. *Interfax*, March 11, 1992. FBIS-SOV–92, March 12, 1992.

32. "Itogi," Moscow Teleradiokompaniya Ostankino, February 23, 1992. FBIS-SOV-92–037, February 25, 1992.

33. Petr Slezko, "Without Light and Heat. One Month of Winter Behind Us. But Two Still to Go," *Pravda*, January 4, 1992. FBIS-SOV-92–005, January 8, 1992.

34. Fyodar Pospelov, *Birzheviye vedomosti*, January 1, 1992. CDSP, February 5, 1992.

35. *Agitator*, November 1988. JPRS-UEA-89–005.

36. *Moscow News*, no. 14, 1990.

37. "Social Portrait of a Phenomenon," *Komsomolskaya pravda*, April 25, 1990. CDSP, June 20, 1990.

38. V. Davydov. "Who Will Be Next? The High Accident Rate in the Country's Highways," *Pravda*, November 16, 1988.

39. Moscow Mayak Radio Network, January 22, 1992. FBIS-SOV-92–016, January 24, 1992.

40. V. Yunisov, "When Visiting God, There Are No Latenesses! *Komsomolskaya pravda*, December 8, 1990. JPRS-UPA-91–001, January 14, 1991.

41. Aleksander Ulitenok, "Minsk Is Counting on 'Gentlemen,' " *Pravda*, April 30, 1992. CDSP, May 27, 1992.

42. Moscow Radio Rossii Network, May 19, 1992. JPRS-SOV–92–099, May 21, 1992.

43. *Kyodo*, June 7, 1992. FBIS-SOV-92–112, June 10, 1992.

44. "On the Nature Watch: From the State Committee's First Session," *Sovetskaya rossiya*, April 28, 1989. [Translation source misplaced.]

45. "Our Time is Up . . . Our Home Is Unclear and Unhealthy. Solutions Must Be Found," *Moscow News*, November 3–10, 1991.

46. "On the Nature Watch: From the State Committee's First Session," *Sovetskaya rossiya*, April 28, 1989. [Translation source misplaced.]

47. "The Baltic Coast Is an Area at Risk," *Izvestia*, July 13, 1991. JPRS-UPA-91–041, September 18, 1991.

48. Nikolay Vorontsov, chairman of Goskompriroda—State Committee for Environmental Protection, *Moskovskaya pravda*, January 18, 1990. JPRS-UPA-90–015, March 22, 1990.

49. Viktoriya Yasnopolskaya, "In Ukraine More Are Dying Than Are Being Born," *Pravda Ukrainy*, October 17, 1991. JPRS-UPA-91–046, November 20, 1991.

50. Moscow Radio Rossii Network, May 19, 1992. JPRS-SOV-92–099, May 21, 1992.

51. Moscow Radio Television Network, June 13, 1992. FBIS-SOV-92–115, June 18, 1992.

4

GORBACHEV'S FAILED RURAL REVOLUTION FROM ABOVE

In 1951, Naum Jasny, the great pioneer of Soviet agricultural studies, wrote his seminal article, "Kolkhozy, the Achilles Heel of the Soviet Regime."[1] Four decades later, the failure of rural perestroika underscored the validity of that observation.

In the early 1930s, Stalin imposed the command system of management on the countryside with the forced collectivization of agriculture. Lenin and his successors were fully committed to industrial fundamentalism, that is, believing that the urban industrial organizational and managerial model, born of the Industrial Revolution, was fully applicable to farming. To a man, even though Nikita Khrushchev was of peasant origin, they were agricultural illiterates when it came to understanding the human setting required for successful farming.

Soviet leaders believed (wrongly) that in agriculture what is big is always good (more efficient and more productive), what is bigger is better, and what is biggest is best of all. With his amalgamation campaign of the early 1950s, Khrushchev carried that illogical conclusion to the extreme. Neighboring collective and state farms were joined together, and the results were rural bureaucratic monstrosities, farms often the size of U.S. counties, inhabited by more than a thousand peasants.

External authorities, especially the rayon (district) party secretaries, constantly imposed their will on the farms, acting in the fashion of the worst of absentee landlords. They routinely told the on-the-farm leaders when to sow and when to reap, more often than not oblivious to real conditions faced in the fields. For example, the record reveals that rayon party secretaries, bent on meeting state delivery plans for grain on time, often ordered the combines into the fields at harvest time, oblivious to the fact that there had been heavy local rains and the machines could not possibly move.

Lenin and his successors were oblivious to the fact that the Industrial Revolution did not have the same fundamental impact on farming that it had on urban industry. As impressive as the modern tractors and combines may be, they are merely extensions of more primitive tools—draft animals and the scythe. Primarily, the successful nurturing of animals and the cultivation of plants is still a struggle with the whims of nature. With rare exceptions, the factory of farming is still the great outdoors as compared to the manufacturing plant, where the production environment is tightly controlled. Living plants and animals require a kind of careful nurturing that is wholly unlike the requirements for monitoring an industrial machine.

Farmers may not love their land—after all, it is inanimate—but successful farmers everywhere must have an intimate commitment to the tasks required (often unpleasant, tedious, and difficult) that is fundamentally unlike the commitment needed by an 8:00 to 5:00 factory worker. Individual attention and initiative are essential.

At the peak of the harvest season, farmers went to bed intending to run their combines the next day. Overnight it rained heavily, however, and the machines could not possibly move in the fields. Under such circumstances, farmers who are combine drivers in the Soviet collective and state farms sighed, rolled over, and slept in that day. Successful independent farmers, however, had long lists of priority tasks, and spent rainy days mending fences, hauling animal feed, fuel, or possibly building flood control dikes, if the heavy rains threatened to wash out some of the crops. Animal husbandry comes by its name for good reason. Livestock and poultry raising is never an 8:00 to 5:00 occupation. The farmers must be constantly monitoring the nutritional and health needs of their animals.

For these reasons, even with the growth in size of modern farms worldwide, most farming is family farming. Members of the family share a commitment to the tasks to be done. Ask any American, European, or other private farmer, and he or she will tell you that a hired hand is never as good as a member of the family. Gorbachev belatedly recognized that reality, stating that a major fault in Soviet collectivized agriculture was that the kolkhoz and sovkhoz peasants were essentially hired hands who were deprived of the initiative that comes from feeling that they were the masters of the land. (See the discussion under "Gorbachev's Agrarian Reforms and After.")

Such was the agricultural environment inherited by Gorbachev, with a determination to achieve a rural perestroika. Before discussing the major elements of perestroika in the countryside, however, we need to appraise the food and agricultural situation that evolved during the Gorbachev era.

MOUNTING FOOD SHORTAGES: 1986–1991

Gorbachev and numerous other internal commentators on the worsening Soviet crises stated repeatedly that by far the most serious domestic problem was the shortage of food. That grim reality was attributable not only to inadequate production on the farms but also, in the twilight years of the USSR, to a breakdown in distribution, especially increased waste of produce between the farms and the citizens' tables.

I [M. Gorbachev] will tell you frankly, the most difficult thing now—and this is what concerns me most of all—is food. Everything must be mobilized, all the state's resources, but the food situation must not be allowed to get worse.[2]

In the final years of the USSR, the food problem was described by Soviet observers as at a crisis level. In the 1990s, for reasons discussed here, some responsible and knowledgeable officials in the independent republics have spoken of catastrophe, and some are even predicting famine.

Since 1986, food availability for the consumer has deteriorated significantly. Especially serious has been the decline in both the quality and the variety of foods available. As documented here, the causes behind the mounting food shortages are many and complex.

One cause of the shortage is the reduced production of many key foods because of several factors. First, the area sown to crops has declined significantly, largely due to pollution of the land and destructive cultivation practices. Also, fuel (especially for planting and harvesting) and other agricultural inputs (e.g., spare parts for machines and equipment) have become increasingly scarce. For such reasons, per capita production of nearly all key foods has declined.

Another cause is the mounting losses of postharvest crops, especially fresh produce and grain. Always inadequate, the infrastructure, including transport and storage facilities, has deteriorated significantly and thus increased waste.

Third, the deterioration of the old command-management system, aggravated by the breakup of the Union, has seriously disrupted the distribution system. As a result, many regions refuse to ship surplus commodities to the cities and other regions deficient in food production.

Fourth, faced with increased food shortages and fueled by prognostications of widespread famine, the people increasingly have turned to hording, which given tragically inadequate private storage capacities, only contributes to an increased spoilage of perishable commodities.

The loss of agricultural land has been serious. For example, in the Russian Federation, "[t]he arable land . . . has decreased by almost 20 percent"[3] in recent years. In the whole of the USSR, an estimated "25–40 percent of the fertile Chernozem lands have been lost over the last decade."[4] As a result, whereas in 1980, 126.6 million hectares were sown to grain, by 1991 the area had fallen to only 108.5 million hectares, a decline during the period of 14.3 percent in grain sowings alone.[5]

Postharvest waste has mounted alarmingly. As reported in *Pravda*, "We ship 5–6 million tons of grain products alone to the dump each year. Because of a shortage of processing capacities, we let up to 1 million tons of meat rot annually.

We throw away a good half of our vegetables."[6] In some areas, the losses reported are even higher. "In storage facilities, we sometimes allow as much as 70 percent or even more [of the vegetables and potatoes] to spoil."[7]

Equally dismal has been the quality of agricultural equipment and machines available and their maintenance once they have been delivered to the farms—for example, spare parts are always in short supply. As a result, the working life of farm machines is several times less than that in Western countries. According to a former Gosplan Department head:

We are already producing six times more tractors than in the United States. . . .

[T]he United States is producing less grain harvesting combines than the USSR by a factor of twelve, while harvesting significantly more grain. . . . [Yet] the lack of proper equipment is a major problem. The production of truck gardening light-duty tractors and motor cultivators in the country totals 65,000 pieces per year. It accounts for 512,000 in the United States.

The energy allocated per agricultural employee in the USSR is four times lower than in the United States.[8]

According to V. A. Brukhnov, former RSFSR minister of highways:

The republic's requirements for good roads [especially rural roads] are ten times greater than they appear to be. An investment of 180 billion rubles is needed in order to raise them to normal condition. Certainly the country does not have such funds at its disposal. This year, 6.4 billion rubles have been allocated to us. Thus we will need thirty years in order to introduce proper order into our network of roads.[9]

As a result of these factors, even though rationing is widespread, shelves in the stores are often empty. Thus, in 1990, according to a national poll by the All-Union Center for the Study of Public Opinion, 43.4 percent of the respondents said they experienced shortages of necessary food quite often; 29.7 percent said constantly. Some 76.8 percent said they could not get enough meat, fish, and poultry, and 63.6 percent not enough vegetables, fruit, and berries. Only 18.1 percent felt that their diet was sufficient in amount and of good quality.[10] Food availability has greatly deteriorated since that poll was taken.

A comparison of average annual per capita production of key food items during the tenth five-year planning period (1976–80) with production levels during the twelfth five-year planning period (1986–90) reveals, as shown in Table 4.1, that grain output per capita declined by 6.0 percent, potatoes by 19.7 percent, vegetables and melons by 1.6 percent, and fruits and berries by 7.2 percent.

Meat production (carcass weight) did reach 67.9 kilograms per capita in 1990. That increase (19.8 percent over the last ten years) would not have occurred, however, without massive imports of feedgrains.[11] Moreover, actual consumption (after waste) was reported to have been only some 45 kgs. per capita, less than half of the consumption level in the United States and most West European

Table 4.1

Population and Soviet Food Production: 1986–90 versus the Previous Two Five-Year Plan Periods (five-year averages)

Years	Grain* Output	Grain** Import Balance	Pota- toes	Vege- tables and Melons	Fruits and Berries	Meat	Popu- lation
Million metric tons							Millions
1976-80	191.8+	20.28	82.6	26.3	9.4	14.8	260.9
1981-85	168.7	40.76	78.4	29.2	10.4	16.2	271.4
1986-90	196.5	31.60	72.3	28.7	9.5	19.3	282.9
Kilograms/capita++							
1976-80	735.1	77.8	316.6	100.8	36.0	56.7	
1981-85	593.4	150.2	288.9	107.6	38.3	59.7	
1986-90	691.2	111.2	255.6	99.2	33.4	67.9	
%Change, 1976-80 to 1986-90							
	- 6.0	+42.9	-19.7	- 1.6	- 7.2	+19.8	

* Weight after additional processing.
**Imports minus exports, based on USDA estimates.
+Estimate based upon the previously reported harvest figures for 1981-85 and the (newly reported) weight after additional process-ing figures, for that period. Thus, the 1971-75 harvest figure was reduced by the same proportion as in 1981-85 --that is, 6.9%.
++The per capita figures were calculated on the basis of the mean commodity output and the import balance during the periods divid-ed by the mean of the official population statistics as of Janu-ary 1 for the years in the periods.

Sources: Narodnoye khozyaistvo SSSR (various volumes since 1970), SSSR tsifrakh v 1989, the report on 1990 plan fulfill-ment, Ekonomika i zhizn, No. 5, January 1991 and various issues of USDA, USSR Grain Situation and Outlook, Foreign Agriculture Circular.

nations.[12] Indeed, according to the calculations of two former Soviet economists, in recent years meat consumption has been less than it was in 1926–27, at the height of the NEP recovery in food production.[13]

FUTURE TRENDS: 1992 AND BEYOND

The weather had been exceptionally good in the USSR in recent years until 1991. Indeed, mother nature was particularly kind in 1989 and 1990. Both years produced new, all-time, back-to-back record yields of grain per hectare. That good fortune cannot continue uninterrupted and, more importantly, the human failures, primarily responsible for the food crisis, continue unabated.

Grain is by far the most important crop since it is used not only for bread but also for animal feed. Production in 1991 was down significantly. As reported in the press, the total grain output was 154.7 million metric tons (558 kilograms/

capita) as compared with 1990 production of 211.5 million metric tons (767 kilograms/capita). Thus, the decline in production per capita was 27 percent. Such production figures need to be put in the perspective of the long-term goal of one ton (1,000 kgs.) of grain per capita in order to supply demand.

Reports on the production of other crops and livestock in 1991 are as follows:

The average yield [of sunflowers] dropped from 1.69 tonnes/ha in 1990 to 1.35 tonnes/ha this year. . . . The average yield [of potatoes] is 9.9 tonnes/ha, or 0.8 ton less than last year. The yield of sugar beets also dropped from 24.7 tonnes/ha last year to 19.6 tonnes/ha this year. . . .

The cotton harvest is 2,674,000 tons, or 36 percent of the planned figure, as against 4,166,000 tons at the same date last year.[14]

[T]he cattle stock in Russia has fallen by 15 percent [due to fodder shortages] and it will take us at least five years to restore it to its former level.[15]

Unfavorable weather was only partially responsible for the 1991 decline in food production. In the words of one observer on the scene, "[e]xperts think that unfavorable weather conditions are only one of the reasons for the poor [1991] harvest. The reduction of area under crops and the general disorganization during harvesting had perceptible consequences. One result was that almost 7 mn. hectares of grain were never harvested."[16]

According to the Russian State Statistic Committee:

The grain harvest [in the Republic] amounted to 89.1 million tons, which is 15 percent lower than the average level of the last five years and is 24 percent down from 1990's figure. . . . In 1991 the volume of oil seed supplies to the state was the lowest in the past six years, vegetables and potatoes—for 18 years.[17]

In Ukraine:

In 1991 the gross agricultural output . . . fell by 12 percent. The gross grain harvest was 38.6 million tons [as received], 12.4 million tons less than in the previous year. The bulk purchases of potatoes reduced by 40 percent and vegetables by 25 percent.[18]

According to Viktor Nikolayevich Khlystun, minister of agriculture, Russian Federation:

[O]ne should not count on there being an abundance of food in the immediate future. Until we change the economic system in the agricultural industry and increase the real output from each hectare of land . . . [and the weather is more favorable], it is doubtful whether we can guarantee to fully satisfy the demand for agricultural products. . . . [F]or this, a certain amount of time, at least a minimum of two years, will be needed.[19]

According to the Russian Ministry of Economics and Finance, "[d]uring the first three months of 1992 the food situation in the republic will remain acute and the output of basic kinds of foodstuffs will fall."[20]

For such reasons, even before he had any way to know that the weather would turn unfavorable in 1991, academician Vladimir Tikhonov flatly stated, "I believe, I am even convinced that unless there are radical changes in agriculture this year, real hunger awaits us next year."[21]

Other commentators have been equally pessimistic in their forecasts for the foreseeable future:

Areas sown with spring corn [grain] have been decreasing year after year. One can be sure the tendency will continue. . . . [Major reasons for the decline in production are] growing disorganization and chaos, lower output of fertilizers, and lack of motivation for increased productivity on collective and state farms.[22]

In the words of former Soviet Deputy Prime Minister Fedor Senko, the agrarian problem is "very alarming. . . . The production slump in main economic sectors has disrupted material and technical supplies to agriculture and the food industry. The situation is critical, and if we fail to rectify the situation dramatically very soon, this year, we shall have no food."[23]

Other reports on the 1991 scene are as follows:

The situation in the agrarian sector has reached a critical point. For the first time in many years production volumes have begun to fall. In January–April this year kolkhozes and sovkhozes sent to state resources 20 percent less milk and 14 percent less livestock than in the corresponding period last year. Food production fell by 7 percent. . . .

[O]ur economic situation is deteriorating so rapidly that we will, I believe, have to have emergency, fire-engine measures aimed at preventing starvation and an energy crisis in the winter of 1991–92.[24]

In mid-summer 1991, recognizing that a poor harvest was under way, Soviet Prime Minister Valentin Pavlov estimated that "it will . . . be necessary to buy [a record] 77 million tons of grain from abroad."[25]

Subsequently, the United States and West European food surplus–producing countries initiated shipments of food aid to the Baltic and several of the CIS republics. What will the future bring?

History may not repeat itself, but there are obviously serious people in the former USSR who are concerned that it might. For example, in February 1992, a *Moscow News* editorial commented on an article in the *International Herald Tribune*, which reported that current commitments by the United States for aid to Russia include 38.4 million tons of food. This contrasts with the 1921 aid of "700 million tons of food, as well as a great deal of medicines and consumer goods." Before the aid arrived, "100,000 people died of starvation every month in Petrograd alone." In total, the aid saved "from 10 to 50 million lives in Russia in three years according to expert estimates."[26]

In mid-1992, evidence indicates that although grain production should be somewhat higher than it was in 1992, on balance food production will be down significantly in both the Russian Federation and the Ukrainian Republic. The sowing campaign was in great disarray. In the Russian Federation, "[i]n the space of two months kolkhozes and sovkhozes in practically all [Russian] oblasts have spent all the profits made on agricultural produce last year and been left without a kopek of money for the sowing campaign." Further, according to a kolkhoz chairman from Krasnodar (sometimes referred to as the Iowa of Russia), "The sowing . . . has already been virtually wrecked. The kray is short of 20,000 tons of gasoline and 30,000 tons of diesel fuel, and the farms have no money."[27]

In addition, "[t]he state of affairs in Kaluga is frightening. Around 2,000 tractors, thousands of trucks, and almost one-third of seeders and cultivators are not ready for operation. Only 269 out of 340 farms have a full supply of seeds. As in Tula, there is a great shortage of pulse crop seeds."[28]

Price changes for commodities have put the farms in a desperate position. Thus, "despite constant talk about the priority of the countryside, [the Russian government] bought up last year's grain harvest for mixed feed at R300–R400 a ton and is now [1992] selling mixed feed to the farms at R6,000–R12,000 a ton."[29]

How serious is the problem in the Russian Federation? According to an *Interfax* report:

The current decline in agricultural production in Russia is caused by two important factors: decreased solvent demand for food products [due to consumer price increases], and forced reorganization of collective and state-run farms. The real threat is that should the rate of declining production exceed 25 percent, the situation may become irreversible. *The agricultural sector may lose its growth base. . . . Agriculture is on the verge of bankruptcy.*[30]

Indeed, at the end of April 1992, another business report revealed that "[f]or the first quarter of 1992, the rate of decline [in processed food in Russia] neared 25 percent (relative to 1991 levels)."[31]

According to agricultural deputies to the Ukrainian parliament, "The farming economy of Ukraine is on the verge of a total collapse—if they do not manage to complete the sowing campaign in a proper manner."[32] The major problem is fuel shortages.

One thing is certain: the availability of livestock products is down and such shortages are destined to worsen. Thus, according to the Russian Federation State Statistical Committee, in January 1992 the sale of cattle and poultry fell by 31 percent compared with that of January 1991. "The gross milk yield decreased by 19 percent, which is the result of the reduction in the number of cattle and their productivity."[33]

Because 1963 was a drought year, the Soviet Union purchased large quantities of grain from abroad for the first time in history. Even that action was not enough, however. For lack of animal feed, one-third of Soviet hogs were slaughtered. Ten years would pass before the hog numbers could be returned to the early 1963 level. As the 1990s unfold, favorable weather would help, but mother nature's blessings cannot repair what human error has destroyed.

GORBACHEV'S AGRARIAN REFORMS AND AFTER

In the raging debate over what is to be done, which carries over to the newly independent republics, there have been essentially three positions: (1) the only way out is full privatization of production, distribution, and market-determined prices; (2) the old command system was the best and it just needed tinkering with to set it right; and (3) a middle ground between the two extremes—for example, promoting some privatization while retaining the kolkhozy and sovkhozy and significant controls over prices.

Gorbachev was staunchly ensconced in the middle, as far as the rhetoric is concerned. Further, his actions exhibited a strong don't-rock-the-boat-too-much position. Essentially, his line was to promote semiprivatization of agriculture through the collective contract (*kollektivnyi podriad*) and lease contracting (*arendnyi podriad*). The kolkhozy and sovkhozy would be maintained, but much of the farming would be turned over to private groups (especially families) who would lease parcels of the land from the collective and state farms.

Collective Contracts, Lease Contracting, Privatization

In its final years, the Soviet Union was, and now the independent republics are, in a state of flux greater than at any other time in the six decades since Joseph Stalin forced collectivization on the peasants in 1929 and the early 1930s. Then and now the organization and management of agricultural production has been the most critical issue. Ironically, however, whereas Stalin forced the peasants into the collective and state farms, Mikhail Gorbachev *seemed to be* reversing the line of march.

Success in Stalin's revolution from above (his own phrase) depended on destroying the entrepreneurial spirit of the individual farmer, but the success of Gorbachev's rural revolution depended on recreating just such an attitude among the peasants.

Following Khrushchev's footsteps, Gorbachev made agriculture his major domestic economic concern. Immediately after coming to power, he started talking about introducing perestroika in the countryside. Repeatedly, he declared that the political-economic changes he attempted to bring about were revolutionary. Moreover, in his book, *Perestroika: New Thinking for Our Country and the World*, a subsection is entitled "A 'Revolution from Above'? The Party and Perestroika." In it he candidly admits, "Yes, the Party leadership started it."[34]

In that section of the book (p. 55 ff.), he also points out that "[t]here is a term in historical science and also in political vocabulary 'revolution from above.' " However, he fell short of crediting the phrase to Stalin, who first used it to describe forced collectivization.

Unfortunately, the revolutionary pronouncements coming from the higher party leadership under Gorbachev were accompanied by qualifications and contradictions that led one to conclude that on the most crucial matters (especially party control), only insignificant changes were envisioned. Specifically, Gorbachev's speeches (particularly on rural perestroika) were masterpieces of obfuscation that could allow readers whose opinions may be poles apart to find support for their diverse views.

A prime example of the obfuscation that characterized Gorbachev's words and actions related to the question of retaining the kolkhozy and sovkhozy. For many observers (including this analyst and some former Soviet authorities), the logic of the Gorbachev reforms suggested abandoning the kolkhozy and sovkhozy. Yet while condemning the errors of the system, the general secretary still did not condemn collectivization as such. Thus, addressing those who called for abandoning the collective and state farms, he said in March 1989, "I believe that this viewpoint is both scientifically and practically ungrounded."[35] Perhaps the clearest message of all was that Gorbachev wanted to preserve Soviet socialism while harvesting the fruits of a free market system. Surely the two are incompatible.

On paper, small groups (most especially families) in the Russian Federation and most of the other republics were and still are encouraged to take over the management of farming. As Gorbachev said over and over, and repeated in the opening sentence of his March 1989 presentation to the special party Central Committee plenum on the agrarian policy of the CPSU, the centerpiece of rural perestroika was "to work out and offer to the nation an agrarian policy that will be able to restore the farmer as the master on the land and [thus] dependably resolve the food problem."[36]

Gorbachev recognized that the kolkhozy and sovkhozy have captured the peasants in a position of working on the farms much like hired hands, in his words "day laborers."[37] As such, they have been deprived of the motivations that are essential to successful farming the world over. Unwilling or unable to go all the way and institute private ownership of the land and break up the kolkhozy and sovkhozy, however, Gorbachev compromised; the collective contract and contract leases were his solution.

The collective contract scheme was experimented with in Stavropol krai when Gorbachev was first secretary of that region. The scheme was said to have resulted in increased production. Moreover, when in 1983 he was still the politburo member responsible for agriculture, he persuaded his colleagues to endorse the scheme for widespread adoption.

Theoretically, collective contracting rests on the personal profit motive and greatly increases individual and small-group responsibility for the livestock, the land, the machinery, and the production. The amount of labor exerted is determined by the degree of commitment by the peasants participating. Most interesting is the fact that violation of one of Marx's most sacred doctrines was discussed. The suggestion was that the groups should be allowed to employ hired labor provided that the wages paid would be comparable to those paid for work in the state sector of the economy.

As the scheme for turning over production management to peasant groups unfolded, its champions came to realize that, before joining in the contracts, the peasants would need assurance that they would be secure in their new ventures. As noted, the discussion included the recognition that a major problem in the USSR was a decline in the quality of the land, especially due to soil erosion and salinization.

Farmers care for the land when they know that their future, and that of their families, depends on it. Land that one controls for only a short period is something to be exploited to the maximum, regardless of long-term consequences.

That reality is joined with the peasants' past experience with failed promises, which give rise to apprehension that what the party (or any central governing group that may take its place now that the republics have become independent) giveth, it can also taketh away. Responding to the problem, the Supreme Soviet issued a decree on April 7, 1989, to allow peasant groups, families, or individuals to acquire long-term leases on the land (up to fifty years) with the provision that surviving family members actively engaged in the work can inherit the leases. Further, the decree called for the Council of Ministers to draft a law on leasing before July 1, 1990. In the ensuing debate, even the sacred doctrine that the state should own the land was challenged.

Beating the July 1, 1990, deadline, the new Fundamentals of Legislation of the USSR and the Union Republics on Land were made public in March 1990. Although stopping short of allowing private ownership of land, and thus its purchase and sale, the law did lay a viable base for the creation of private farming in the USSR, if that was to be the path that the peasants chose.

Key provisions of the law were as follows:

Article 5: Land is granted to citizens for heritable life tenure. . . .

Article 23: . . . Agricultural land is granted: (1) to USSR citizens—for personal subsidiary plot farming and individual horticulture, truck farming, and livestock raising. . . .

Article 25: . . . USSR citizens expressing the desire to run a peasant farm based primarily on personal labor and the labor of members of their families are granted land plots, including a farmstead plot, for heritable life tenure or on a lease, as they wish. . . . [However, the maximum size of a land plot was to be determined by regional and local authorities.] Also, the land plots of citizens engaging in peasant farming may not be divided."[38]

Beyond the production management arena, the creation of markets and, inseparably, prices determined by the supply of, and demand for, foodstuffs was in the wind and now have been adopted in most of the republics, with some exceptions—for example, a regulated price for milk.

Where such reforms have been adopted in the now-independent republics, central production planning, which from Stalin to the present has dictated what the farms must produce through the decreed delivery of specific produce to state collection depots, has been abandoned in theory. Practice is another matter, however. Thus, in the Russian Federation, "mandatory" contracting volumes for sale of produce to the state have been established for all farmers.

Of course, with the breakup of the internal empire, agricultural policy has been the responsibility of the independent republics. What assurance is there, however, that new centralized controls at the republic level will not be imposed? As we will see, old ways of doing things die hard.

"Mines Laid by the Past"

Many Soviet commentators, including the former editors of *Pravda*, were aware of the dimension of the problems involved in the attempt to achieve reform. Thus, in "The Principles of Restructuring," one editorial stated that there were quite a few "obstacles ahead," particularly from "mines laid by the past."[39]

As we have tried to document here and elsewhere, the obstacles in the way of solving the food problem are of Herculean proportions.[40] As suggested, in the former USSR among the major obstacles were qualifications imposed by Gorbachev himself and now by the new leaders.

Although the rhetoric that Gorbachev used was astoundingly fresh, including the admission of faults in the system that could not have been publicly recognized a few years earlier, he left no doubt that he was a Marxist-Leninist, unable or unwilling to abandon most of the sacred doctrinal baggage. How many of the new leaders, even Boris Yeltsin, have fully cast off the baggage of Soviet socialism that they have carried all their lives? Clearly, Gorbachev wanted to enjoy the advantages of free enterprise while strengthening socialism. Thus, the kolkhozy and sovkhozy were not to be abandoned, only transformed.

At first glance, in the post-Soviet era, the kolkhozy and sovkhozy seem destined to oblivion. Thus, "[i]n accordance with a decree [On Urgent Measures to Implement the Land Reform in the Russian Federation] signed by Russian President Boris Yeltsin on December 26, 1991, members of collective farms and workers on state-owned farms are given the right to leave them in order to create individual farms."[41]

Specifically, according to the *ukaze* (decree), the land will be transferred to former farm workers according to their shares. The new owners will have "the right to exchange their land and property shares, lease them or mortgage in banks for credits."[42] The land can be sold if the proceeds are "invested into creating enterprises in rural areas." Prices for the land will be fixed by the government, however, and maximum size of plots are to be established. Land not transferred to individual former farmers will be sold, giving preference to such people as rural teachers.

The ukaze also states that the kolkhoz and sovkhoz members have four choices: "The first is to change into an association of peasant farms. The second is to change into a joint stock company. The third is to change into a production cooperative with the share form of ownership. Finally, the fourth is to leave everything as it is.[43]

A law on private ownership of land was introduced in the Ukrainian Supreme Soviet in January 1992. "The document states that land in the Republic may be owned collectively, privately, and by the state.[44]

Assuming that the peasants are really able to choose freely the form of tenure they prefer and are not subject to pressure by local officials, which option are the vast majority most likely to select? As documented in the section "Private Resistance to Private Farming," the evidence points to a conclusion that their most likely action will be to "leave everything [essentially] as it is."

Even more important than the ideological millstone that the top leaders cannot cast off easily is the burden of the party-state apparatus (now primarily the state apparatus, since the party has been virtually disbanded) from which the central leaders draw their power. Specifically, at the local level, the major figure responsible for the abuses of the command-management system in the past was the district party secretary.

Unless the post of rayon party secretary is abandoned, in fact and not just in name, truly independent farming cannot be realized. If that view is correct, a passage in Gorbachev's March 1989 speech could have signaled the most important of all agricultural reforms in the former USSR. He stated that restructuring agriculture required "eliminating the existing administrative (departmental and territorial) system of management of agriculture and of the agrarian sector of the economy as a whole."[45] Unfortunately, given the prospects for genuine reform, that statement must be seen in the broader context of both the political system (old and new), Gorbachev's own position then, and now the position of the newly powerful republic leaders.

As stated, more than any other external force, the power wielded by the rural district party secretaries prevented any significant on-the-farm initiative. Under the command system of management, fulfillment of plans was the prime measure of success. Thus, given the hierarchy of party secretaries that stretched in the past from the general secretary in the Kremlin to local secretaries, when production plans were not met, the blame traveled down the line of command and was directed, particularly, at the district secretaries. It was they who suffered most if plans were not fulfilled; their careers could be ruined and, at an earlier time, they faced even worse consequences. As a result, although theoretically they were primarily responsible for political matters, from Stalin forward they were not able to refrain from acting like absentee landlords, determined to manage all affairs, even though they were ignorant of on-the-farm conditions.

Typical must have been V. Korolkov, first secretary of the Piterskiy Rayon CPSU Committee in the Saratov area, who insisted in a 1989 interview, "We do not get into technological matters or engage in petty supervision" over the farms but then, in the face of contrary evidence, explained, "I am supposed to control. . . . [M]y intervention greatly speeds up the discussion. . . . The people have become accustomed to the old and firmly mastered procedures. Who in the rayon could make careless workers do that which they should? Only the party raykom [rayon party committee]."[46]

A brigade leader in the same region pointed out that his brigade council "does not even discuss any somewhat serious matter without 'running it by' the party group in advance, and without the group's agreement. . . . The party's influence is the party influence. It is the foundation," he explained.[47]

In a 1991 interview, Yuriy Chernychenko, USSR people's deputy, publicist, writer, and president of the new Russian Peasant party, said: "[A]t present, collective farms are just miserable fragments of the 'agroGULAG.' A hair cannot fall from the head of a cow without a resolution of the rayon party committee. . . . There are 230 million hectares of arable land in the USSR and all of it, to the last hectare, belongs to the CPSU."[48]

Undoubtedly, Gorbachev's call for "eliminating the existing administrative system" at the local level had its impact, but such changes were not intended to include district party secretaries, on whom his power ultimately rested. Surely, he knew well that Khrushchev, who on that score probably saw the problem even more clearly, made the mistake of firing more than half of the rayon party secretaries in the USSR and Ukraine in 1960–61.[49] Given the Soviet *nomenklatura* system (i.e., patron-client relationship), the fired party secretaries probably played an important role in Khrushchev's ouster in 1964.

In a major June 1987 speech on perestroika, Gorbachev stressed: "[I]t is the command-and-administer forms of managing society that are breaking our movement."[50] Furthermore, he repeated the call for decentralizing decision making and unleashing the initiative of the family farmers via the contract groups. Yet near the end of his long address, he stated, "Comrades, it is now especially necessary to increase party influence in all aspects of our work."

When it comes to practical matters at the local level, no better example of the built-in contradictions in Soviet socialism that impeded agricultural reform in the past can be found than in a passage in Gorbachev's March 1989 address. Although stressing the need to unleash local initiative, he addressed the "pressing" problem of food supply in several industrial centers, calling the situation "outrageous" and asking "Where are the party organizations and Communist managers?"[51]

As of mid-1992, there is important evidence that, at best, the old system of local administration in most of the newly independent republics will be dismantled only partially. Obviously, the party's overt monopoly over power has been destroyed. Nevertheless, the party potentially is by far the most powerful political group and, unless it is totally rooted out, the district party secretaries (or their state counterparts, answerable to a new higher leadership) will continue to thrive because without them the central leadership's levers of power would be disabled.

Academician Vladimir Tikhonov, a major proponent of agricultural privatization, was asked in 1988 if he was optimistic about the success of rural perestroika. Of course, he had to say yes, but the qualifications that he added at the end of the interview were most sobering. "The forces opposing perestroika are still considerable: [The] 18 million bureaucrats . . . objectively . . . cannot but oppose perestroika." Moreover, he concluded, "a change of at least two generations of leaders, i.e., practically twenty-five years will be needed."[52]

Subsequently, Tikhonov observed that "[a]t the present time, the government assumes that the introduction of leasing at kolkhozes and sovkhozes constitutes radical changes. This is a myth. It is an illusion. The leading of land and the economic independence of peasants at kolkhozes are impracticable."[53]

The land is formally assigned to a kolkhoz or sovkhoz, but under the old scheme only the state organs could establish the plan, the timing of planting and harvesting operations, and the prices. Thus, for all practical purposes, a peasant was "deprived completely of the opportunity of managing in an independent manner. . . . [T]he requirements for presenting economic independence to the peasants remain merely as unrealized slogans."[54]

Under the old scheme of things, a major obstacle to on-the-farm planning was the requirement to fulfill state-imposed purchase orders. According to much of the post-Soviet rhetoric, all such constrictions are to be removed. Not so in practice, however. According to the Russian Federation minister of agriculture, "[M]andatory contracting volumes are being established for output [of all farmers]: 25 percent for farming [crops]; 40 percent for animal husbandry (except meat and milk); and 50 percent for meat and milk. What is fundamentally new is that the purchases will be made at market prices."[55] Market-set prices would be new. There is much discussion, however, of the need to regulate prices for such crucial commodities as milk.

Given the enormous downgrading of the party due to the revolutionary events of 1991, in most of the republics, the power of the rayon party committees and, thus, that of the rayon party secretaries has been eliminated, at least on paper. In July 1991, however, I discussed the changing situation in the rural rayons with a Soviet professor of agricultural economics, whose primary interest is agrarian reform. I asked him what has happened to the deposed rayon party secretaries. He replied that for the most part, they have moved into rayon Soviet offices where they continue business as usual—for example, telling the kolkhozy and sovkhozy when and what to sow and when to reap.[56]

The actions of Russian Federation President Boris Yeltsin have confirmed the old adage that "the more things change, the more they stay the same." As he stated:

In every oblast now there is a presidentially appointed head of administration who has the power to appoint the heads of cities and rayons, right down to the most remote ones. They all form their own administration. . . . Their direct task is to promote the progress of the reforms, follow their course, and help the Russian Government and the president.[57]

In the words of a *Pravda* reporter, whatever their new titles, the nomenklatura are very much in business:

The life of private farmers in the Russian heartland is no sweeter: The agro-industrial monster is diligently stifling them. And the trail leads to the RSFSR Ministry of Agriculture and Food, where apparently the inveterate nomenklatura is running the show. The management system in the agro-industrial complex is still dictatorial. There is no sign of imminent land reform for this reason. Furthermore, ministerial officials have set traps for commercial structures. . . . In Russia as a whole the proportion of former party workers occupying local organs of power is between 30 and 90 percent.[58]

The following is but one example of the ways the local authorities resist those who choose to privatize:

Erich Liske, a private farmer from the north Russian city of Pskov, is suing the nearby collective farm for robbery. One morning he found out that all locks on his farm were broken and 140 calves and all farming vehicles stolen.

The collective farm authorities admit their blame, claiming they could not accept that a nearby private farmer, called "kulak" in Russia, could produce more than they did. And since they learned in school that the property of all kulaks was expropriated under the Bolshevik rule and the farmers were exiled to Siberia, they acted accordingly.[59]

As Alexandr Yakovlev, long-time adviser to Gorbachev, has observed:

A new nomenklatura is in the making. The same people, having failed to pay the bills presented to some by the electorate and to others by parliament, are going round the circle, changing their official positions. Old games are being played again by the old rules in Staraya Ploshchad (Old Square), in the former building of the CPSU Central Committee which now houses Russia's government.[60]

When a Dutch farmer who spent most of 1990 on a Soviet farm near Moscow was asked "What's wrong with our agriculture?" he answered, "A high official tells farmers what to do, and they have to obey him."[61] Again, whatever their new titles may be, off-the-farm officials are still in business as usual.

From the peasants' immediate point of view, however, a major reason that the lease scheme has faltered for those who have selected to follow such a route lies in the kolkhozy and sovkhozy themselves, according to a study conducted in the RSFSR:

Why hasn't the high level of effectiveness of lease contracts become one of the main forces of the agricultural branch? On what level, where, is the greatest opposition to the development of lease relations? On the oblast level? Rayon? Enterprise?

The answer turned out to be unanimous—on the level of the enterprise.

It is becoming clear that today the administration [on the kolkhozy and the sovkhozy] is utilizing the contract more often than not to confuse the lessee, to invalidate the essence of the lease and to deprive the individual of incentives for labor productivity.[62]

In the words of another observer of the rural scene, "[A]s a rule, leasing subdivisions remain completely at the mercy of kolkhoz and sovkhoz offices, which very reluctantly give up the methods of management to which they are used."[63]

Peasant Resistance to Private Farming

In his book, Gorbachev wrote that "everything depends upon the people." He noted further that "[a] drastic change must be made in social and political thought." And again, "One more conclusion—the most important one I would say—is that we should rely on the initiative and creativity of the masses; on the active participation of the widest sections of the population in the implementation of the reforms planned."[64]

Finally, spelling out the bottom line of his reforms, Gorbachev delivered the message again in a speech on "Socialism through Democratization" to the CPSU Central Committee: "[T]he key to everything is democratization. . . . Therefore, the aim of perestroika is mobilization of the human potential."[65]

As noted, Gorbachev was guided by the belief that the key to mobilizing the peasants is to make them the masters on the land. Although he did not say it, from the human point of view, what is needed is the restoration of a kulak class. As the rural sociologist and academician Tatyana Zaslavskaya stated in an interview, however, if the collective contract scheme is to be successful, production initiative must pass to the individual production groups. Unfortunately, as she observed:

[I]n seventy years of Soviet power, . . . sixty years . . . of state-run agriculture, generations have changed, and the people who today work in the kolkhozes and sovkhozes not only were never independent peasant farmers, but their parents were not independent peasants, and their grandparents even joined the kolkhozes. [Thus, the peasants lack the] psychological prerequisites [for the transition to private farming.] I have been to many kolkhozes and talked to many people . . . those . . . who dream of working individually . . . just do not exist.[66]

Yet Viktor Nikhonov, who held the agricultural portfolio on the politburo in the mid-1980s, reported that by 1987 the bulk of the farms had adopted the collective contract scheme.[67] What is not recorded is how many of the contracts existed only on paper and how many were abandoned after they were formed. As early as 1983, there were reports of contracts adopted by peasant workers only to be abandoned later for the former guaranteed minimum wage system.

Still, the mind-set of a people who went almost directly from tsarist serfdom to Stalinist state serfdom is the major obstacle to rural reform. Although the end of serfdom in 1861 freed the peasants politically, most did not abandon their communal ways. The Stolypin reforms under Nicholas II never really succeeded in the goal of creating a yeoman Russian farmer, and the NEP was only a brief interlude in a period of a thousand years during which entrepreneurial individual farming was discouraged, indeed largely prohibited. Old habits are difficult to break.

Not surprisingly, on a farm near Moscow, a family rebuilt a private hog operation three times, each time to be burned out by resentful neighbors.

Gorbachev knows about peasant apathy and resistance to change. Obviously, he listened to Tikhonov, Zaslavskaya, and their colleagues. As he said in his March 1989 speech, "Leasing is . . . received with caution by that part of collective farmers and workers who have lost, over many years, the habit of working conscientiously and got used to steady incomes irrespective of the end results of their work."[68]

In 1989, academician Tikhonov made the point even more strongly, indicating that only a small percentage of the peasants are willing to undertake full-scale private farming.

Over a period of 60 years, we have destroyed the social type of peasant and created something completely different. Initially, . . . he was a bonded worker with a plot of ground. But today he is a hired worker with a definite guaranteed wage. A peasant knows that, regardless of the results of his labor, he will receive his salary and one which will satisfy his minimum requirements. And the peasants do not wish to undertake the risk of receiving income based upon vague results of labor realized earlier. Studies [for example] conducted by my Siberian colleagues reveal that roughly [only] 20 percent of the peasants questioned by them are prepared to willingly undertake leases.[69]

Alexandr Yakovlev made the same point:

We have created a society that has the mentality of the lumpen. The lumpen only waits for other people to stuff something into his mouth, even if it is nothing but a beggar's pittance, as long as he has to do nothing in return. The most important thing for the lumpen is that he does not have to work. . . . Look, we are all a product of these old structures. . . . The old ways are in the genes of even the most democratic and progressive new leadership forces. They are used to ordering others around, they are used to permitting or prohibiting things. . . . In our minds, we are still the Bolsheviks of yesterday. The human psyche cannot be changed overnight. That takes time. . . .

Why is our agriculture unproductive? It is unproductive because half of all those who are employed in a kolkhoz are in the administration. They are all chiefs and hardly any of them really works.[70]

What then is one to make of the 1987 claim by Viktor Nikhonov that a majority of the farms had converted to the contract scheme?[71] Surely the answer lies in the findings of a USSR Academy of Sciences study. Many, probably most, of the leases have been only on paper.

According to academy surveys in "several" oblasts, "only 16 percent of the lessees polled entered into a lease on their own conviction." Further, another study by sociologists in Belorussia revealed that "72 percent of leasehold collectives in the republic were created at 'initiative from above.' Only 18 percent of those polled [in one oblast] turned out to be genuine leases."[72] Nor is it surprising to learn that "about 70 percent of the kolkhoz farmers and sovkhoz workers think that a new 'dekulakization' is possible."

When Stalin destroyed the kulaks during forced collectivization, he eliminated the nation's best farmers and, thus, those with entrepreneurial spirit and training.

A 1990 study of Russian Republic collective and state farm workers indicated that "[p]rivate ownership of land was advocated by [only] 17 percent and 12 percent respectively."[73]

A reading of the rhetoric of those in favor of conversion to leasing might lead to a conclusion that the privatization of agriculture is advancing. The number of peasant farms reached only 29,500, however, as of July 1, 1990. As one Soviet observer wrote, "Obviously, the independence of peasant farms has so far only been declared and does not exist in practice."[74] Indeed, in making his claim that by 1987 the majority of the farms had adopted the leasing scheme, Nikhonov admitted that each year a number of the contract groups are abandoned.

The truth is now out. Privatization has hardly made a dent in the rural scene. "As of 1 January 1991 there were [only] 40,600 peasant farms to which were assigned about 700,000 hectares of land [17.2 hectares each]." According to the same report, this in contrast with the fact that there are some 20 million workers on the kolkhozy and sovkhozy, cultivating nearly 210 million hectares.[75]

As the Report of the Committee for Farm and Food Policy of the USSR Supreme Soviet observed, "According to figures as of 15 April 1991, 55,400 peasant farms have been created in the country, and 1,463,800 hectares of land have been transferred to their possession and use." That is 26.4 hectares each. Further, given the various factors involved, the committee calculated that, under optimum conditions over the next three to four years, private possession of the land, including private plots, "could increase from 9 million to 40–45 million hectares, which is 7–8 percent of all the farmland in the country.)"[76] Given the evidence offered here, that is a most optimistic forecast.

Reading the lines and between them and taking into account Baltic history, this analyst believes that a widespread reestablishment of private farming in the now independent Baltic states is possible in the near future. No such prognostication is offered for Russia, Ukraine, and most of the other republics, however, whatever the new political configuration.

As noted, in Gorbachev's attempt to gain the benefits of private entrepreneurial initiative, he insisted that the Soviet Union could, indeed must, keep its socialist cake of collective and state farms. Not all internal observers of the rural scene agree with this view, however, a point underscored in an *Izvestia* editorial:

At thousands of collective and state farms living off state subsidies, the habit of living beyond their means for decades and producing less than they receive has led to the formation of the collective morality of an exploiter who lives off other people's labor. This is a harsh truth. But these tragedies have wiped the last greasepaint off the rosy assurances about the progressiveness of keeping leasing within the framework of the farms.[77]

Alarmingly, there is indication that the exodus from the countryside is accelerating. In many rural areas, there is a shortage of labor and, especially at harvest time, part of the army, along with numerous urban dwellers, has been needed to help bring in the harvest.

The results of a 1991 representative poll of rural inhabitants, 71.6 percent of whom work on kolkhozy and sovkhozy, are the following:

[A]bout 15 percent of the respondents said they had . . . intentions [to leave the country-side] and 3.3 percent had already firmly decided to do so. . . . [O]nly 9.9 percent of the respondents want their children to stay and work on collective farms. 14.4 percent want to see them become independent farmers, and 22.2 percent recommend that their children leave the countryside and get a job in the city. . . . [F]or every one respondent who has faith in the Union Law on Land, four believe it is likely to be repealed.[78]

During the spring and summer of 1989 two other pieces of evidence that surfaced indicate the depth of the resistance to private farming.

First, both academician Tikhonov and academician Zaslavskaya were elected as people's deputies to the new Congress of the USSR from the Moscow district. The new Supreme Soviet Council of the Union voted on May 27, however, to reduce the Moscow delegation from fifty-five to the required number of twenty-nine. Tikhonov and Zaslavskaya, among the most vocal and severe critics of the old agricultural system, were *the two most soundly defeated* by their fellow Supreme Soviet deputies—many of whom play important roles in the now-independent republics. The vote was for 591, against 1,558, for Zaslavskaya and for 630, against 1,519, for Tikhonov.[79]

Second, *Moscow News* in recent years has been extremely critical of the old agricultural scene, frequently running articles by, and interviews with, Tikhonov and Zaslavskaya. In June 1989, it featured the article "How They Stamped out a Farmer's Co-Op" subtitled "A Co-op in Novosibirsk was declared 'capitalist' and dissolved." Beyond describing how the local bureaucrats destroyed the farmer's co-op, the article included two tables. The first, reproduced here, reveals an increasingly negative attitude in recent years toward the essential elements of the agricultural reform. Table 4.2 summarizes the number of positive and negative articles about attitudes of state farms (state farm officials) to family farms, leaseholders and co-ops between 1986 and 1989, based on an examination of six national newspapers.

As shown in Table 4.2, whereas the 1986–1987 articles reflected overwhelming support for the key elements of Gorbachev's rural reforms, by 1988–1989 there had been a complete reversal, with more than half of the commentaries being negative, including nearly a three-to-one rejection of the crucial lease-holding scheme.

The second table listed the nine specific criticisms found in the articles and the number of times they were repeated. At the top of the list was "price of product and wages," twenty-one times; second was "lease requests denied and length of leases," eleven times; and third was "limited independence," ten times. Second from the bottom was "arson of farms and damage to equipment," three times.[80]

Table 4.2
Press Support for Rural Perestroika

	7/1/86 to 6/30/87		7/1/87 to 6/30/88		7/1/88 to 6/1/89	
	Positive	Negative	Positive	Negative	Positive	Negative
Family farm	17	0	10	4	2	3
Lease holding	1	0	9	4	13	30
Co-ops	0	0	2	3	7	13
Total:	18	0	21	11	22	46

Source: Alexandr Bekker, Moscow News no. 28, 1989.

Gorbachev repeatedly said that just throwing more rubles at agriculture, which was the essence of Brezhnev's food policies, will not solve the problem. Gorbachev placed his confidence in glasnost and perestroika to bring about the revolution from above. Glasnost would provide the knowledge because something cannot be fixed if one does not know what is broken, and perestroika would provide the necessary tools. Now, thanks to glasnost, everyone knows what is broken, but paper reforms seem unable to fix it.

Gorbachev placed his major wager to solve the food problem on making the peasants masters of the land by transforming the countryside into a private farming system, Soviet style. Alongside glasnost as a prime tool of perestroika, however, was democratization, with the clear implication that under the new order, the will of the people must be followed. Yet according to the surveys of public opinion reported here, the resistance to privatization remains enormous.

As numerous Soviet, and now republic, commentators have observed, an agrarian reform that would end the food crisis could not be isolated to the countryside alone. Furthermore, as demonstrated again and again in studies of the agricultural problems in the Third World, as important as land reform may be in itself, distribution of the land to those who farm it is never a solution in itself to a nation's food problems.[81]

Successful resolution of the food production problem in nations deficient in food availability and where the farmers have not been the masters of the land requires much more than land redistribution. Successful agrarian reform requires investment in the local infrastructure, new tools, and so on, most especially retraining the farmers. Thus, for example, where the "green revolution" succeeded in increasing food production in the Third World, the scientists who carried out the work discovered that the increased yields offered by the new seeds depended as much on education of the farmers in their cultivation as it did on planting the "miracle seeds" in the ground.

Realizing the full fruits of agrarian reform also requires a basic change in ᴴic relations and an end to off-the-farm rule of the farmers—in short, ₘₑₙₙₑ revolutionary changes in both society and the system.[82]

A CATALOG OF NEEDED AGRARIAN REFORMS

A catalog of seemingly insurmountable obstacles to satisfactorily resolving the food crisis in the former Soviet republics in any foreseeable future exists. Although the problem is rooted primarily in deeply ingrained attitudinal, organizational, and managerial habits and practices, there also are some enormous impediments in the economic realm, especially as related to the need for reinvestment and/or new investments in the food-agricultural complex, that are not easy to alleviate. Specifically, untold hundreds of billions of rubles are drastically needed, but probably impossible to obtain for years to come, to be invested in the food and agriculture infrastructure, including the following:

1. Producing or importing from abroad machines and equipment necessary for small-scale farming.
2. Building new homes and outbuildings required for individual farming.
3. Constructing roads, transportation, and storage facilities necessary to reduce the enormous losses of produce that now occur.

According to an estimate made by a Soviet farmer in 1989, to set up a private lease operation on 50–100 hectares the cost for machinery, buildings, and other capital expenses would "exceed 200,000" rubles.[83] In 1989, the estimated average annual income for each member of a kolkhoz family was 1,528 rubles.[84] An average family of four, making a total income of 6,112 rubles, would require thirty-three years of accumulation of this total annual income to establish such a private farm.

As discussed, the human impediments to fundamental change of the nature called for are even more formidable. What must be done to create a true market system along with a production system wherein the farmers feel that they truly are the masters of the land?

1. State orders, which continue to dictate what crops are to be cultivated and livestock to be husbanded, must be eliminated. In that regard, the rural bureaucracy that continues to dominate local decision making must be eliminated.
2. If the experiment in creating parliamentary systems is to succeed, thereby eliminating authoritarian rule, it must provide a means to allow peasant views to be genuinely heard and accounted for.
3. The peasants somehow must be convinced that their welfare would improve if the production responsibility were in their hands, even if this meant giving up the past guarantee of a minimum income and a place to live.
4. The peasants somehow must be convinced that, whether by long-term leases or by

outright purchase of the land, some future reconstituted authoritarian leadership will not reverse policy and take the land from them as was done at the end of the NEP.

5. The attitudes of the urban populace must somehow be changed to end its opposition to private farming.

6. The urban population somehow must be convinced that the creation of a market place for food will eventually result in lower food prices and end shortages, thus eliminating the need for rationing.

In 1989, Allan Mustard, who had served as U.S. agricultural attache in Moscow, noted in assessing the possibility that Gorbachev's rural perestroika would solve the food problem that "[t]he odds against Gorbachev are great, the obstacles many, and if one judges by Russian/Soviet history, his chances of success are virtually nil."[85] As we have seen, most all of the problems faced by Gorbachev have been inherited by the new republic leaders.

Indeed, in the fall of 1991, when Gorbachev conferred in Moscow with farmer representatives on ways to promote agrarian reform in the country, his observations underscored the dim future for agrarian reform. In the meeting,

Mr. Gorbachev admitted that the land reform had been grinding to a halt, with people in the rural areas obviously fearing to be left tête-à-tête with a free market. . . . He added that he no longer insisted on holding a national referendum on the private ownership of land, since it was a matter not to be decided by voting: the urban population might support the idea of private property and the rural residents reject it, or vice versa. The main thing was to ensure that the problem be decided not by the center but by the republics which would proceed from their specific living standards and economic practices.[86]

NOTES

1. *Soviet Studies*, October 1951. For an appraisal of Jasny's pioneering contributions to Soviet studies, see Betty A. Laird and Roy D. Laird, *To Live Long Enough: The Memoirs of Naum Jasny, Scientific Analyst* (Lawrence, Kans.: The University of Kansas Press, 1976), pp. x, 190.

2. Viktor Andriyanov, Oleg Kulish, and Vadim Raskin, "On the Main Point: Comradly, Frank Discussion between the Country's Leaders and Representatives of Labor Collectives," *Sel'skaya zhizn*, July 1991. FBIS-SOV-91–147, July 31, 1991.

3. S. Skorokhodov, "A Ration of Bread," *Sovetskaya rossiya*, March 28, 1991. JPRS-UEA-91–017, April 8, 1991.

4. V. Chernyak, doctor of economic sciences, Kiev, "Opinion of a Candidate for People's Deputy: Are Price Increases Inevitable," *Argumenty i fakty*, March 4–10, 1989. JPRS-UEA-89–018, June 26, 1989.

5. *World Grain Situation and Outlook*, circular series FG 6–91 (Washington, D.C.: U.S. Department of Agriculture, Foreign Agriculture Service, June 1991).

6. A. Klimenko, "There's a Question: Fleecing . . . the State," *Pravda*, June 11, 1991. FBIS-SOV-91–113, June 12, 1991.

7. V. A. Nikolayenko, "Supreme Soviet Committee Chairman Veprev Interviewed

on Agricultural Development," *Zemlya sibirskaya, Dalnevostochnaya*, May 1990. JPRS-UEA-90–030, August 24, 1990.

8. N. Borchenko, Gosplan Department head, "The Material-Technical Base of the Agroindustrial Complex: The Need for Structural Change and Qualitative Renewal," *Planovoye khozyaystvo*, June 1989, pp. 48–59.

9. V. Parvenov, "Roads for the Harvest," *Pravda*, July 6, 1990. JPRS-UEA-90–030, August 24, 1990.

10. *Ogonek*, no. 5, 1990; *Report on the USSR*, May 25, 1990.

11. Ibid.

12. All-Union Research Institute of the Trade Conditions and Population Demand for Consumer Goods, estimate, and USSR State Committee for Statistics, preliminary estimate, *Moscow News*, no. 10, 1989.

13. Vladimir Tikhonov, "Land for the Peasants," *Yunost*, October 1989. JPRS-UPA–90–001. "Comparison of U.S. Soviet Living Standards," *SSHA: Ekonomika, Politika, Ideologiya*, December 1988, pp. 12–22. JPRS-USA-89–007, April 14, 1989.

14. Soviet Business Report," *Interfax*, October 2, 1991. FBIS-SOV-91–194, October 7, 1991.

15. Lyudmila Aleksandrova, TASS, October 30, 1991. JPRS-SOV–91–211, October 31, 1991.

16. "Soviet Business Report," *Interfax*, January 21, 1992. FBIS-SOV-92–104, January 22, 1991.

17. Igor Agabekov, TASS, January 24, 1992. FBIS-SOV-92–017, January 27, 1992.

18. TASS, February 3, 1992. FBIS-SOV-92–023, February 4, 1992.

19. Moscow Central Television, January 23, 1992. FBIS-SOV-92–026, February 7, 1992.

20. "The Food Market," *Izvestia-Interfax*, February 8, 1992. FBIS-SOV-92–030, February 13, 1992.

21. "Economist-Deputies on Radical Economic Reform," *Voprosy ekonomiki*, no. 9, 1989. *The Soviet Review*, July–August 1990.

22. Andrei Sizov, "Smaller Harvests Create Imports for 1991," *Moscow News*, no. 8, 1991.

23. TASS, June 11, 1991. FBIS-SOV-91–113, June 12, 1991.

24. N. Shmelev, "Where I See an Opportunity for Salvation," *Izvestia*, March 30, 1991. JPRS-UEA-91–017, April 8, 1991.

25. *Interfax*, July 2, 1991. FBIS-SOV-91–128, July 3, 1991. In December, after the harvest was completed, the USDA estimate of total Soviet grain production was only 175 million metric tons. See *World Grain Situation and Outlook*, circular series FG 12–19 (Washington, D.C.: United States Department of Agriculture, Foreign Agricultural Service, December 1991).

26. "Not the First Round of Aid," *Moscow News*, February 23–March 1, 1992.

27. Yevgeniya Pishchikova, "They Might Not Even Sow," *Rossiyskaya gazeta*, March 13, 1992. FBIS-SOV-92–053, March 18, 1992.

28. "Peasants Hoarse from Shouting," *Pravda*, March 12, 1992. FBIS-SOV-92–053, March 18, 1992.

29. Sergey Zhigalov, "Man with Gun in Stockyard," *Izvestia*, March 18, 1992. FIBS-SOV-92–054, March 19, 1992.

30. "Interfax Business Report," *Interfax*, March 9, 1992. FBIS-SOV-92–049, March 12, 1992.

31. "Business Report," *Interfax*, April 23, 1992. FBIS-SOV-92–080, April 24, 1992.

32. Radio Kiev, March 4, 1992. FBIS-SOV-92–045, March 6, 1992.

33. Moscow Radio Rossii, March 11, 1992. FBIS-SOV-92–059, March 26, 1992.

34. Mikhail Gorbachev, *Perestroika: New Thinking for Our Country and the World*. (New York: Harper and Row, 1987), pp. 55–59.

35. Mikhail Gorbachev, *On the Agrarian Policy of the CPSU in the Present Conditions*, Report . . . at the Plenary Meeting of the CPSU Central Committee, March 15–16, 1989 (Moscow: Novosti Press Agency, 1989), p. 25.

36. Ibid., p. 3.

37. Ibid., p. 11.

38. *Izvestia*, March 7, 1990.

39. *Pravda*, April 5, 1988.

40. Roy D. Laird, "Perestroika and Agriculture," *Problems of Communism*, November-December 1987, pp. 81–86.

41. "Politics," *Postfactum*, December 28, 1991. FBIS-SOV-91–250, December 30, 1991.

42. *Postfactum*, December 28, 1991.

43. *Sel' skaya zhizn*, January 7, 1992. JPRS-UEA-92–002, January 17, 1992. Interview with Viktor Nikolayevich Khlystun, Russian Federation minister of agriculture.

44. *Moscow Mayak Radio Network*, January 30, 1992. FBIS-SOV-92–021, January 31, 1992.

45. Gorbachev, *On the Agrarian Policy*, p. 33.

46. A. I. Leshchevskiy, *Kommunist*, October 4, 1989, pp. 40–45.

47. Ibid.

48. Vitaliy Korniyenko, "Party of the Peasant House," *Molod Ukrayiny*, October 25, 1990. JPRS-UEA-91–004, January 23, 1991.

49. Alexandr Yanov, *The Drama of the Soviet 1960s: A Lost Reform* (Berkeley: University of California Institute of International Studies, 1984), p. 75.

50. *Pravda*, June 26, 1987.

51. Gorbachev, *On the Agrarian Policy*, p. 40.

52. *Moscow News*, February 1988.

53. Ibid.

54. "Vladimir Tikhonov: Land for the Peasants," *Yunost*, October 1989. JPRS-UEA–90–001.

55. *Izvestia*, December 31, 1991. JPRS-UEA-92–002, January 17, 1992. Interview with Viktor Nikolayevich Khlystun, Russian Federation minister of agriculture.

56. A private conversation in July 1991 with Professor Vladimir M. Yefimov, USSR Academy of National Economy Agribusiness Department.

57. A. Lugovskaya, "Boris Yeltsin: Rapid Reforms Are Russia's Only Chance," *Izvestia*, November 30, 1991. FBIS-SOV-91–233, December 4, 1991.

58. S. Razin, "But There Is a Long Way to Go," *Komsomolskaya pravda*, October 19, 1991. JPRS-UEA-91–041, November 25, 1991.

59. "They Come to Steal," TASS, December 6, 1991. FBIS-SOV-91–238, December 11, 1991.

60. Alexandr Yakovlev, "Seven Ds or How Many Steps We Must Make into the Future," *Moscow News*, January 5–12, 1992.

61. "Dutch Farmers Make Points on Soviet Farm," *Moscow News*, no. 8, 1991.

62. I. Yelistratove, "Leasing through the Eyes of the People's Control Committee,"

Sovetskaya rossiya, March 14, 1989. A study by the RSFSR KNK, People's Control Committee.

63. V. Nefedov, "In the Vise of the 'Coverage,' " *Sovetskaya rossiya*, October 18, 1989. JPRS-UEA-89–040, December 20, 1989.

64. Gorbachev, *Perestroika*, pp. 44, 48, 76.

65. *Pravda*, May 11, 1988.

66. Bohdan Nahaylo, "Interview with Tatyana Zaslavskaya," Radio Free Europe: Radio Liberty, RL 365/87.

67. *Sel'skaya zhizn*, January 25, 1987.

68. Gorbachev, *On the Agrarian Policy*, p. 26.

69. Vladimir Tikhonov, "Land for the Peasants," *Yunost*, October 1989.

70. Vienna ORD Television Network, December 3, 1991. FBIS-SOV-91–234, December 5, 1991.

71. *Sel'skaya zhizn*, March 25, 1987.

72. A. Moregachev, "Does the Peasant Need Emancipation," *Sel'skaya zhizn*, October 12, 1989. Interview with the director of the Institute for Socioeconomic Problems in the Agroindustrial Complex, USSR Academy of Sciences.

73. "What People Are Talking About: Enough Shows, Give Us Bread!" *Pravda*, November 27, 1990. CDSP, January 9, 1991.

74. V. G. Pinegin. " 'Course of Perestroika' Rubric: 'How to Carry Out Land Reform? (Notes from the VASKHNIL Meeting),' " *Zemledeliye*, December 1990. JPRS-UEA–91–011.

75. "The USSR Economy in 1990," *Ekonomika i zhizn*, January 1991. FBIS-SOV-91–023, February 4, 1991. *SSSR v tsifrakh v 1989 godu*, pp. 234, 247, 249.

76. "On Realization of the Bases of Legislation of the USSR and the Union Republics on Land and on Progress in Land Reform," *Delovoy Mir*, June 22, 1991.

77. *Izvestia*, January 5, 1990.

78. Liliya Babayeva, "Land: Why no Takers?" *Moscow News*, no. 11, 1991.

79. *Izvestia* stenographic coverage of the Congress' sessions. An extensive translation of the condensed version of the debate is presented in *The Current Digest of the Soviet Press*, June 21 and 28 and July 5 and 12, 1989.

80. Alexander Bekker, *Moscow News*, no. 28, 1989.

81. For a discussion of the requisites of genuine agrarian reform, see, for example, Roy D. Laird and Betty A. Laird, "Food Policies of Governments," in *Dimensions of World Food Problems*, ed. E. R. Duncan (Ames: The Iowa State University Press, 1978), pp. 233–249.

82. Ibid.

83. N. Avdeyev, "Do Not Call Me to the Homestead," *Pravda*, November 13, 1989. JPRS-UEA-89–041, December 21, 1989.

84. I. Kukhar, "Kolkhozes in a Multi-Layered Economy," *Sel'skaya zhizn*, March 15, 1991. JPRS-UEA-91–027, May 31, 1991.

85. Allan Mustard, "Ruminations on Gorbachev's Agricultural Policy, or Two years Observing Perestroyka," *Newsletter for Research on Soviet and East European Agriculture*, March 1989, pp. 2–3.

86. *Interfax*, October 4, 1991. FBIS-SOV-91–194, October 7, 1991.

5

HOMO-SOVIETICUS: THE CRISIS
OF THE MIND

In March 1992, a citizen of Archangel, Russia, told a Western reporter the following joke: "Here we have two paths to development: reality and fantasy. . . . Reality would be if Martians came down and did everything for us, . . . Fantasy would be if we managed to do everything ourselves."[1]

The Soviet Union has been cast into the trash bin of history. In 1992, and for the foreseeable future, its bequest is fifteen sovereign republics, all of which are in a state of catastrophe, engaged in a momentous struggle between forces for fundamental economic, political, and social reform and those that resist such change. The obvious question arises: Which of the forces seems to be most powerful? In searching for an answer to that question, we cannot overstate that the mind-set of the people, the leaders, and most especially the masses more than anything else will determine the future of the new central Eurasian states.

Of course, the limitations of social sciences are such that predicting the future course of nations and societies is always a precarious enterprise. For example, in the early 1980s, no Sovietologist of repute foresaw the fatal convulsion that was to grip the Soviet Union by the end of the decade. Be that as it may, information about forces that will shape the future, which previously was unavailable, is now out in the open, deserving careful attention.

Therefore, this analyst has devoted many months to searching the Soviet and post-Soviet communications media for measures of the physical state of affairs (i.e., gross national product, standards of living and, especially, clues to attitudes, beliefs, and values that can be expected to shape the people's behavior in the foreseeable future. Specifically, based on the assumption that more than any other force, people make their own history, most of the effort has been devoted to identifying and appraising the nature and depth of the support for, and resistance to, needed fundamental change.

Given the approach of the analysis, most of what follows depends on an interpretation of public opinion surveys. As such, the author is very much aware that opinion polls must always be read with great skepticism. For example, in mid-1992, the most recent reminder of how misleading such measures can be is the outcome of the April 1992 British elections. The polls indicated that Labour would win or, at least, there would be a hung parliament. Instead, the Conservatives were returned to office with a solid, but reduced, majority that ensures their rule for another five years. Such failures in reading the voters' intent are not proof that such surveys are worthless, however. Repeated polls revealing that the overwhelming majority of the citizens of the former Soviet Union view their situation as desperate, yet are not psychologically prepared to accept needed changes cannot be ignored.

All of the evidence is not in. On the basis of present survey analysis, however, one may conclude first that roots of the ever-worsening crises inherited by the former Soviet republics are deeply planted in the minds of the leaders and, especially, a people born of seventy-four years of Soviet rule. Second, if that finding is valid, and the assumption that individuals and, collectively, nations strongly resist challenges to deeply entrenched values also is true, then one can safely predict that, at best, the catastrophe bequeathed by the Soviet experience will take, at best, many years to resolve. Third, as a corollary to the second conclusion, the longer the crises continue, the louder will be calls for emergency measures and, thus, most probably, some form of authoritarian rule in the newly independent republics will prevail for years to come. Fourth, although the rise of strongly anticommunist regimes cannot be ruled out, a wholesale abandonment of the asserted verities of Marxism-Leninism seems unlikely.

The preceding conjectures are supported not only by an extensive analysis of Soviet public opinion but also by an awareness of tsarist-Soviet history—for example, a millennium of unbroken authoritarian rule. Further, the words and actions of the individuals and groups currently contending for leadership and power support these predictions. Most important of all, however, is the mind-set of the people unveiled by the advent of glasnost, which, after years of darkness, has opened up a window into the souls of the people.

In his attempt to achieve perestroika, Gorbachev in effect called for the release of information that would result in the creation of a Soviet value system akin to what has been identified in the West as the Protestant work ethic. The hope was to unleash the creative initiative of the masses. Unfortunately, however, the evidence is that the desire of the people to captain their own destiny was, and still is, largely lacking. A school teacher in Moldavia asked Gorbachev: ''Do you think it is easy to wake up a nation . . . lulled to sleep for decades? Do you think it is easy to promote initiative when many people have to look up the meaning of this word in the dictionary?''[2] The question surely identifies the greatest obstacle of all that blocks the attempt to unravel the Gordian knot bequeathed by the Soviet Union.

The weighty baggage of old Soviet socialist values and behavior and the deepening mood of despair fuel a mounting call for desperate (thus authoritarian) solutions. Obviously, any attempt to test the winds of change must include a sounding of the mood of the people as influenced by the more tangible indicators of the nation's health—for example, measures of economic performance, the crime rate, and the physical well-being of the population. How then, at the beginning of the 1990s, do the former Soviet masses view their lot? What are their hopes and fears for the future? Most importantly, are they prepared to make the changes, often sacrifices, necessary to eliminate the social and economic crises that brought the Soviet Union to self-destruction?

Until recent years, any attempt to divine the mind-set of Homo-Sovieticus depended largely on anecdotal evidence, informed appraisal by outside observers, and interviews with emigrants from the Soviet Union. Prior to the glasnost era, the "index" of forbidden fruits of knowledge, under the supervision of GLAV-LIT (Chief Administration of Literary and Publishing Affairs), ensured that any internal appraisal of Soviet affairs was always positive. Anything that cast a negative light on the Soviet Union was suppressed as not being fit to print. That is no longer the case, and, as a result, public morale has plummeted. Two pieces from the Soviet press in the final years of the Union reflect the frustration of the masses.

A group of youngsters at a rally held this banner: "Let's catch up with and surpass Africa." This may be their ironic way of stating the sad fact that the USSR's economy is slipping to the level of a developing country.[3]

Poignantly but eloquently, an essayist for *Literary Gazette* has written:

In order to understand what we are missing, in order to understand what human hands can do, in order to understand what the earth gives us, our people should tape a four-hour TV program in a [U.S.] supermarket. This most military of military secrets should be exposed. It isn't a secret anymore. We should stop playing imagination games and look at just what they sell in an American store. It's the only thing that can shake up our people; it's the only thing that will give them confidence in themselves. It will not break them or amaze them. Our tourists behave differently: some cry, some faint, some try to hang themselves, some don't want to leave. There's nothing special there—just everything. Absolutely everything that we know, heard, read somewhere, saw in pictures.[4]

At least as early as May 1989, Gorbachev was aware of the serious deterioration in public morale. In that connection, it is appropriate to repeat here his words in the speech to the Soviet Congress in which he attempted to "dispel the illusion" that he was not aware of the mood of the people: "I even know about the following instance: Veterans riding the last bus in Moscow carried with them some 'visual aids'—Brezhnev's portrait covered with medals and Gorbachev's portrait covered with ration coupons."[5]

Now everyone knows nearly everything. Glasnost has brought forth an abundance of measures of the woeful state of affairs inherited from the failed Soviet experiment, not only measures of deplorable economic performance and social welfare but also a plethora of public opinion polls that bare the tormented soul of Homo-Sovieticus. As a result, in recent years students of Soviet affairs, and now post-Soviet affairs, have had an embarrassment of measures of values, attitudes, and goals with which to appraise the changing scene.

At this time of national convulsion, what do the citizens of the former Soviet Union believe in? What do they want? If change is imperative to ending the crises inherited from the old system, what changes are the people and the leaders prepared to make?

As expected, the polls reveal a complex society whose members hold a considerable disparity of views. The myth of a contented people happily marching in step to a communist utopia has been totally destroyed. Perhaps the greatest commonality is dourness. Indeed, for more of the people in the republics than not, there seems to be a sense that doomsday is near at hand.

Near the end of the Soviet experiment in building communism (April 1991), sociologist and academician Tatyana Zaslavsakay painted the following picture:

The gap between policy and social expectations is more dangerous today than ever before. It will only add to the radicalization of both right- and left-wing forces in society. In the absence of a stable political center the hopes of achieving consensus may be finally extinguished. . . .

Our polls have demonstrated that 60 percent of the people feel uncertainty about the future. Over 50 percent expect mass unemployment, 40 percent—famine, a third—the stoppage of railways. . . . First-mentioned were concern and uncertainty, with malice and aggressiveness coming second, and terror—third.[6]

A month before, in a longer article, she summarized the most important characteristics of current Soviet public opinion as follows:

[There is] social pessimism: disappointment with the actual results of perestroika, and a loss of confidence in its rapid success; frustration as manifested in deep concern over events taking place, alarm, weariness, a lack of confidence in the future, and the expectation of all sorts of disasters (inflation, monetary reform, economic catastrophe, nationwide famine and civil war); suspicion and aggression as the reverse side of that alarm, widespread perceptions of "plots by secret enemies" (of perestroika, democracy, the Russian people," the CPSU and so on), heightened attention to "who is to blame," and a desire to immediately punish the "culprits"; a profound value and moral vacuum resulting from the collapse of communist ideology and the destruction of traditional Soviet values, such as the belief in Soviet society's "great historical mission" in building communism; the grandeur, power and security of the Soviet "empire," and its economic and military power; heroic labor "for the benefit of the motherland" and "without regard for recompense"; a constant readiness to work to accomplish great feats and to stoically endure daily hardship; scorn for material benefits, comsumerism, and so forth; a return to previously rejected religious and moral values, the growing authority of various religions, the attraction of all manner of mysterious phenomena and mysticism for a sizable number of people; paternalism and egalitarianism that date back to our communal mentality; these traits flourished in the nutrient medium of "real socialism" and are nourished today by people's poverty and depressed situation. Outspoken and aggressive envy of the status of any groups that are materially well off, and especially if they enjoy privileges. The view that people's material prosperity is a direct index of their dishonesty, in the form of involvement in the shadow economy, the appropriation of unearned income, and so on.[7]

As discussed previously, perhaps the greatest human impediment to building a better future for the people of the former Soviet Union lies in the very low level of civil consciousness; they are a people who "believe in a state society, not a civil society."[8] That observation is substantiated by the public opinion surveys.

In a 1989 nationwide survey, those polled were asked:

What about responsibility to society? According to the sociologists' data, this problem is of concern to only 28.6% of workers and 28.2% of executives. . . . Only 14.7% and 17.7%, respectively, of those polled are seriously interested in our social policy. . . . Only half of the respondents to the questionnaire are concerned about problems of morality, and a third about questions of family relations.[9]

In a Congress speech a few years ago, a young Ukrainian deputy said:

I am pained by ration coupons in the seventy-second year of Soviet power, I am pained by the breakdown of the economy, by the ravaged countryside, by the sometimes barbarous relations between nationalities, by the rivers without fish and by the cities with chemical smog. . . .

But what hurts the most is that you older comrades, our fathers and grandfathers, haven't left us young people any acceptable ideals on which we can build our life, toward which we can strive, for which we can fight and which we can instill in young people.[10]

A 1990 editorial in a Russian journal contained the following passages:

It is difficult to cite any other period in our Homeland's past when our national dignity and our national pride were reviled with frank sadism.

The rubbing of "blank spots" in our history until they become "black holes" is aimed at instilling a persistent inferiority complex in Russians and all Soviet people. . . .

Bureaucrats, both central and local, and corrupted elements are heightening social tension. Crime has spilled out into the streets and permeates the sphere of production and distribution. It now threatens the safety of every person and is giving rise to an atmosphere of fear in society. . . .

The fatherland is in danger! That is the sober and honest conclusion to be drawn from an analysis of what is going on.[11]

On more than one occasion, Gorbachev referred to the dour state of mind among the Soviet people. For example:

We cannot help but see that . . . uneasiness is growing in society. People are reacting badly to shortages, to the waiting in lines that take up time, and frankly, are humiliating to people. People perceive this situation as a gap between word and deed, as a discrepancy between promises and the real changes in life.[12]

Table 5.1
Public Trust in Institutions

	Trust completely	Trust	Not very much	Don't trust
Church	17.5	46.8	24.1	4.8
Green movement	12.9	41.6	16.3	8.5
Armed Forces	12.3	44.1	33.9	8.0
Judiciary	2.0	18.3	52.1	20.7
Government	4.0	24.3	42.1	22.5
CPSU (The Party)	5.4	33.4	37.0	17.3
Young Communist League	2.8	23.5	38.0	28.4
Trade Unions	3.8	33.4	39.4	18.7
Militia	3.0	19.9	53.3	20.5

Source: <u>Moscow</u> <u>News</u>, no. 22, 1990.

One senses that among the very few optimists who live in the former USSR, and among most well-wishers without, there is a belief that since some changes (e.g., to a parliamentary democracy and a market system) seem so self-evident, they surely will be realized because the people innately want them. Unfortunately, the evidence offered here does not support such a sanguine conclusion. Specifically, public opinion surveys strongly support the observation that more than seven decades of Communist rule have deeply embedded many Marxist-Leninist-Stalinist values in the psyche of most of the people.

True, far from all of the myths that bind the people together are of Marxist-Leninist origin. For example, according to a 1990 public opinion poll of Muscovites (Table 5.1) jointly conducted by the Houston-based Institute of Sociological Research with the USSR Academy of Sciences, the respondents placed the church at the top of the list of institutions enjoying their trust.

Still, the lessons taught during seventy-four years of Communist rule are not easily erased. Even though confidence in Gorbachev's leadership plummeted during his final years in office, in his 1990 speech on the occasion of the seventy-third anniversary of the 1917 revolution, he expressed a view that was shared, and probably still is, by most citizens when he said, "[O]ur October Revolution [was] the greatest revolution of the twentieth century, unequaled in scope and impact on people's destiny. The values that the socialist revolution brought the masses of the people are everlasting."[13] Certainly those values were hammered into the minds of every Soviet person from the cradle to the grave.

One of the most astounding and sobering indicators of the depth that Soviet communist values have penetrated popular thinking was revealed in a 1990

Table 5.2
Public Sympathy or Antipathy for Remembered 1917 Leaders

Sympathy?		Antipathy?
27	Bukharin	3
41	Dzerzhinsky	7
5	Kerensky	18
4	Kolchak	21
64	Lenin	8
10	Makhno	18
3	Milyukov	5
5	Nikholas II	10
7	Stalin	50
15	Trotsky	12
13	Hard to say	22

Source: "The Russian Revolution: As Judged by Its Descendants," Moscow News, no. 44, 1990.

nationwide poll by the All-Union Center for the Study of Public Opinion of 1,848 persons in seventeen regions of the country. Under the rubric of heroes and villains, the respondents were given a list of prominent personalities of the time of the revolution and asked to indicate which of the names evoked the greatest sympathy and which the greatest antipathy (Table 5.2).

The respondents were allowed to choose more than one person. That Lenin was ranked first is no great surprise, but Dzerzhinsky's strong second is most sobering for anyone harboring hope that the people are mentally prepared to abandon their authoritarian shackles. He, of course, was the founder of the CHEKA, the extraordinary commission that imposed rule by terror. That the response was no fluke was underscored by the respondents' answer to another question in the poll.

The question called for an evaluation of the creation of the extraordinary commission and its being given the broadest rights. As shown in Table 5.3, the response in percentage terms was 51 percent in favor of the Cheka.

The evidence that the Leninist past is deeply, and positively, embedded in the minds of the masses is strong. For example, as noted previously, the Moscow branch of the Soviet Center for Public Opinion and Market Research (VCIOM) on September 14–15, 1991, randomly polled 2,302 people (Table 5.4). The question was: "If Lenin's body is buried [in St. Petersburg according to his wish], what should we do with the Mausoleum?" Sixty-six percent said "leave it."

If the future of a nation belongs to its youth, what do today's youth foresee for tomorrow? In a representative national poll, 7,730 young people were asked, "Toward what social system is humanity headed over the long term?" While only 8.4 percent replied "communism," 48 percent said a "mixture of socialism and communism." Only 13 percent said "capitalism," and 31 percent replied "I do not know."[14]

A University of Kansas Ph.D. candidate spent most of the summer of 1991

Table 5.3
In Retrospect Was the CHEKA Necessary?

```
51 there was a need for this
23 this was unnecessary
23 hard to say
```

Source: "The Russian Revolution: As Judged by Its Descendants,"
Moscow News, no. 44, 1990.

Table 5.4
What Should Be the Fate of Lenin's Mausoleum?

```
Leave it      66%
Remove it     20%
Don't know    14%"
```

Source: Moscow News, no. 39, September 29-October 6, 1991.

in the Soviet Union in advanced Russian language training, which brought him
into close contact with Soviet university students. One of the strongest impres-
sions the Kansas student received was how deeply collectivist behavior had
penetrated the psyche of his Soviet counterparts. As he told this author on his
return to the university in the fall of 1991, they were reluctant to take individual
initiative. Whatever they did was group determined. Were they representative
of the new leaders who are destined to guide the Commonwealth of Independent
States—or whatever system(s) arises from it—into the future?

Such an observation on the behavior of Soviet students in 1991 would hardly
surprise Professor Urie Bronfenbrenner. In the 1960s, in an unprecedented col-
laboration between U.S. and Soviet academies of science, he and his colleagues
were able to conduct extensive empirical studies comparing attitudes and behavior
of junior high youth in the USSR, the United States, and several West European
nations. The major finding of the work was that Soviet youth, compared with
that of other countries, reflected a high degree of collective behavior. Peer
pressure, not individual initiative, dominated.[15]

As widely reported, confidence in the Gorbachev leadership declined precipitously. Although there are no reliable pre-1985 polls to tell us what the attitude
of the people was toward the party then, there are ample indicators that today
the masses are highly critical of its past performance. Yet the gauges of opinion
on the establishment (i.e., party and government leaders) provide a mixed message. Table 5.5 summarizes the results of a nationwide poll taken during July
1990.

Not too surprisingly, most of the respondents would not like for their offspring
to be party members. After all, the vast majority of the population were not
members. More revealing, however, is that with all of the recent revelations of
the party's past sins, a plurality disagreed with the proposition that the CPSU

Table 5.5
The CPSU: People's View

	Agree	Disagree	Hard to say
Do you agree that the CPSU must be made responsible for all of its errors over the 70 years of Soviet rule?	74	15	11
Do you agree with those who say the CPSU should be disbanded?	31	41	28
	Yes	No	Can't say
Would you like your children (grandchildren) to be members of the CPSU?	15	54	31
	Positive	Negative	Can't say
What is your attitude towards the growing criticism of Mikhail Gorbachev?	64	19	17
What is your attitude towards the growing criticism of the USSR government?	75	9	16

Source: A national poll conducted by the All-Union Center for the Study of Public Opinion, July 7-17, 1990, reported in <u>Moscow News</u>, no. 30, 1990.

should be abandoned. That finding is supported by the responses to another 1990 poll (Table 5.6) to which the respondents were asked to identify who is "primarily responsible" for the continuing crisis. Since the column in the table adds up to more than 100, some of the respondents obviously felt the responsibility to indict more than just one group.

If the party is down but not totally out in the minds of the people, what about their faith in, hope for, and support of a possible transformation to an open, pluralistic, democratic system?

In a 1989 survey of 2,462 Soviet people from seventeen provinces in sixteen republics, only 31 percent said they believed that the new parliament "will be able to alter the course of our history. . . . Half (52 percent) of the respondents take a doubtful view of this possibility."[16]

During 1990, the attitude toward the new Soviet governmental institutions drastically deteriorated. As reported in *Izvestia*: "[I]n March [1990] 30 percent of those polled in a survey still believed in the possibilities of the Soviets, while in July that figure was only 11 percent." Commenting on the findings, the *Izvestia* journalist wrote:

[S]ociety has entered a very risky phase of development. In essence we have a threefold crisis of power. First the process of peeling the Party skin off state mechanisms is proceeding slowly and painfully. . . . Second, . . . political institutions created after restructuring began are also in a state of crisis. Third, . . . a crisis of the Soviets as a system of power has begun and is deepening.[17]

Table 5.6
Who Is Responsible for the Crisis?

Today one often hears it said that the country is in a state of crisis. Who do you believe are primarily responsible for this?	
The country's former leaders	37
The present-day party leadership	29
The CPSU as a whole	17
Ministries and government departments	12
The people as a whole	11
Ideologues of socialism	11
Ideologues of the `shadow economy'	7
Extremists and nationalists	6
Others	1
Hard to say	6

Source: _Moscow News_, no. 21, 1990.

In a 1989 national survey, [only] 26 percent of the polled say that there must be no subjects closed for discussion.''[18] So much for support for a truly free press.

Indeed, glasnost was not accompanied by either First Amendment guarantees of press freedom or sunshine laws. In the heat of the debate in the Second Congress of the new Supreme Soviet over the 1989 bloodletting in Nagorno-Karabakh, Georgy Arbatov, director of the Institute for the Study of the USA and Canada and Congress deputy, said:

[T]he passions that are flaring up here [are most troubling]. I can imagine what will happen in [Azerbaijan and Armenia] and Nagorno-Karabakh when all this is shown on television. I propose that the whole part of the debate involving Nagorno-Karabakh, Armenia and Azerbaijan not be shown on television. The same should be done in the future with respect to all nationality-related questions.[19]

The proposal passed 1,437 for, 443 against, and 95 abstentions.[20]

In mid-January 1991, a random telephone survey of Muscovites was taken by a group working for the RSFSR Supreme Soviet during the height of bloodletting events in the Baltic republics. As compared to a similar survey taken a year earlier, the 1991 survey revealed a growing disenchantment with the nascent move to democratic ways. The following is a summary of the findings:

The growing dissatisfaction of the population with the democrats, who have not been able to halt the deterioration of the situation in the country; a reduction in the ratings of all leading figures, including the recent idols; deep disappointment with the activity of the parties and movements that recently developed; appearance of a significant social basis for the possible establishment of an authoritarian regime.[21]

According to the Moscow poll, in November 1990, 20 percent agreed with the proposition that order should be quickly established, having halted democracy and glasnost, contrasted with 39 percent who responded in January 1991 in favor of establishing authoritarian order.[22]

A year earlier, in a speech to the February 1990 Central Committee Plenum, Central Committee member and Ambassador to Poland V. I. Brovikov said:

[R]estructuring . . . in less than five years has plunged the country into the abyss of a crisis and has brought it to a point at which we have come face to face with a rampage of anarchy, the degradation of the economy, the grimace of general ruin and a decline in morals. In this situation, to claim that the people are "for" all this, that it pleases them is politically indecent, to say the least. The people are against this, and they are saying so more and more loudly.[23]

If Gorbachev is right that all efforts to end the economic crisis inherited from the USSR will fail if the people's attitude toward their work cannot be changed, what then are their attitudes about work and related matters, especially the creation of a market economy through privatization?

Published studies indicate that popular support for moving toward the private sector is limited, unstable, and declining. "In January 1990 the idea of developing that sector had the support of 59 percent, while in March [of that year] this number was 57 percent and in May and June approximately one-half of those surveyed."[24]

Moreover, when asked questions concerning issues that affected their pocketbooks, consumers have been even more skeptical of a move to a market economy. In another national poll, 55 percent of the respondents said they would "agree to have smaller earnings in exchange for easier work or a guarantee of their condition's stability. And only 37 percent would like to earn well [more] by working their hardest. Only 7.3 percent favor lifting all bans on enterprise and all 'ceilings' on wages, and [only] 24 percent deem it necessary to revive independent farming."[25]

In the words of one Soviet writer, "Wage leveling . . . has impregnated all the cells of society and has become deeply rooted in mass consciousness. For decades we had a lenient attitude toward loafers and clods and redistributed in their favor what sloggers earned."[26] As another observer wrote, "[T]he people are not prepared to abandon [wage] equalization all of a sudden, although many of them are displeased with it. We shall need a rather lengthy period of psychological adaptation."[27]

A psychological stereotype is said to exist, rooted in the Soviet past and strengthened over the years. It goes as follows: "I would rather die than let *him* live better than *I* do. The fact that *he* was more talented and that *he* could invent something for the general good, something which no one else could do, was unimportant."[28]

According to still another survey, "70 percent of those polled associate the higher cost of living, cheaper goods being washed out of trade and finally the sharp growth in crime with the appearance of the cooperatives."[29] The co-ops are synonymous in the mind of most former Soviet people with private enterprise. Moreover, there is a widespread belief that the co-ops are controlled by the mafia (co-op owners).

In 1990, the average salary of co-op workers was reported to be about 500 rubles per month, as compared to salaries of 240 rubles, in state-run industry and incomes of 196 collective farmers.[30] Given their wage-leveling mentality, most people regard the incomes earned by co-op workers as indecent, indeed, undoubtedly criminal.

According to a Supreme Soviet debate,

One esteemed deputy put it bluntly. The cooperatives, he said, are the cancerous tumor of the people. . . . The following simple thought could also be heard at the session. . . . There were no cooperatives before, and there was something in the shops then. Now there is nothing at all. . . . Apart from shortages, the growth of cooperatives has raised the number of divorces, increased the accident rate on railroads, and brought AIDS into the country. They say that the ozone hole is also due to them.[31]

Not surprisingly, an elderly woman teacher "swears that she would better starve to death than go and peddle cooperative merchandise."[32]

Such attitudes were supported by the answers in a 1991 national poll (Table 5.7) to the question "Who now has the real power in the country?" The mafia scored higher than any other source of power.

In a study of views linked directly to adopting a market economy and the effects on the consumer, responses to the question "How will the market economy affect the position of [various social groups]?" are recorded in Table 5.8.

Fundamental to the healthy operation of a market economy are free prices determined largely by changes in supply and demand. In the former Soviet Union, according to a national survey, however, "[M]ost people oppose the proposed changes in state retail prices . . . only 10 percent of the respondents [were positive] to free-floating prices. . . . [S]even out of every ten respondents . . . [expressed a belief] that transition to a market economy will worsen the material status of families."[33] So much for popular support for a move to allow supply and demand to determine prices.

Given these attitudes, a new law adopted in November 1990 must have been one of the most popular pieces of legislation enacted near the end of the old regime. According to it, anyone profiting from selling goods above retail prices would be sentenced to ten years in prison.[34]

As noted, following the major January 1992 price rises, which were not accompanied by comparable wage increases, 93 percent of the population were

Table 5.7
Who Held Real Power in the Spring of 1991?

The USSR president	30%
Nobody	25%
Mafia and bosses of the shadow economy	42%
Difficult to give an answer	12%
The CPSU	12%
Army, military industrial complex, Supreme Soviet	8%
Council of Ministers	2%

Source: "Question: Who Has the Power?" Nezavismaya gazeta, March 9, 1991. JPRS-UPA-91-021, April 18, 1991.

Table 5.8
Who Will Benefit or Lose from Creating a Market Economy?

	Workers	Co-op members	Intellectuals	Pensioners	Managers
Better	16	53	18	6	26
No change	6	18	16	5	39
Worse	69	13	48	83	18
Undecided	9	16	18	6	18

Source: Moscow News, no. 20, 1990.

Table 5.9
Public Support for Anti-Price-Rise Strikes

Do not support	43%
Support	25%
Ready to join	20%
Hard to say	12%"

Source: "Express Poll," Moscow News, February 2-9, 1992.

estimated to have fallen below the poverty line.[35] Not surprising, then, was the response to a random poll taken January 25–26, 1992, in thirteen Russian cities (Table 5.9), when the respondents were asked "Do you support appeals for anti-price-rise strikes?"

As discussed in detail in chapter 4, peasant resistance to privitization of agriculture is enormous. That reality, plus the evidence offered in this chapter, strongly underscores the conclusion that fundamental reform, especially in the economic realm, is most unlikely to be acceptable by the populous in any foreseeable future. That perspective is mirrored by a substantial majority of the people in their views of the future. According to a national public opinion poll conducted August 19 to 21, 1991, while 46 percent of the population had hopes "for the country's better future, . . . sixty-four percent of the respondents believe that worst times are still ahead.[36] Not surprisingly, in March 1992, public opinion surveys "indicate that every fifth person in the Russian Federation would want to emigrate."[37]

The Soviet leadership failed to produce the ideal new Soviet man. Nevertheless, the evidence offered here supports the conclusion of the editorial writers for *The Literary Gazette International*: "Alas, seventy years of unprecedented, cruel social experiment really did succeed in developing a new genus of person: Homo-Sovieticus."[38]

NOTES

1. Justin Burke, "Western Food Shipments Buy Time for Reformers in Russian Cities," *The Christian Science Monitor*, March 2, 1992.

2. Mikhail Gorbachev, *Perestroika: New Thinking for Our Country and the World* (New York: Harper and Row, 1987), p. 76.

3. Anatoly Druzenko, "Still No Freedom of Information?" *Moscow News*, no. 51, 1989.

4. Mikhail Zhvanetsky, "I'm Playing America," *The Literary Gazette International*, February 1990.

5. Mikhail Gorbachev, speech to the Soviet Congress of Deputies, May 25, 1989.

6. Tatyana Zaslavskaya, "When the 'Powers that Be' Err," *Moscow News*, April 1991.

7. Tatyana Zaslavskaya, *Poisk*, March 22–28, 1991. JPRS-UPA-91–033, July 2, 1991.

8. Fyodor Buriatsky, chairman of the Subcommittee on Humanitarian, Scientific and Cultural Cooperation of the Supreme Soviet Committee on International Affairs, *Meeting Report Kennan Institute for Advanced Russian Studies*, January 1990.

9. L. Ponomarev and V. Shinka, "There's Happiness and There's Happiness," *Pravda* April 5, 1989. CDSP, vol. 41, no. 14, 1989.

10. S. V. Chervonopisky, first secretary of the Cherkassy City ZUCL Committee, Cherkassy, Ukraine Republic, Congress Deputy, Congress speech, *Izvestia*, June 3, 1989.

11. "For a Policy of National Accord and Russian Rebirth," *Literaturnaya rossia*, December 29, 1989, pp. 2–3. CDSP, vol. 42, no. 1, 1990.

12. "M. S. Gorbachev's Closing Remarks at the Plenary Session of the CPSU Central Committee on April 25, 1989," *Pravda*, April 27, 1989. CDSP, June 7, 1989.

13. TASS, November 8, 1990.

14. Marina Mulina, "Do Young People Believe in Socialism?" *Sobesednik*, February 1990, JPRS-UPA-90–025, May 8, 1990.

15. Eurie Bronfenbrenner, *Two Worlds of Childhood: U.S. and USSR*, (New York: Russell Sage Foundation and Basic Books, 1970).

16. *Argumenty i fakty*, October 21–27, 1989. CDSP, vol. 41, no. 46, 1989.

17. L. Shevstova, "Crisis of Power—Why It Arose and How to Get out of It," *Ivzestia*, September 17, 1990. CDSP, October 31, 1990.

18. "Homo-Sovieticus: A Rough Sketch," *Moscow News*, no. 11, 1990.

19. Second Congress Debates, *Izvestia*, December 14, 1989. CDSP, vol. 41, no. 50, 1989.

20. Ibid.

21. Leontiy Byzoyev, "Democracy Is Losing Popularity: A Shift of Public Opinion in Moscow," *Nezavismaya gazeta*, February 16, 1991.

22. Ibid.

23. *Pravda*, February 7, 1990. CDSP, vol. 42, no. 16, 1990.

24. Vladimir Boykov and Zhan Toshchenko, "In the Mirror of Sociological: So as Not to Be like Jourdain." *Partiynaya zhizn*, September 1990. JPRS-UPA-90–069, December 14, 1990.

25. "Homo-Sovieticus: A Rough Sketch."

26. Aleksey Kiva, "Wage Leveling," *Sovetskaya Kultura*, October, 1988. JPRS-UEA-89–003.

27. Conversation with the director of USSR Gosplan Scientific Research Economics Institute, *Kommunist*, November 1989. JPRS-UKO-90–002.

28. Viktor Sergeyevich Rozov, writer and playwright "Negating Negation," *Kommunist*, November, 1989. JPRS-UKO-90–002.

29. "Are Business and Law Compatible?" *Moskovskaya pravda*, January 7, 1990. JPRS-UEA-90–010, March 21, 1990.

30. "Under Threat," *Moscow News*, no. 6, 1990.

31. "Cooperatives, Law and Emotions," *Moscow News*, no. 41, 1989.

32. Lyudimila Saraskina, "Capitalism Is for the People to Choose," *Moscow News Fax Digest*, March 24, 1992. FBIS-SOV-92–060, March 27, 1992.

33. V. Kirichenko, "People and Prices," *Pravitelstvennyy vestnik*, July 1990. JPRS-UEA-90–028, August 15, 1990.

34. "Law of the Union of Soviet Socialist Republics: On Increased Liability for Speculation and Illegal Trade Activities and Abuses in Trade. *Izvestia*, November 3, 1990. CSSP, vol. 42, no. 44, 1990.

35. "Vesti," Moscow Russian Television, March 18, 1992. FBIS-SOV-92–054, March 19, 1992.

36. "Viewpoint," *Interfax*, October 21, 1991. FBIS-SOV-91–203. October 21, 1991.

37. *Interfax*, March 26, 1992. FBIS-SOV-92–060, March 27, 1992.

38. "To Our Readers," *The Literary Gazette International*, November 1990.

6

PROGNOSTICATIONS

The Soviet Union died in December 1991, but the people who had inhabited the empire did not. The people cannot be seen as reborn democrats. Nor are they a people imbued with entrepreneurial drives, prepared to establish a market economy. Democracy and market-set prices were not part of their historical experience. Any attempt to follow such a path requires traveling over uncharted, often hostile territory.

The prosperity of nations is determined in part by their natural resources. The country that was the Soviet Union possesses a great wealth of minerals, fuels, and land. Unfortunately, in some cases unfavorable natural environmental factors make utilization of these resources difficult. For example, Soviet crop yields could never have rivaled those achieved in West Europe and North America because of climate. Nevertheless, according to an estimate made by the agricultural division of the Academy of Sciences, because of human shortcomings, Soviet "agriculture 'withdraws' annually from nature not more than two-thirds of the total amount of gross output that could be obtained."[1]

Many nations that are small and relatively poor in natural resources (for example, Japan, Switzerland and South Korea) are surely proof that the wealth of nations is influenced largely by the human factor. The actions of governments, the organization and management of economic enterprise and particularly the attitudes of the people toward their work are primary determinants of the economic health of a nation.

Perhaps, it is hoped, in some distant future the new post-Soviet states will be transformed into prosperous civil societies. The evidence strongly suggests, however, that such a transformation could well take several decades and then only if there has been a perestroika of the mind-set of peoples whose attitudes were shaped by a millennium of tsarist and Soviet authoritarianism.

Table 6.1
Public Support for the Breakup of the Union

	Approve of republics' secession	Against republics' secession	Hard to say
Ukrainians	55	26	19
Belorussians	42	41	17
Indigenous residents of Central Asia	24	54	22
Indigenous residents of the Baltic republics	91	1	8
Georgians	92	1	7
Russians in the Russian SFSR	44	41	15

Source: Yury Levada, "Social Barometer," Moscow News, October 14, 1990.

As noted previously in discussing the forces opposed to agrarian reform, academician Vladimir Tikhonov concluded that for true reform to occur, "a change of at least two generations of leaders, i.e., practically twenty-five years will be needed."[2] Echoing a similar point of view, one of the proponents of major reform, Leonid Albalkin, stated that "creating an effective economy will take no less than a decade and perhaps the life of a whole generation."[3]

Concerning the democratization of the former USSR, the British philosopher Sir Karl Popper, author of *The Open Society and Its Enemies*, has suggested that even a whole generation probably would not be time enough for such change to occur. In an interview, he stated, "I find it perfectly conceivable that it will take fifty years or more before it [the USSR] gets over the first steps [of ridding itself] of authoritarianism."[4] Surely, Popper's observation is applicable as well to the newly independent regimes with the possible exception of the Baltic republics, which had some limited experience with democracy in the memories of some of their citizens.

In propagandizing the advantages of independence in the final months of the USSR, the ethnic leaders almost universally promised that the major fruit of such an achievement would be democracy. Not surprisingly, then, an August 1990 All-Union Center for the Study of Public Opinion survey on attitudes toward secession revealed strong support for independence, especially among the Georgian and the Baltic populations and, to a lesser extent, the Ukrainians. Even a plurality of the Russians responded in favor of independence. Table 6.1 summarizes the published results of the poll.

Two years later, after the fact of independence, another survey of public opinion suggested a marked shift in the views of the Russian people, however. Reflecting back on earlier sentiments for independence, a March 1992 poll (Table 6.2) taken in the Russian Federation asked "If you were faced with the choice again today, which decision would you make: 'Yes' to [saving] the Union or 'No' to the Union?"

Table 6.2
After the Fact Most Russians Regret Breakup of the Union

```
Yes to the union --70.5 percent
No to the Union --22 percent
Other opinion --2.8 percent
Hard to say --4.9 percent.
```

Source: A. Khlopyev, "`Yes!' To Union: Russians Confirm Their Choice of 17 March Last Year," Sovetskaya rossiya, March 19, 1992. FBIS-SOV-92-055, March 20, 1992.

At the least, one can conclude that in early 1992, looking back over their shoulders, a substantial number of the inhabitants of the Russian Federation yearned more for the security they felt they had under Soviet authoritarianism than they did for a nebulous, uncertain democratic future.

According to Vice President A. Rutskoy of Russia in January 1992,

Now we have anarchy instead of democracy. It is impossible to make a transition from dictatorship to democracy bypassing the process of firm authority, the power of the law. Therefore, we are now in the most vulgar, banal dictatorship—the dictatorship of the street and that of street leaders. . . . We do not have a real power today. Power is where the laws are observed. Everybody disregards them these days.[5]

At the time of the failed August 1991 coup, many Western news commentators asserted that the actions (really inactions for the most part) of the people demonstrated their deep desire for democracy. Sadly, the evidence offered here contradicts such a conclusion. Indeed, in summarizing the results of an all-Russia opinion poll taken in January and February 1992 on attitudes toward democracy, Professor Boris Grushin (of the Service for the Study of Public Opinion) stated:

[M]ore than half the population has no real conception of what democracy is. The key element of democracy [for the respondents] is rigid control, order and the absence of conflict. . . . It is a myth that democracy has completely triumphed in the hearts of the former Soviet people. This view is held by only 3 percent of Russia's population.[6]

A. Latynina, a contributor to *Novy mir*, quoted the writer Yu. Burtin as having asked "How many generations would it take just to repair, in some way, the damage from all that slaughter of the past few decades, to restore what had been accumulated over centuries?" Expanding on that question, Latynina continued, "The demand of freedom for oneself presupposes the recognition of freedom for others. If we do not recognize intellectual freedom as a principal value (and codify the right to it in law), we will not become an open society. So far, we are just at the beginning of the path toward one."[7]

In many of the independent republics, new "democratic" constitutions are being written. Unfortunately, such documents (e.g., the pre-Nazi Weimar Constitution of Germany) often are not even worth the paper on which they are written. A democratic constitution is of value only if it reflects attitudes set deeply in the minds of most of the people. It must be an understood social contract that recognizes the other person's nose as a sacred boundary and that rule by law, not by men, is the essence of civilized society. Democratically elected parliaments, such as the 1987 Supreme Soviet of the USSR, do not guarantee democratic rule.

An absolute requirement of open, democratic rule, without which authoritarian rule always exists, is the freedom to criticize publicly the actions of the government and political leaders. The only exception is during nation-threatening wars when, by necessity, the best of democracies revert to authoritarian rule. For example, censorship was practiced in the United States during World War II under the slogan, "A slip of the lip may sink a ship." What hope, then, exists for the realization of democracy in the Russian Federation, if a February 1992 draft law is enacted? The draft "proposes . . . to establish criminal liability of up to seven years' deprivation of liberty for acts, in other words action or inaction, committed for any purpose flagrantly contravening the interests of the Russian Federation."[8] Who is to decide what these interests are? Ultimately, in a democracy the voters must decide. By their votes and expression of opinions, they must dictate that nation's interests.

Creating an open, democratic society requires widespread tolerance of differences. Beyond the widespread manifestations of extreme ethnocentrism in the newly independent republics, including erratic civil war in Azerbaijan, Armenia, and Georgia, there is other evidence of widespread intolerance. In a national poll concerning attitudes toward Jews taken in 1991, "Forty-four percent said that Jews are 'sly and hypocritical.' "[9] Most sobering, an August 1991 "sociological survey . . . provides evidence that about 30 percent of Soviet citizens favor the death penalty for homosexuals. Thirty percent said they were in favor of imprisonment for them, 30 percent were for forced medical treatment, and only 10 percent were in favor of their free existence."[10] Surely, these views have not been abandoned since independence.

For Homo-Sovieticus, deviation from the prescribed socio-political norm was the greatest of sins.

Tragically, former Soviet President Mikhail Gorbachev was right when, in a March 1992 interview with *The Washington Post*, "he likened the atmosphere in the country to 'an insane asylum.' "[11]

There is much food for thought in the words of a *Moscow News* editorial writer: "History does not repeat itself, of course, but in some respects present-day Russia still looks like the Weimar Republic of 1932."[12] Russians, Ukrainians, Georgians, and so on are not Germans, but their plight today does exhibit many similarities to that of Germany at the beginning of the 1930s. Hyperinflation has devastated the economy; social order has broken down, and the masses are increasingly desperate for a solution to their plight.

What the American cartoon character Pogo once said surely applies to the current post-Soviet scene: "We've met the enemy and they is us!"

NOTES

1. *Izvestia*, December 17, 1987.
2. *Moscow News*, February 1988.
3. V. Dolganov and A. Stepovoi, "Izvestia Parliamentary Correspondents Report from the Kremlin," *Izvestia*, October 19, 1990. CDSP, vol. 42, no. 42, 1990.
4. " 'The Best World We Have Yet Had' George Urban Interviews Sir Karl Popper," *Report on the USSR*, May 31, 1991.
5. *Argumenty i fakty*, January 1992. FBIS-SOV-92–015, January 23, 1992.
6. Alexander Rubtsov, "Democracy as Understood in Modern Russia," *Moscow News*, January 26–February 2, 1992.
7. A. Latynina, "The Tolling of the Bell Is not Prayer," *Novy mir*, August 1988. CDSP, January 4, 1989.
8. Sergey Kornilov, "Press Conference," *Rossiyskaya gazeta*, February 24, 1992. FBIS-SOV-92–037, February 25, 1992.
9. "Viewpoint," *Interfax*, June 19, 1991. FBIS-SOV-91–125, June 28, 1991.
10. V. Gushchin and V. Buldakov, "Sex, AIDS . . . and Human Rights," *Argumenty i fakty*, August 1991. JPRS-UPA-91–038, August 26, 1991.
11. TASS, March 24, 1992. FBIS-SOV-92–058, March 25, 1992.
12. Dmitry Kazutin, "What I Have Read, Heard or Seen," *Moscow News*, January 5–12, 1992.

Part II

Revelations of Glasnost: The Soviet and Post-Soviet Mind

A work such as this could not have been produced prior to the advent of glasnost in the former Soviet Union in the mid-1980s. Censorship and editorial control in the name of "socialist realism" still existed. Prior to glasnost, the Soviet press and other communications media played a role fundamentally different from that of the open societies of Europe and North America, for example. Much, indeed, most of what composes news in the West was judged unfit to print in the USSR. Almost all news that reflected negatively on Soviet affairs was not allowed for public consumption. As one would expect, glasnost opened an entirely new information world for Soviet citizens. That world is reflected in the chronologies that follow.

During the final years of the Soviet Union, the content of the press became even more negative than that of typical U.S. or West European newspapers. As the opening up of public information revealed the severe, increasingly cata-strophic problems facing the country, frustrations were vented in the press and other media, eventually to a point of shrill masochism. From the latter 1980s on, an unending stream of accusation and expose has been printed and/or broad-cast in the Soviet Union—and now in the independent states—refecting the malaise that has gripped the people, the economy, and the polity.

What appears here is only a minute selected sample of the commentary that reflects the physical and, especially, mental health of the people at the end of the Soviet era and the onset of the post-Soviet world. The material is presented because it reflects the central thesis of this work in greater detail than is possible in Part I. People shape their own destiny. More than anything else, the mind-set of the people and the leaders determined the death knell of the Soviet Union, and the mind-set of the inhabitants of the new republics will be the primary determinant of what unfolds in the future.

Specifically, most of the materials that follow are extracts of articles that have appeared in Soviet and post-Soviet periodicals or broadcasts by radio or television since the mid-1980s. The presentation is divided into two broad categories: (1) Social well-being, including physical and mental health, the rise in crime, strikes and disruptions and (2) the mind-set of both the masses and the leaders toward economic and political reform in general and, especially, attitudes toward privatization of farming.

The material is organized in chronological order in the belief that such an approach will allow the reader to gain a blow-by-blow sense of the mounting force of the shifting winds of change that destroyed the Soviet Union and are now shaping the future of the independent republics.

7

SOCIAL WELL-BEING

As discussed in Part I, the economy, which was always seriously defective, has fallen into a deep depression. Production in many sectors has declined. The distribution system is in disarray. Fuel has become scarce in many regions. Housing shortages have mounted. Consumer goods shortages are rampant. Food is scarce and rationing is widespread. Inflation has skyrocketed. Poverty has reached astronomical levels. As a result, the physical and mental well-being of the people has deteriorated, and there has been an alarming increase in strikes, crime, and civil strife.

POVERTY, INCOMES, COST OF LIVING, AND INFLATION

December 1988

"In 1927 the worker's family spent 43.8 percent of its budget on food (excluding alcohol), but now the figure is over 60 percent. Furthermore, in the past there were many more dependent family members. . . .

"Expenditures on food (not counting alcohol) represented 59 percent of the consumer spending of a family of four with two working members who earned 380 rubles a month (before taxes) in 1985. . . . [T]he indicator for the United States calculated according to the same procedure, was 15.2 percent in 1984. . . .

"[T]he average worker (in a city) in the USSR has to work 1.23 hours to pay for each square meter of actual living space for a month, with the state subsidizing part of the cost, but this costs the worker in the United States only 0.87 hours (and only out of his own pocket)."[1]

Table 7.1 compares the cost of food in the United States and the USSR as measured in work hours.

Table 7.1
Relationship of Work Hours Required in the USSR (Russia until 1917) for Purchase of 1 Kilogram of Food to U.S. Level (U.S. Indicator is 1)

Year	Meat (beef)	Milk	Butter	Bread	Sugar	Potatoes
1913	1.5	1.4	1.8	0.5	6.5	---
1927	1.9	2.1	2.7	0.7	6.1	1.6
1960	4.4	4.6	8.9	2.0	18.2	2.3
1985	10.0	4.5	10.1	2.8	10.2	3.0

Source: "Comparison of U.S. Soviet Living Standards," SSHA: Ekomomika, Politica, Ideologiya, December 1988, pp. 12-22 JPRS-USA-89-007, April 14 1989.

Table 7.2 compares the cost of goods and services in the United States and the USSR.

March 1989

"[I]n order to buy one kilogram of meat of the same quality as that bought by his American counterpart, a Soviet citizen must work at least 10 times more, . . . for one square metre of state housing he or she must work 1.5 times more."[2]

August

According to a study by a Soviet economist, "In the developed countries the percentage of average income families is about six times higher than here, while in the GDR, Czechoslovakia and Hungary, it is about four times higher."[3]

September

"This is the fifth year of restructuring. . . . The working people and pensioners are now living worse rather than better. More than 45 million Soviet people in our country live below the poverty line. There are empty shelves at the stores, and unchecked rise in prices, inflation, speculation. And there is rationing."[4]

December

"Today, about 9 million people in the republic [of Tajikistan] have a per capita income of less than 75 rubles [a month], which does not provide a subsistence minimum. One-fourth of the able bodied population is not employed in the sphere of social production."[5]

Table 7.2

Percent of Worker's Budget Spent on Goods and Services: United States versus USSR

	USA	USSR	USSR % of USA	USSR X USA
Food	15.2	59 %		3.9
Housing	26.6	6 %		
Hours	45			
" per square meter	0.87	1.23		
Housing available			14	
Consumption of men's haberdashery items			12	
Worker time to buy clothing, footwear, and household items, especially electrical appliances				10-20
Availability of durable goods			14	
" furniture & carpeting			27	
" motor vehicles			5	
" of public transport				2.5
Per capita volume of public & private transport			11.8	
Cost of travel across city	$2.00	5 kopeks		
Consumption of services, all			20	
Municipal & utilities			21	
Recreational			44	
Repairs, laundry, etc.			48.2	
Income spent on services. USA over half USSR 21%				
Per capita expenditure (all sources) on medical services			33	
Number of telephones one-tenth of USA				
Total money spent on education			77	

Source: "Comparison of U.S. Soviet Living Standards," SSHA: Ekomomika, Politica, Ideologiya, December 1988, pp. 12-22. JPRS-USA-89-007, April 14, 1989.

January 1990

In the USSR "40 million of us live below the poverty line. . . . According to studies and polls the average person needs some 260 rubles a month to live well. . . . " But studies reveal that the "average per capita income of Leningraders is just R138 a month. . . . A family of four, two children, husband an engineer R130, wife a librarian R90 a month."[6]

According to the calculations of a Latvian reporter, Latvian "investigators and criminal investigators earn for their work slightly less than $50 a month compared with an American patrolman's salary of $2000 a month."[7]

"There are 40 million individuals waiting for housing throughout the country."[8]

March

"The aggregate per capita income for industrial as well as office and professional workers increased in the last year by 8 percent. But their outlays for the purchase of non-food-stuffs rose by 13 percent, and expenditures on foodstuffs rose by 4 percent. . . .

"[U]nder the conditions prevailing at the beginning of 1990, . . . an average of 97–99 rubles per month per person [is required at a] minimum."[9]

October

According to *Izvestia*, more than 40 million of the Soviet Union's 288.8 million live below the official poverty line of 78 rubles a month and if, as many believe, the real line is 100 rubles, the number would be 70.9 million.[10]

"Living standards have begun falling sharply. Only 11 percent of the people indicated that they live comfortably, while 65 percent said that they have only enough money to make it from one pay day to the next."[11]

April 1991

"[M]ore than 90 million people, or almost 32% of the country's population, have a per capita income of less than 105 rubles a month, and hence the status of being below the poverty line."[12]

Calculations of the real cost of living—for example, purchase of food at levels recommended by the nutritionists, and purchasing it from the kolkhoz market when not available in the state stores—reveal that "the poverty line in our country now comes to R250."[13]

"[I]n 1989 the average per capita total income for the families of manual and office workers amounted to 159 rubles. This is the amount, on average (average statistical), a worker spent for life. In the process, 30.6 percent of his income, or 48.7 rubles, was spent for food. . . .

"[Following the March 1991 price increases, the cost of food jumped 113 percent. Overall, according to official statistics] . . . the living expenses for an individual have increased on the average by 102 rubles, or by 64 percent. . . .

"How did our standard of living decline?

"Based upon the fact that the average wage, following the introduction of compensation (60 rubles), increased by 25 percent and the cost of living index by 64 percent, we drew the conclusion that the standard of living for manual and office workers declined by 24 percent (compared to 1989)."[14]

May

According to a study by independent Soviet economists, "The quality of life over a five-year period [i.e., since 1985] has declined 10 percent, labor activity, 30 percent, and satisfaction with the living standard, 35 percent (this figure is determined by the ratio of indicators of the degree of development of society and the minimum living standard). . . .

"By 1995, the [economic] situation will have deteriorated sharply."[15]

In commenting on President Gorbachev's decree "On the Minimum Consumer Budget," an *Izvestia* writer stated: "The USSR Ministry of Labor and Social Questions has reported that the nationwide average for the proposed minimum consumer budget is estimated at 227 rubles [a month]. In actual fact the average consumer budget throughout the Union is 140 rubles. . . .

"[T]here are zones of outright destitution. Here are some calculations, which, . . . were made before April 2, 1991: In Estonia, only 3% of residents had an income of less than 100 rubles a month; in Belorussia, 7%; in Russia and the Ukraine, 11%, but in Kirgizia, 47%; in Turkmenia and Azerbaizhan, 49%; in Uzbekistan, 57%; and in Tazhikistan, 69%."[16]

June

"Consumer prices in the RSFSR rose by an average of 96 percent in May compared with May 1990, according to Western and Soviet reports of official RSFSR statistics. Food prices went up 127 percent on average with meat up 180 percent, fish 193, and sugar 155. Textiles and clothes prices increased by 166 percent and building materials by 132 percent."[17]

July

According to a poll taken by the National Public Opinion Studies Center (VCIOM) in May and June:

"Forty percent of the people polled said that they spend more than one half of their income on food products.

"Twenty-eight percent said food consumed nearly all of their family budget.

"Twenty-one percent said . . . roughly one-half of the money they earned [went on food]. . . .

"Six percent admitted they spent less than 50 percent of their incomes on food. Five percent said 'I don't know.' The error margin was at 3 percent."[18]

"Prices of agricultural produce have more than doubled in Moscow and Leningrad kolkhoz markets compared with the same period last year. . . . Grapes and watermelons [now] cost 40 rubles . . . and R5 per kilogram. Tomatoes range between R6 and R10, chicken R25, meat from R30 to R40."[19]

August

According to figures "announced at a recent session of the cabinet [the average minimum subsistence income is] 210 rubles a month. . . . In fact, *the average per capita income* in this country in Soviet families is 212 rubles a month."[20]

"The inflation level in 1990 . . . [was] 24 percent. . . . [D]uring the first three months [of 1991] . . . it will be 23 percent."[21]

September

"In September, the ruble began to be devalued by 2 to 3 percent per week or 96 to 144 percent annually."[22]

"According to the [RSFSR] State Committee for Statistics, grocery prices have increased by 181 percent in 1991 compared with the same period in 1990."[23]

"The overwhelming majority of analysts predict a sharp intensification of the economic crisis, a swift growth of gross unemployment, an acceleration of hyperinflation and a fall in the standard of living to the point beyond which a limitless number of hunger riots will begin."[24]

October

"The decline in the standard of living, or more exactly in real income, has been observed in all of the republics without exception, but to the greatest degree—in Kirghizstan and Georgia (25 and 26 percent), and to the least degree—in Belorussia and Uzbekistan (14 percent). . . .

"[O]n the whole, one third of the population (97 million individuals) subsist on a figure that is lower than the living wage established by the sovereign republics. . . .

"[I]f we take as a reference point the monthly monetary income of a family member, then the smallest figures are for Tajikistan (123 rubles), Uzbekistan (143), Turkmenistan (156), and the largest—in Belorussia and Russia (297 and 277). In the Ukraine—246 rubles."[25]

November

Food prices in 1992 are projected to increase much more than wages. Estimated past and present average monthly wages and the quantities of food that can be purchased by such wages, under free retail prices are introduced in 1992 (Table 7.3).

"Last year, when our respondents [to a national poll] estimated their subsistence minimum at 120 rubles, the number of people earning less than that constituted 52 percent of those polled. The situation has changed over the past twelve months. In August 1991, the subsistence minimum was estimated at 328 rubles. And, even though the population was compensated for the price rise, the

Table 7.3
Prices and Inflation

	1950	1991*	1992**		1950	1991*	1992**
	(in rubles)				(in kilograms)		
Average wage		117	330	700			
	State retail prices (per kg.)				Quantity of products purchasable (Average wage)		
Beef	3.00	7.00	30.00		39	47	11
Milk	0.35	0.50	3.00		343	660	110
Butter	6.40	9.70	63.00		18	34	5
Eggs(10)	1.40	1.80	5.00		84	183	66
Rye Bread	0.30	0.48	1.70		390	687	194
Wheat Flour	0.80	0.94	0.94		146	351	94
Maca-roni	1.00	1.20	4.00		117	275	82

*As of April 2, 1991, when new state prices were introduced.
**Forecast price after introduction of free prices.

Source: _Interfax_, November 10, 1991. FBIS-SOV-91-219, November 13, 1991.

number of citizens who found themselves below the poverty line increased to 84 percent.''[26]

''[T]he new price for bread [in Moscow] significantly exceeds the old price for meat. Moreover, it is a jump of several hundred percent: 3.60 rubles for certain types of black bread (a quarter of all output), and R5.40 for specific types of white (2 percent).''[27]

According to an October 1, 1991, survey, ''12 percent of Soviet families can afford less than 1 kilo of fresh meat per member a month.''[28]

''Average monthly inflation rates in the Soviet Union have increased 4-fold as compared to the beginning of the year, it is revealed in the latest issue of the _Kommersant_. . . .

''The weekly forecasts that the rates of inflation in the country may grow to 650–700 percent at the end of the year.''[29]

December

In Latvia, the ''general cost of living has increased at least three times in comparison with the last year.''[30]

"Living standards in all the sovereign states within the former Soviet union are on the decline due to reduced production and soaring prices. In the first nine months of this year, consumption of material benefits and services by the people fell by 17 percent."[31]

January 1992

"In the Donbass, prices [for food] lept 10-fold on average. Cooked sausage, which had been R [ruble] 9 before the beginning of the year, now costs R136, butter has jumped from R11 to R179 and sour cream from R3 to R50. More curious and disturbed people have begun to gather in front of the shelves."[32]

According to Russian Vice President A. Rutskoy, "Before the great perestroika started we had 20 million people below the poverty line; now we have 100 million."[33]

According to the Russian State Statistic Committee, "Between June and May in 1991, a family of four spent 310 rubles on each person to provide the minimal living standing, by the beginning of February 1992 the sum rose to 1300–1500 rubles."[34]

"The Lithuanian Government has again increased prices for power, heat, and gas. All consumers will now pay 35 kopeks per kilowatt-hour of power. Prices of heat and natural gas have quadrupled, the price of furnace fuel has tripled, and the price of hard coal has doubled."[35]

In Russia, according to Goskomstat, "Subsistence wage per member of the family per month [was] 144 rubles (R) in 1990; R430 in 1991; R1,300 in February 1992 (forecast). Naturally, retail prices doubled as well.

"The monetary income of the population rose by the same amount—by 216 percent. The average monthly wage amounted to R530, but this growth was entirely cancelled out by inflation."[36]

"The municipal authorities of Vilnius have issued an ordinance to raise twenty-fold the rent for apartments of the state housing stock. . . .

"Municipal bus and trolley-bus fare has also increased from February 1—80 kopeks, 20 times as high as the fare a year ago."[37]

February

As compared with January 1991, "[t]he composite index of consumer prices is tentatively about 350 percent. The average index of food prices in January was 396 percent and that of nonfood items—250 percent, and charges for services of all types including rent—230 percent."[38]

"According to informed sources, after the first stage of price liberalization, the subsistence minimum in Armenia was estimated at 1,450 rubles and the average consumer basket was estimated at 8,280 rubles. The sum needed to sustain a living standard comparable to that of the European States is 20,400 rubles."[39]

Table 7.4
Cost of Living Index

	1913	1990	Dec. 1991
Standard of living index*	1	1.83	0.41
Cost of daily food basket (rbls)**	0.70	2.88	18.60

*The ratio between the wages index and the prices index.
**A conventional food basket, family of two parents, three children."

Source: Andrei Tkachenko, "Wages and Prices: Living as we did 45 years ago, if not worse," Independent Newspaper, March 20-21, 1992.

March

According to a computer model created by The Din-Prognoz Scientific Center and the Russian Supreme Economic Council, "The inflation may amount to monthly 30–40 percent in the next three or six months."[40]

"By the end of 1991 the standard of living . . . was flung back to the level of 1946—a time when almost all of the people went hungry."[41]

Table 7.4 compares the cost of living in 1913 with that in 1990 and 1991.

According to a poll of Muscovites, 97 percent said that in order to "live normally," the income for each member of the family should be R1,000 or more. Indeed, 20 percent said the required income would be R5,000 or more. Yet the same respondents said the actual income per capita was only R547.08 a month. That compares with the average income per capita of R160.58 in January 1990.[42]

"According to Russian Goskomstat figures, . . . about 90 percent of the republic's population is living below the poverty line. The population's average monthly income is now 895 rubles. Goskomstat considers the minimum sufficient income to be 1,500 a month. Only 7 percent of the population receive this amount."[43]

"From 1 April, food subsidies are being introduced [in the Ukraine] for disabled single people and families whose income per capita—average combined income per member of the family—is less than 50 percent of the minimum wage."[44]

According to data provided by the Georgian Committee on Social Economic Information, "In 1991, . . . real income of the population dropped by 30 percent."[45]

Due to the loss of purchasing power born of inflation, in Ukraine "[p]er capita sales of food and other consumer goods . . . is half as much as in February 1991."[46]

"Overall inflation has been calculated by Kommersant Data Service at more than 1,000, rather than the 250 percent or 350 percent suggested by the Gaidar team."[47]

According to Audrius Misevicius, Lithuanian deputy social security minister, "The subsistence minimum in the republic is these days 1,150 rubles."[48]

April

According to official statistics, "Over four-fifths of the Georgians have found themselves beyond [below] the poverty level."[49]

"The minimum wage in Georgia will be 500 rubles from 1 May. . . . The wages of employees in publicly financed organizations will rise to 1,500 rubles from 1 May."[50]

The Russian Supreme Soviet decided that "[t]he minimum old-age pension will beginning 1 May be equal to 900 rubles."[51] The minimum wage for workers on the state budget also will be 900 rubles, the Soviet determined.

According to Russian Federation Goskomstat figures, "The consumer price index for Russia as a whole in the first quarter of 1992 stood at 619 percent compared with December 1991."[52] Whereas the minimum per capita income should be 1,200 rubles per month, Goskomstat reported that "more than 50 million people—one third of Russia's population—had incomes of less than R900 a month."

May

"Experts say the cost of living went up by 14 percent last month [April] against 36 in March."[53]

According to a decree issued by Russian President B. Yeltsin, "The minimum wage at organizations and establishments funded from budgetary sources shall be raised in the second quarter of 1992 to 900."[54]

"Mosenergo [Moscow Energy Company] is increasing its electricity charges on average by 300 percent, and its heating charges by almost 200 percent."[55]

In Armenia, "[a] 20-liter can of gasoline now costs drivers R700; a kilogram of butter costs over R200 and a kilogram of cheese more than R100. Meanwhile the average monthly pay in Armenia stands at around R470."[56]

"The life of Russians is continuing to worsen. Food prices in retail trade increased by an average of 25.6 percent in April, although in March they had increased by only 21 percent. . . . The State Committee for Statistics also points out that the physical mass of goods sold in April fell 40 percent compared with the same period last year."[57]

According to Grant Bagratyan, vice premier of Armenia, "at present the average wages in the republic are R600, whereas the subsistence minimum is R2,230."[58]

According to the economist Pavel Bunich, "Monthly inflation [in the Russian

Federation] is 30–40 percent. If the bank pays 80 percent a year, bank deposits will depreciate by 700 percent a year."[59]

In the first three months of 1992, "goods [in the Ukraine] increased in price by 30 percent."[60]

In Prokopyevsk in the Kuzbass, miners' wages run from 15,000–25,000 rubles a month.[61]

June

"According to Estonia's statistics department, the cost of living has increased by 10.67 times in the republic compared to May 1991. Compared to April 1992, the cost of living increased five times."[62]

"The Kazakh President Nursultan Nazarbayev . . . said a sharp price rise has been successfully curbed. In January the prices leaped 16 times, and in June they have edged up by 8%."[63]

FOOD AVAILABILITY: CONSUMPTION, SHORTAGES, AND NUTRITION

September 1985

In 1985, Gorbachev said that "meat production is an element of the greatest strain. . . . We are lagging behind in this field. . . . Demand for some . . . [foods] exceeds their supply." Moreover, he deplored the need "to spend sizable hard-currency reserves" to import grain.[64]

September 1988

"[T]he daily calorific value for nutrition in the country even exceeds the recommended rational level and amounts to approximately 3,000 calories. However, the ration is poor in proteins of animal origin and vitamins. At the same time, we are consuming more grain products and sugar than are deemed necessary."[65]

March 1989

Table 7.5 compares the consumption of foods in the USSR with that in other nations.

May

"Let us be honest. Our average per capita consumption [of meat and meat products] does not amount to 64 kilos a year; at best it varies from 45 to 50 kilos."[66]

Table 7.5
Consumption of Staple Foods: USSR versus Other Nations (kilograms per capita)

	USSR 1988*	Soviet goals 2000	USA 1987	West Germany 1987	Netherlands 1987
Meat and meat products	45	78	120	104	81
Milk and dairy products	355**	370	271	366	299
Eggs (number of)	275**	274	243	268	184
Fish and fish products	18.0	20.0	7.6	4.1	7.0
Sugar	36	38	28	35	39
Vegetable oil	10.0**	13.0	22.4	14.1	28
Potatoes	99	105	57	76	89
Vegetables and melons	95	140	126	77	104
Fruits and berries	40	75	97	140	182
Breadstuffs	131	115	97	78	57

*All-Union Research Institute of the Trade Conditions and Popula-
tion Demand for Consumer Goods, estimate.
**USSR State Committee.

Source: Aleksandr Shinkin, "Cheap Promises Grow More Expensive, But Our Purses Get No Heavier," Pravda, May 21, 1989.

October

"[Today the most vital problem is] food, the situation in the countryside."[67]

"[I]t turns out that the country was fed better in 1926 than is the case at the present time, notwithstanding today's modern technologies, colossal technical pool and so forth."[68]

December

"Recently, deliveries of agricultural output to all-Union and republic stocks have been disrupted, to all intents and purposes. Many industrial centers, ... and a number of areas in Siberia and the Far East, are in a critical situation with the respect to the supply of meat and certain other foodstuffs. Apparently, urgent and, I would say, even emergency measures are a must here."[69]

''[Food] production should be increased to 205–210 billion rubles a year, or by nearly one-third of the present level, if we want to eliminate food shortages.''[70]

January 1990

''Practically everywhere, sugar was sold by ration cards. . . . [In a survey of 146 cities] meat and foul were distributed by ration cards in 33, butter—20, and tea—in 16. . . . [In the kolkhoz market the price of potatoes rose by 8 percent and vegetables 10 percent.] In November, flour was unavailable for sale in 5 percent of the cities studied, porridge—47 percent, and macaroni—in 48 percent of the cities.''[71]

March

''[T]he majority of Turkmenian children today do not get enough to eat.''[72]

May

According to a poll by the All-Union Center for the Study of Public Opinion, 22.1 percent of the respondents said they spend almost all of their income on food, 38.2 percent more than half, and 24.6 percent approximately half. Of the respondents, 43.4 percent said they experienced shortages of necessary food quite often and 29.7 percent said constantly; 76.8 percent said they could not get enough meat, fish, and poultry, and 63.6 percent not enough vegetables, fruit, and berries. Only 18.1 percent felt that their diet was sufficient in amount and good quality.[73]

January 1991

According to Radio Moscow on December 29, ''Food shops in Erevan the Armenian capital are virtually empty, receiving only 40–50% of food provisions, public transport had stopped operating.''[74]

July

''So far this year, Moscow has failed to receive 54,000 tons of meat products and 250,000 tons of dairy products; Leningrad—8,000 and 150,000 tons respectively; Central Asia—31,000 and 20,000 tons; and the Transcaucasus—6,000 and 120,000 tons. Why? Because the Ukraine, Belorussia, Kazakhstan, the Baltic republic, Moldava, and Kyrgyzstan have failed to fulfill their obligation for deliveries to all-Union stocks.''[75]

According to *Argumenty i fakty*, a special meat shop still exists in Moscow for the ''higher party and government bodies located in the capital.''[76]

''I [M. Gorbachev] will tell you frankly, the most difficult thing now—and this is what concerns me most of all—is food. Everything must be mobilized, all the state's resources, but the food situation must not be allowed to get worse."[77]

August

In the first seven months of 1991, "[p]roduction of flour from state resources was up 2 percent, production of pasta articles was up 6 percent, but production of meat and butter was down again—by 13 percent, and production of whole milk and edible fish products was down 9 percent."[78]

October

"The study of families [nationwide] revealed that for the most part they are purchasing fewer products and consumer goods. For example, bread, meat and meat products—18 percent less, milk and dairy products—17 percent less, including butter—27 percent less. . . .

"Following the increase in prices, the population's food structure shifted even more towards an irrational carbohydrate model and this undoubtedly will have an effect on the populations health. . . .

"It is easy to understand that 30 million individuals with incomes that are lower than the living wage by a factor of 2–3 will endure a half starved and pitiful existence. . . .

"How is it possible to discuss rations today when the ration cards for bread in a number of regions are even more severe than they were during the war?"[79]

"The collapse of the food market is largely due to the breaking of economic ties between republics and regions. Traditional deliveries are being broken off and new ties have not yet been established. . . .

"It must be taken into account that food prices are rising. And food will become simply unaffordable for some population categories. Therefore, it is high time to think about organizing charity canteens and other means of providing free or concessionary food to pensioners, especially those living on their own."[80]

November

"Talinin is suffering from acute shortages of milk and milk products. Mayor Hardo Aasmae . . . [said] 'unless the situation improves within the next few weeks, we'll have to introduce coupons, so that milk can reach at least those needing it most.' "[81]

"In Moscow, bread, meat, sausage, eggs, butter, and vegetable oil will be rationed starting with the first of next month."[82]

"St. Petersburg Mayor Anatoly Sobchak has announced today, Wednesday, his intention to introduce in the city and the region 'stringent food rationing at certain shops in the localities' beginning with December 15."[83]

"St. Petersburg, . . . suffers a serious food shortage currently because the Baltic nations and the Ukrainian Republic have virtually halted food shipments, the city's mayor said Saturday [November 24]."[84]

December

On December 23, the Russian Deputy Prime Minister Yegor Gaydar reported that the foodstuffs supply in Moscow was down by 30–40 percent below the 1990 level.[85]

January 1992

"Statisticians analyzed the budget of 75,000 families. . . . In the first three months after the [April 1991 price] reform 18 percent fewer bread products, meat, and meat products were acquired than in the corresponding period of last year, 17 percent fewer dairy products and 27 percent fewer animal fats. . . .

"In Georgia, Uzbekistan, and Azerbaijan one family in three, consumed less than 1 kilogram of meat and poultry per person per month. . . .

"The statisticians' conclusion is clear: 'The reduction in the proposition of biologically valuable food products will undoubtedly have a negative effect on the population's health.' "[86]

February

"The present amount of food stocks in Russia is barely enough to meet half the demand, Russia's Goskomstat (statistics) committee has reported."[87]

"Yesterday, it was announced that total Western aid to the CIS was $89 billion. That includes past, present, and future aid. This is of course principally food aid. But somehow we do not particularly feel its impact. Maybe we see its benefits for children, who get tinned meat and milk at school, but we do not see it in the stores. Where is this food aid?"[88]

Moscow News commented on an article in the *International Herald Tribune* stating that current commitments by the United States for aid to Russia include 38.4 million tons of food. This contrasts with the 1921 aid of "700 million tons of food, as well as a great deal of medicines and consumer goods . . . [when] 100,000 people died of starvation every month in Petrograd alone, saved from 10 to 50 million lives in Russia in three years according to expert estimates."[89]

April

According to data provided by the Georgia Committee on Social Economic Information, "In 1991, the per capita meat consumption reduced by 23 percent (as against 9 percent in the [former] USSR), milk and dairy products—by 29 percent (6 percent) and sugar—by 35 percent (10 percent). In 1991, purchases of cattle and poultry reduced 2.5 times and purchases of milk and eggs—40 percent."[90]

"Shortages of such [most] foodstuffs are due to deepening disruptions of inter-republican and inter-regional ties, breaches of contact between wholesalers and retailers, and a dangerous drop in the food industry's productivity. More and more food is changing hands through barter deals, bypassing the retail sector."[91]

June

"Russian Vice-President Aleksandr Rutskoy, . . . warned that Russia may be threatened with a severe food crisis in several months."[92]

PHYSICAL HEALTH: ABORTIONS, INFANT MORTALITY, MALNUTRITION, ENVIRONMENTAL POLLUTION, AND LIFE EXPECTANCY

November 1988

According to Goskomstat statistics, infant mortality in 1987 in the USSR was 25.4 per 1,000 births. As compared to France, the United States, Great Britain, Japan, and the Federal Republic of Germany, "[i]nfant mortality in the USSR is currently 2.5–5 times higher than in these countries. . . . " The life expectancy in 1986–87 for the urban population was men 65.8, women 74.3, and the rural population, men 63.5 and women 72.8.[93]

January 1989

"The heaviest blow during the stagnation years was dealt to public health. . . . By 1984, life expectancy in the Soviet Union decreased by 2 years; general and infantile mortality rose."[94]

April

"Theoretically, it is impossible to live in every seventh city of the 273 RSFSR cities which conduct observation of atmospheric air conditions. . . . [For example] there is 20 times as much of nitrogen oxides as the norm in the air of Gorky, Smolensk, and Omsk; . . . and the benzopyrene content in Novokuznetsk's air is 598 times as much as the maximum possible norm!"[95]

November

"Every year on the nation's highways, about 40,000 people are killed and 260,000 are maimed, as the result of which half of those suffering become invalids or die prematurely. . . . [T]hree-fourths . . . are personal vehicles. For every 100 people who have suffered on our highways, 13 have died. In the GDR and the ChSSR—3–4 persons, in the FRG—2 and in the United States—1.3 persons. . . . In other words, the severity of the results . . . in the United States is 10-fold lower than in our country.''[96]

January 1990

According to Soviet scientists, each year 100,000 ''hereditary sick children are born,'' due to heavy metal poisoning of their mothers.[97]

April

According to *Komsomolskaya pravda*, there is starvation among children in Turkmenia, largely because of the malnourishment of infants born to mothers with inadequate diets.[98]

January 1991

''Since in our country there are 52 million women of child-bearing age, i.e., between ages 15 and 44, and it is a well-known fact that of every 1,000 women 180 have an abortion each year (in Germany this figure is 7 per 1,000), then that means that each year 9.5 million children are murdered in their mother's womb. . . .

''In terms of average life span the Soviet Union is in 34th place—last place—in Europe.''[99]

February

In an interview, Inga Ivanovna Grebesheva, chairman of the RSFSR State Committee for Family Affairs and Demographic Policy, stated, ''In the Russian federation the death rate today outstrips the birthrate so much that, according to the prognoses of sociologists, if things continue to go this way in the future in 25 years the republic's population may decrease to half of what it is now. The reason lies in the disregard of the interests of the family.''[100]

July

''[T]he public health services of Latvia continue to prohibit—or at the very least to recommend against—swimming in the Baltic Sea. The reason is a concentration of bacillus coli so high that it exceeds the permissible norms more than 10-fold and in spots even 100-fold.''[101]

September

"Particular concern is evoked by the almost total absence of medicines, first of all those needed by patients suffering from diabetes, cardiovascular disorders and other ailments requiring uninterrupted treatment. This already has very grave consequences. For instance medicine shortages have led to serious social complication in some cities of Western Siberia, such as Omsk."[102]

According to the RSFSR minister of health, "The supply of medicaments to the public and hospitals in the RSFSR continues to be in a disastrous state."[103]

October

"It is theoretically possible that 1.5 million people will die prematurely next year because of the shortage of medicines. . . . [There is a] catastrophic situation regarding supply of medicines and medical equipment: [only] 35–38 percent of required demand."[104]

November

According to the medical authorities in the Ukrainian Academy of Sciences, "The increment in the birth rate in the republic (according to 1991 data) is zero. Many more of us are dying than are being born. . . .

"Already ineluctable statistics indicate that in some regions only 20–30 percent of school-age children can be considered healthy. On the whole, the disease rate for Ukraine's population has increased by a factor of 2.12 for all classes of disease."[105]

According to the Institute of Geography of the Soviet Academy of Sciences, "On the Soviet Union's territory they have identified about 300 areas in regions whose environment is now unfavorable for human population. These territories occupy 3.7 million sq. km. or 16 percent of the country's total area. Including the reindeer pastures ruined in the tundra, however, this figure rises to 20 percent."[106] The area involved is equal to 39 percent of the area in the fifty United States.

January 1992

According to Aleksey Vladimirovich Yablokov, state counselor of the Russian Federation for Ecology and Health, "[T]he average life expectancy in Russia reached its maximum in the mid-60s when it amounted to 70.4 years and then it fell to 67.6. In the United States, the average life expectancy is now 6 years more than ours, and in Japan it is 8 years more. Forty percent of the men who died in Russia in 1990 were of working age."[107]

March

"Only 38.9 percent of those questioned in a public opinion poll carried out in March by the Russian Academy of Sciences Sociopolitical Research Institute can afford to pay for essential foodstuffs. Of those polled 56.9 percent said that they already have to deny themselves many things. Almost 4 percent of the respondents admitted that they sometimes have to go hungry."[108]

April

According to *Pravda*, land affected by radiation from the "Chernobyl catastrophe . . . makes up 1% of the total area in Russia and 4% in Ukraine, the figure is 24% in Belarus."[109]

May

According to the "head of the Moscow State University Population Studies Center, . . . mortality has topped Russia's birth rate for the first time in Russian history. . . . [T]he birth rate dropped by 30 percent during the past few years. . . . Mortality figures are also very high. Their peak was recorded last year."[110]

"Archangel oblast is an ecological disaster zone, scientists of the Archangel Medical Institute have concluded on the basis of twenty years research. . . . [It revealed] that 95 percent of children in the Archangel oblast are born in a weakened condition. That is four times more than in the first postwar year of 1946.

"Over the past three years, the number of instances of children falling ill with blood diseases and cancer has tripled.

"Professor Pavel Sidorov noted that the cause of such a dramatic situation is also a consequence of global nuclear tests, the pollution of the White and Barents Seas by toxic radioactive waste, the appearance of an ozone hole over the region and destructive emissions from local industrial enterprises."[111]

June

"Nuclear waste discharges from a Russian military facility from 1949 to 1967 irradiated half a million people, according to a report by Russian experts.

"The planned and accidental discharges from the Mayak facility in the southern Urals dispersed 150 million curies of radiation into the environment, 'apparently . . . higher than the quantities discharged in Hiroshima and Chernobyl.' [The report says] 28,000 were 'severely irradiated' and 8,015 died over a 32-year observation period as a result of the discharges."[112]

"In the period between 1987 and 1991 [in Russia] the birth rate decreased from 17.1 to 12.1 per 1,000 of the population, while the death rate went up from 10.5 to 11.4. Infant mortality remained unchanged at 17.4 per 1,000. The three first months of this year brought the figure up to 18. The population growth in 1991 was 0.7, the lowest ever during the past 20 years.''[113]

In a CBS interview, Lesley Stahl ''asked Yeltsin about a St. Petersburg children's hospital where she said she saw two babies die because the facilities had no antibiotics.

''Then why don't you give us antibiotics?' responded the Russian president. 'You are a rich country. . . . My own mother who had a heart attack . . . there is no medicine to treat her . . . and this is the mother of a president.' ''[114]

In an interview, Aleksey Yablokov, ecology adviser to President Yeltsin, said that enormous amounts of radiation have been leaked from two Central Siberian nuclear reactors. ''For hundreds of kilometers along the Yenisy [River] below Krasnoyarsk, the radiation contamination is in places higher than in the most dangerous regions of Chernobyl, up to 160 curies per square kilometer. That is incredible radiation. There are small patches, of course, perhaps 100 square metres, where there is no contamination, but this information is [has been until now] secret from the people who live there.''[115]

''This is a 1982 map of Moscow. The red spots—and there are 630 of them—are areas of radiation pollution. Top-secret burials of dangerous waste had been carried out by institutes and plants since the fifties. . . . We find 50–60 radiation pollution hot spots in Moscow every year. . . . Despite the fact that we're doing this work [decontaminating previous finds] in areas that we've covered before.''[116]

''[St. Petersburg] has started to 'glow.' It is polluted by radioactive waste sites; moreover, one of the most dangerous is situated next to the hard currency hotel 'Pribaltiyskaya'. . . . No less than nine extremely dangerous centers of radioactive contamination emitting beta-radiation of up to 50,000 particles per square centimeter per minute, are situated less than 300 meters from the Gulf of Finland.''[117]

''The growth of the death rate . . . [since] the second half of the eighties has by now affected all the three Slav republics of the former Soviet Union. Russia has been the worst hit. . . . Russia ranks with the developing countries. The main reason is the increasing death rate among able-bodied men, a high-risk group in Russia. Chronic diseases claim ever more lives, shifting towards ever younger age groups.''[118]

MENTAL HEALTH: ALCOHOLISM, ACCIDENTS, AND SUICIDE

November 1989

''An atmosphere of extreme disregard for traffic rules reigns on the roads today, an aggressive style of interaction between drivers and pedestrians has taken hold. . . . The principle of 'anything goes' is becoming ever more firmly established.''[119]

December

"In our country today,... 9% to 11% of the people are chronic alcohol-ics,... drug addiction is increasing at a catastrophically rapid rate.... Whereas in 1987, 19% of respondents in a poll did not believe that our work [against alcoholism and drug addiction] would be successful, last year the figure was 26%, and this year it is 58%."[120]

In the first half of 1989, there were thirty-two major accidents in the coal industry as compared to twenty-four for the same period in 1988, an increase of 33 percent.[121]

January 1990

"[T]he deaths per 10,000 vehicles in the USSR is four to six times as high as in countries with a high level of vehicle ownership and operation—the FRG, Great Britain, the United States."[122]

"Every year some 60,000 persons commit suicide in our country."[123] That is 30/100,000 compared to the U.S. rate of 12/100,000.

CRIME: SOURCES, RATE, AND NO LAW-GOVERNED STATE

July 1988

"The shaping of law-governed state cannot be separated from the process of democratization. Socialist self-governing can be put into effect only under the rule of law which excludes tyranny as well as anarchy, probable results of the self-will of officials."[124]

"[O]ur country lacks clear-cut standard rules for the preparation of draft legislative acts.... [M]any sensible proposals regarding the improvement of current laws have been published in our press and especially recently. But do these proposals reach the legislator?... Unfortunately, this is not certain.... Another... dangerous brake is to be found in the actual 'kitchen' where laws are made. A more-or-less finished draft appears from 'nowhere....' There are numerous obstacles at the next stage. Commission members work on the draft from early morning until late at night..., examine almost with magnifying glasses every norm proposed by the legal act.... And when the law appears it is almost unrecognizable: complex provisions have been erased 'for clarity,' contentious issues have been smoothed over, and the only norm that is left out of the several alternatives is the one that most rigidly curbs the rights of the individual. It is disappointing. At the last stage some 'functionary' who always remains anonymous has deleted something from the draft by a stroke of his pen and has substituted something else.... According to our constitution lawmaking is the function of the USSR Supreme Soviet and its Presidium. *But the party organs' desire to cover everything and everybody has not bypassed this sphere either.*''[125]

August

''Let us be frank: There is as of yet no firm legal order in the country, no stable law and order. Today in many aspects we still have the political and legal situation that V. Gilyarovskiy described at the beginning of the century as follows: 'In Russia there are two disasters: below—the power of darkness, above—the darkness of power.' ''[126]

July 1989

''During the first six months of this year, internal affairs agencies and prosecutors offices recorded 1,102,509 crimes, which is 267,650 more crimes than during the same period last year. The percentage increase is also quite 'spectacular'—32.1%.''[127] Moreover, if unsolved crimes are compared for the same two periods—168,262 in 1988 and 340,790 in 1989—they have more than doubled.

September

''[W]hile during all of 1988, only 600 incidents of racketeering were discovered, in the first four months of 1989 alone, [there were] 1,107 criminal cases.''[128]

November

''On the average compared to the same period of last year, the number of murders is up 27 percent . . . , the number of severe bodily injuries up 47 percent . . . , rapes up 22 percent.''[129]

''In the past five years the number of crimes committed by minors has risen by 15 percent . . . , and for the first six months [of 1989] 21 percent. . . .

''Negative phenomena in the sphere of the economy [primarily associated with the expansion of cooperatives said to be controlled by the 'mafia'], have been increasing. Wheeler-dealer embezzlers, racketeers and speculators have been preying parasitically on mismanagement and exacerbated shortages.

''It should be noted that it is precisely the activities of cooperatives functioning as middleman-type cooperatives and buying-and-selling cooperatives that cause the greatest discontent among the public.''[130]

January 1990

''Internal affairs agencies and agencies of the prosecutors office recorded 2,461,692 crimes in 1989; that is 31.8 percent more than in 1988.''[131]

February

As compared to those recorded in 1988, in 1989 recorded crimes were up 31.8 percent and grave crimes up 42.3 percent.[132]

March

"Unlike the American mafia, which . . . developed on the basis of prohibited trade (control of prostitution, games of chance, sale of alcohol and narcotics); in our country, the 'godfathers' were born . . . on the basis of mismanagement and gross violation of distributive relations. . . .

"Organized crime is developing primarily on the basis of the shadow economy. . . .

"[F]or the most part [organized crime groups] act as parasites on the problems of the economy, especially on the notorious deficits. . . .

"The term 'chemist' is used widely as a slang synonym for probationer or parolee with a mandatory labor assignment. . . . This year there are approximately 140,000 of them in the country. According to predictions by legal experts, the number of 'chemists' will soon be almost twice that."[133]

May

"Society is greatly alarmed about the increase in crime among young people and juveniles. Persons aged fourteen to twenty-nine years comprise nearly 60 percent of those involved in crimes, and for certain kinds up to 90 percent. During the years 1977–1988 crime among 14-to-15-year-olds doubled. Crime among juveniles and young men continued to climb in 1989 and 1990."[134]

June

According to the deputy chief of the CPSU Central Committee Ideological Department, "[T]wo serious mistakes have been made in the pursuit of perestroika. First, 'the economy was sacrificed to politics' and second 'behind the general discussions about a law-governed state, we have forgotten to ensure elementary law and order.' "[135]

July

As compared to 1989, during the first six months of 1990 the rate of increase of recorded crimes was up 14.6% and of serious crimes 21.6%. Among the categories listed the highest increase was 23.9% in "crime on means of transportation."[136]

"We have not been given information concerning the sources for the financing of the governmental and department dachas, the housing funds, the security organs, the personnel staff, and many other departments. . . . [W]e cannot get all the joint resolutions of the CPSU Central Committee and of the Council of Ministers concerning advantages and privileges that are given to the Party apparatus. And even the few which we have gotten are terribly distorted!''[137]

February 1991

In an interview, Boris Karlovich Pugo, minister of interior, stated, ''[I]n 1990 [the crime rate was] 13.2 percent higher than the previous year. . . . [T]he number of violent personal assaults has grown by 11 percent, while crimes involving use of firearms has increased by a third.

''An increase in crime has been noted in all union republics, especially in Armenia (43.9 percent), Estonia (24.4), Lithuania (18.6), and Latvia (16.9 percent). The growth rate of property crime is increasing rapidly in Armenia (64.5 percent), Georgia (42.1), Estonia (33.0) and Lithuania (31.0 percent).''[138]

July

''In the first half of the year [1991], over 1.5 million crimes were recorded, or 20 percent more than in the corresponding period last year.''[139]

In an interview with the chief of the Transport Internal Affairs Main Administration and the chief of the Armed Security Administration of the MPS (Ministry of Railways), the officials said, ''The crime wave that has overwhelmed the country has rolled on to railroad transport. . . . [A]lmost everyday: policemen and armed security guards are killed in skirmishes with armed robbers. . . .

''We are particularly alarmed by the increase in losses including those from theft, on the Transcaucasian, Central Asian, North Caucasus, Volga, Alma-Ata, Azerbaijan, Moscow, October and West Siberian railroads.''[140]

September

''The rumors of a coming lean winter, chaos, and unrest in the country are making people scared and spiteful and pushing them into crime. Pilfering has assumed threatening proportions. People are removing whatever they can from kolkhoz and sovkhoz fields in broad daylight—cabbages, potatoes, tomatoes. . . . And not in bags, but on trucks. It is no longer astonishing to hear of sheep, cows, and horses being taken from farms. . . . In short, it's every man for himself.''[141]

November

''There were 7,500 crimes against foreigners reported last year. This is five times the average level a decade ago.''[142]

A representative poll taken in Russia, the Ukraine, Moldova, Georgia, Uzbekistan, Tajikistan, Turkmenia, Latvia, and Lithuania asked the question: "Is it possible to live in the Soviet Union without violating the law? . . . The answers throughout the country were as follows: 'Yes'—30 percent; 'No'—51 percent; 'Don't know'—20 percent."[143]

December

According to Goskomstat data, "In a year, from 1989 through 1990, the turnover of the shadow economy has significantly increased from 59.0 to 68.8 billion rubles. Even if we had no other data on the state of affairs in the national economy, this alone would have been sufficient for the most alarming diagnoses. . . .

"In absolute expression, the largest article of shadow business remains the production and sale of moonshine: R23 billion! Let us compare: In 1990 the state produced R55.2 billion worth of alcoholic beverages."[144]

January 1992

"According to General Vladislav Massimovskiy of the interior service, for the first time the number of registered crimes in Russia exceeded 2 million, which was an 18 percent increase as compared with 1990."[145]

According to Russian Supreme Soviet Chairman Ruslan Khasbulatov, the situation in the markets is chaotic. For example, he said that in Moscow almost all of the markets are effectively "under the protection of criminal groups. We will establish control," he said; "if our law enforcement agencies cannot cope, we will replace them with the military."[146]

February

A draft law in the Russian Federation proposes to "establish criminal liability of up to seven years' deprivation of liberty for acts, in other words action or inaction, committed for any purpose flagrantly contravening the interests of the Russian Federation."[147]

As reported by Alexander Rahr, "The former USSR KGB chairman Vladimir Kryuchkov, now in prison for his part in the attempted coup, alleged in a recent interview that the KGB could never have dreamt of exerting the kind of power under former Soviet leader Mikhail Gorbachev that the Russian state security organs now have under Yeltsin."[148]

March

"Semferopol, 3 Mar—A group of homeless officers from the Black Sea Fleet division . . . seized fifteen rooms in a hotel owned by the Intourist joint-stock company."[149]

" 'The most awful threat now facing Russia,' Academician Osipov, director of the Sociopolitical Studies Institute, repeats yet again, 'is disintegration. Unless the government stops theft and corruption, the country will perish sooner than might be expected.' "[150]

April

"Permission to acquire smooth-barreled firearms has started to be given to private farmers in the [Russian Federation] Jewish Autonomous Oblast.

"They are being forced to arm themselves by the need to defend their property from thieves and robbers."[151]

"According to data from the Russian Ministry of Internal Affairs, crime increased by 36% in the first of 1992."[152]

May

"Moscow—The founding conference of the Non-Governmental Council has come to the conclusion that honest business in Russia today is impossible."[153]

June

"The Constitutional Court [CC] of the Russian Federation declared that 'the constitutional system in Russia is in threat.' The statement distributed in Moscow on Friday [27 June] stresses that 'separate official persons and political leaders of different orientation stand for abolishing the constitutional bodies of power.' . . .

"At the same time the CC statement says that the institutions responsible for security of the constitutional order, the rights and freedoms of citizens 'shows inadmissible passivity' and do not use the powers granted them."[154]

STRIKES AND DISRUPTIONS

December 1989

According to Prime Minister Ryzhkov, "[L]ast August . . . undesirable phenomena that seriously complicate economic development began to show up. This included a fall-off in production and labor discipline, and a decline in responsibility for fulfilling commitments to consumers and to the state. Nationality-based clashes, strikes at enterprises, 'blockades' and long interruptions in traffic on main rail lines are causing enormous, difficult-to-predict damage. In the first 11 months of this year, losses from strikes alone totaled 7.5 million man-days, and output shortfalls in the national economy came to more than 2 billion rubles."[155]

January 1991

"The increased losses of work time were affected by the strikes and interethnic conflicts. In 1990, 1,800 enterprises and organizations had strikes, losses of work time exceeded 10 million man-days, and approximately 40,000 people were absent from their work places each day."[156]

March 1992

Social tension remains in a number of regions in Russia, Belarus, and Ukraine, where strikes staged by workers in some key industries and in the social sphere are continuing.[157]

April

Russian health workers are on strike, demanding wage increases to "3100 to 3200 rubles a month instead of the 940 rubles they are receiving now. . . . Russian medical workers report full collapse of national health care service."[158]

May

"The oilmen's strike already caused the daily output of oil at the northern Fields in the Komi SSR to fall by 3,000 to 4,000 tons."[159]

NOTES

1. "Comparison of U.S. Soviet Living Standards," *SSHA: Ekonomika, Politica, Ideologiya*, December 1988, pp. 12–22. JPRS-USA–89–007, April 14, 1989.

2. *Moscow News*, no. 10, 1989.

3. M. Berger, "Who Owes Whom, or the Banker's View of Personal Savings," *Izvestia*, August 23, 1989. JPRS-UEA-89–031, September 15, 1989.

4. A. Gamov, "Follow-Up on an Event: . . . " *Sovetskaya Rossiaya*, September 13, 1989. CDSP, vol. 41, no. 43, 1989.

5. Second Congress Debates, *Izvestia*, December 16, 1989. CDSP, vol. 41, no. 52, 1989.

6. A. Manilova, "Social Accounting: Does Everyone Poor Mean Everyone Equal?" *Leningradskaya pravda*, January 23, 1990. JPRS-UEA-90–013, April 12, 1990.

7. I. Upmacis, "Crime Statistic, Or the Crime of Statistics," *Admoda*, January 9, 1990. [Translation source misplaced.]

8. Lyubova Ulyanova, "The Purchase of an Apartment," *Pravitelstvennyy vestnik*, January 1990. JPRS-UEA-90–010, March 21, 1990.

9. A. Kormilkin, "The Subsistence Wage: Some Observations on Different Ways of Calculating It," *Trud*, March 7, 1990. JPRS-UEA-90–020, June 14, 1990.

10. *Izvestia*, October 17, 1990. Radio Liberty Report on the USSR, October 26, 1990.

11. V. Boykov, "On the Threshold of the Market: Concerns and Hopes," *Ekonomika i zhizn*, no. 39, 1990. JPRS-UEA-90–039, November 23, 1990.

12. Tatyana Yarygina, "A Nonessential Item," *Moscow News*, April 21, 1991.

13. Yu. Rytov, "A Good Beginning Makes a Good Ending...; Price Reform in the Context of Perestroika," *Pravitelstvennyy vestnik*, April 1991. JPRS-UEA-91–027, May 31, 1991.

14. L. Pronina, "How Much Has the Cost of Living Increased," *Argumenty i fakty*, April 1991. JPRS-UEA-91–024, May 17, 1991.

15. Ye. Melnikova, "Where Our Armored Train Is Crawling," *Literaturnaya gazeta*, May 1, 1991. JPRS-UEA-91–022, May 14, 1991.

16. V. Romanyuk, *Izvestia*, May 22, 1991. CDSP, July 26, 1991.

17. "Saturday, June 22, 1991," *Report on the USSR*, July 5, 1991.

18. "Viewpoint," *Interfax*, July 2, 1991. FBIS-SOV-91–128, July 3, 1991.

19. "The USSR Economy in the First Half of 1991: USSR State Statistics Committee Announcement," *Ekonomika i zhizn*, July 1991. FBIS-SOV-91–147, July 31, 1991.

20. "Living Standard in Free Fall," *Moscow News*, August 11–18, 1991.

21. Vasiliy Selyunin, "What Is Happening to Our Money?" *Rossiyskaya gazeta*, August 1, 1991. JPRS-UEA-91–034.

22. Gennadiy Petrov, TASS, September 23, 1991. FBIS-SOV-91–185, September 24, 1991.

23. "Moscow Radio Rossii," September 22, 1991. FBIS-SOV-91–184, September 23, 1991.

24. "Hyperinflation: Today or Tomorrow," *Delovoy mir*, September 6, 1991. JPRS-UEY-91–039, October 25, 1991.

25. G. Gorbey, "Free-Fall into the Abyss of Poverty," and B. Golovachev, "These Are Still Not Records," *Trud*, October 30, 1991. JPRS-UEA-91–042, November 20, 1991.

26. "Nation & Society: Poverty in the USSR," *Interfax*, November 22, 1991. FBIS-SOV-91–229, November 27, 1991.

27. M. Berger, "Old Mistakes with New Bread Prices," *Izvestia*, November 24, 1991. FBIS-SOV-91–223, November 19, 1991.

28. Radio Moscow, November 19, 1991. FBIS-SOV-91–225, November 21, 1991.

29. TASS, November 18, 1991. FBIS-SOV-91–223, November 19, 1991.

30. Radio Riga, December 2, 1991. FBIS-SOV-91–233, December 4, 1991.

31. Radio Moscow World Service, December 31, 1991.

32. Boris Sverdlov, "Recoiling from the Shelves," *Rossiyskaya gazeta*, January 11, 1992. FBIS-SOV-92–011, January 16, 1992.

33. *Argumenty i fakty*, January 1992. FBIS-SOV-92–015, January 23, 1992.

34. Igor Agabekov, TASS, January 24, 1992. FBIS-SOV-92–017, January 27, 1992.

35. "Newsbeat," *Pravda*, January 14, 1992. FBIS-SOV-92–011, January 16, 1992.

36. "Vesti," Moscow Russian Television Network, January 29, 1992. FBIS-SOV–92–020, January 30, 1992.

37. Kazys Uscila, TASS, January 23, 1992. FBIS-SOV-92–018, January 28, 1992.

38. Alexander Dzyublo, TASS, February 13, 1992. FBIS-SOV-92–031, February 14, 1992.

39. Moscow Mayak Radio Network, February 23, 1992. FBIS-SOV-92–038, February 26, 1992.

40. TASS, March 26, 1992. FBIS-SOV-92–060, March 27, 1992.

41. Andrei Tkachenko, "Wages and Prices: Living as We Did 45 Years Ago, if not Worse," *Independent Newspaper*, March 20–21, 1992.

42. "Capital's Rich and Poor People," *Rossiyskaya gazeta*, February 27, 1992. FBIS-SOV-92–040, February 28, 1992.

43. "Vesti," Moscow Russian Television, March 18, 1992. FBIS-SOV-92–054, March 19, 1992.

44. Moscow Programma Radio Odin, March 19, 1992. FBIS-SOV-92–056, March 23, 1992.

45. "Domestic Market," *Postfactum*, April 4, 1992. FBIS-SOV-92–067, April 7, 1992.

46. "Domestic Market," *Postfactum*, March 18, 1992. FBIS-SOV-92–055, March 20, 1992.

47. Kommersant, March 2, 1992, as cited by Keith Bush, "Russia: Gaidar's Guidelines," *RFE/RL Research Report*, April 10, 1992.

48. *Baltfax*, March 31, 1992. FBIS-SOV-92–063, April 1, 1992.

49. Moscow Radio Moscow World Service, April 8, 1992. FBIS-SOV-92–071, April 13, 1992.

50. Moscow Mayak Radio Network, April 18, 1992. FBIS-SOV-92–077, April 21, 1992.

51. Ivan Novikov, ITAR-TASS, April 21, 1992. FBIS-SOV-92–078, April 22, 1992.

52. "Goskomstat Reports," *Rossiyskaya gazeta*, April 24, 1992. FBIS-SOV-92–080, April 24, 1992.

53. Moscow Radio Moscow World Service, May 6, 1992. FBIS-SOV-92–088, May 6, 1992.

54. *Rossiyskaya gazeta*, May 1, 1992. FBIS-SOV-92–087, May 5, 1992.

55. Viktor Belikov, "Heat and Water in Moscow Homes to Go up in May," *Izvestia*, May 1, 1992. FBIS-SOV-92–087, May 5, 1992.

56. Moscow Mayak Radio Network, May 1, 1992. FBIS-SOV-92–087, May 5, 1992.

57. Aleksandr Shinkin, "Cheap Promises Grow More Expensive, But Our Purses Get No Heavier," *Pravda*, May 21, 1992. FBIS-SOV-92–099, May 21, 1992.

58. *Postafactum*, May 28, 1992. FBIS-SOV-92–103, May 28, 1992.

59. Vtacheslav Goncharov, "One Lot of Wages, Two Lots of Wages," *Kuranty*, May 22, 1992. FBIS-SOV-102, May 27, 1992.

60. Kiev Radio Ukraine World Service, May 20, 1992. FBIS-SOV-102, May 27, 1992.

61. A. Kolpakov and P. Budanayev, "Vesti," Moscow Russian Television, May 13, 1992. FBIS-SOV-92–096, May 18, 1992.

62. "Politics," *Postfactum*, June 14, 1992. FBIS-SOV-92–119, June 19, 1992.

63. "Kyodo," *Interfax*, June 20, 1992. JPRS-SOV-92–120, June 22, 1992.

64. *Pravda*, September 11, 1985.

65. A. L. Pern, "Family Budget in the Mirror of Statistics," *Organizatsiya promyshlennogo proizvodstva*, September 1988. JPRS-UEA-89–003.

66. Vladimir Tikhonov, "Do We Need Ration Cards?" *Moscow News*, no. 24, 1989.

67. Viktor Shirokov, "Person without a Job," *Pravda*, October 31, 1989. CDSP, November 29, 1989.

68. "Vladimir Tikhonov: Land for the Peasants," *Yunost*, October 1989. JPRS-UPA-90–001.

69. Second Congress Debates, *Izvestia*, December 15, 1989. CDCP, vol. 41, no. 52, 1989.

70. Nikolai Ryzhkov, *Pravda*, December 29, 1989.

71. *Kommunist*, January 1990. JPRS-UKO-90–005, April 16, 1990.

72. *Moscow News*, no. 14, 1990.

73. *Ogonek*, no. 5, 1990. Radio Liberty, May 25, 1990.

74. *Report on the USSR*, January 11, 1991.

75. Grennadiy Yastrbtsov, "Topical Subject: Discrepancy of 300 Billion Rubles. Why Is It Beyond Us to Supply Enough Goods, Even After Raising Prices," *Pravda*, July 1, 1991. FBIS-SOV-91–132, July 10, 1991.

76. V. Buldakov, "Readers Only," *Argumenty i fakty*, July 1991. FBIS-SOV-92–146, July 30, 1991.

77. Viktor Andriyanov, Oleg Kulish, and Vadim Raskin, "On the Main Point: Comradly, Frank Discussion between the Country's Leaders and Representatives of Labor Collectives," *Sel'skaya zhizn*, July 1991. FBIS-SOV-91–147, July 31, 1991.

78. V. Romanyuk, "Statistics and Our Economy," *Izvestia*, August 15, 1991. FBIS-SOV-91–159, August 16, 1991.

79. G. Gorbey, "Free-Fall into the Abyss of Poverty," and B. Golovachev "These Are Still Not Records," *Trud*, October 30, 1991. JPRS-UEA-91–042, November 20, 1991.

80. "The Battle for the Harvest Always Includes Plans for Casualties," *Komsomolskaya pravda*, October 30, 1991. JPRS-SOV-91–211, October 31, 1991.

81. *Baltfax*, November 5, 1991. FBIS-SOV-91–2115, November 6, 1991.

82. Radio Moscow World Service, November 6, 1991. FBIS-SOV-91–215, November 6, 1991.

83. *Interfax*, November 20, 1991. FBIS-SOV-91–225. November 21, 1991.

84. *KYODO*, November 24, 1991. FBIS-SOV-91–229, November 27, 1991.

85. "Domestic Market," *Postfactum*, December 23, 1991. FBIS-SOV-91–247, December 24, 1991.

86. Aleksander Dzyuhio, TASS, January 16, 1992. FBIS-SOV-92–012, January 17, 1992.

87. TASS, February 4, 1992. FBIS-SOV-92–024, February 5, 1992.

88. *Moscow Central Television*, January 23, 1992. FBIS-SOV-92–026, February 7, 1992.

89. "Not the First Round of Aid," *Moscow News*, February 23–March 1, 1992.

90. "Domestic Market," *Postfactum*, April 4, 1992. FBIS-SOV-92–067, April 7, 1992.

91. "Trade and Investment," *Interfax*, April 23, 1992. FBIS-SOV-92–080, April 24, 1992.

92. "Kyodo," *Interfax*, June 21, 1992. JPRS-SOV-92–120, June 22, 1992.

93. *Agitator*, November, 1988. JPRS-UEA-89–005.

94. A. G. Aganbegyan, "On the Conception of Long-Range Socioeconomic Development," *Izvestia akademii nauk SSSR: Seriya ekonomicheskaya*, no. 1, 1989. JPRS-UEA–89–010.

95. "On the Nature Watch: From the State Committee's First Session," *Sovetskaya Rossiya*, April 28, 1989. [Translation source misplaced.]

96. V. Davydov. "Who Will Be Next? The High Accident Rate in the Country's Highways," *Pravda*, November 16, 1988.

97. Nikolay Vorontsov, chairman of Goskompriroda, the State Committee for Environmental Protection, *Moskovskaya pravda*, January 18, 1990. JPRS-UPA-90–015, March 22, 1990.

98. "Social Portrait of a Phenomenon . . . ," *Komsomolskaya pravda*, April 25, 1990. CDSP, June 20, 1990.

99. Vadim Grigoryevich Pervyship, "What Next? A Real Threat to the People's Genetic Stock Has Emerged," *Liternaturnaya rossiya*, January 25, 1991. JPRS-UPA–91–014, March 11, 1991.

100. N. Barabash, "In the Name of the Unborn," *Sovetskaya rossiya*, February 8, 1991. JPRS-UPA-91–013, March 11, 1991.

101. "The Baltic Coast Is an Area at Risk," *Izvestia*, July 13, 1991. JPRS-UPA-91–041, September 18, 1991.

102. *Interfax*, September 9, 1991. FBIS-SOV-91–175, September 10, 1991.

103. Moscow Radio Rossii Network, September 22, 1991. FBIS-SOV-91–184, September 23, 1991.

104. Vladimir Zaynetdinov, "A Validol Tablet, Citizens!" *Nabochaya tribuna*, October 30, 1991. JPRS-UEA-91–042, November 20, 1991.

105. Viktoriya Yasnopolskaya, "In Ukraine More Are Dying Than Are Being Born," *Pravda Ukrainy*, October 17, 1991. JPRS-UPA-91–046, November 20, 1991.

106. "Our Time is Up . . . Our Home Is Unclean and Unhealthy. Solutions Must Be Found," *Moscow News*, November 3–10, 1991.

107. Moscow Mayak Radio Network, January 22, 1992. FBIS-SOV-92–016, January 24, 1992.

108. *Moscow Teleradioveshchatelnaya Kompaniya*, March 21, 1992. FBIS-SOV-92–059, March 26, 1992.

109. Aleksander Ulikenok, "Minsk Is Counting on 'Gentlemen,' " *Pravda*, April 30, 1992. CDSP, May 27, 1992.

110. Ivan Novikov, ITAR-TASS, May 19, 1992. JPARS-SOV-92–099, May 21, 1992.

111. Moscow Radio Rossii Network, May 19, 1992. JPRS-SOV-92–099, May 21, 1992.

112. *Kyodo*, June 7, 1992. FBIS-SOV-92–112, June 10, 1992.

113. Galina Vinitskaya, ITAR-TASS June 9, 1992. FBIS-SOV-92–112, June 10, 1992.

114. "Impatient Yeltsin Cuts off Interview for American TV," *The Kansas City Star*, June 15, 1992.

115. Moscow Radio Television Network, June 13, 1992. FBIS-SOV-92–115, June 18, 1992.

116. Ye. Blokhin and V. Mikosha, "Novosti," Moscow Teleradiokompaniya Ostankino Television, June 16, 1992. FBIS-SOV-92–122, June 24, 1992.

117. "Briefly and Clearly," *Pravda*, June 16, 1992. JPRS-SOV-92–121, June 23, 1992.

118. Veronika Romanenkova, ITAR-TASS, June 25, 1992. FBIS-SOV-92–124, June 26, 1992.

119. "The USSR State Statistics Committee Reports," *Argumenty i fakty*, November 11–17, 1989. [Translation source misplaced.]

120. Second Congress Debates, *Izvestia*, December 16, 1989. CDSP, vol. 42, no. 1, 1990.

121. *Trud*, December 12, 1989. JPRS-UEA-90–010, March 21, 1990.

122. "People on the Roads," *Pravda*, January 21, 1990. CDSP, vol. 42, no. 3, 1990.

123. V. Yunisov, "When Visiting God, There Are No Latenesses! *Komsomolskaya pravda*, December 8, 1990. JPRS-UPA-91–001, January 14, 1991.

124. V. Kudryavtsev and Ye. Lukasheva, "A Socialist Law Governed State," *Kommunist*, July 1988, p. 44. [Translation source misplaced.]

125. V. Voronetskiy, "The Difficult Path to New Laws. Democratization of Legislative Process on Agenda," *Argumenty i fakty*, July 9–15, 1988, p. 56. [Translation source misplaced.]

126. G. Ovcharenko, "The Legal State: What Should It Be Like?" *Pravda*, August 2, 1988, p. 1.

127. "A briefing with Lt. V. Bakatin, USSR minister of internal affairs," *Izvestia*, July 11, 1989. CDSP, vol. 41, no. 28, 1989.

128. Aleksandr Ivanovich Gurov, SSR MVD administrations chief, "Organized Crime," *Agitator*, September 1989. JPRS-UPA-90–003.

129. "The USSR Ministry of Internal Affairs' Press Center Comments," *Chelovek i zakon*, November 1989. [Translation source misplaced.]

130. "The USSR Ministry of Internal Affairs' Press Center Comments," *Chelovek i zakon*, November 1989. [Translation source misplaced.]

131. "Interview with the head of the USSR Ministry of Internal Affairs' Chief Information Center," *Izvestia*, January 10, 1990. CDSP, vol. 42, no. 2, 1990.

132. "Our Safety in the Mirror of Statistics," *Soyuz*, February 19–25, 1990. JPRS-UPA-90–023, May 1, 1990.

133. Dmitry Radyshevsky, "Plus 'Chemicalization,' " *Moscow News*, no. 12, 1990.

134. "USSR MVD Press Center Comments," *Chelovek i zakon*, May 1990. JPRS-UPA-90–048, August 16, 1990.

135. G. Zyuganov, "Realism of Actions," *Sovetskaya rossiya*, April 13, 1990. JPRS-UPA-90–029, June 4, 1990.

136. A. Illesh and V. Rudnev, "Statistics and Our Commentary: The Fight Against Crime—Illusion and Reality," *Izvestia*, July 24, 1990, CDSP, vol. 42, no. 31, 1990.

137. Vladislav Starchevsky, "They Will Fight for Their Privileges," *Nedelya*, July 2–8, 1990. JPRS-UPA-90–058, October 9, 1990. An interview with Ella A. Pamfilova, a member of the Supreme Soviet of the USSR, the secretary of the commission concerning privileges.

138. S. Ovsienko, "From a Position of Law," *Veteran*, February 1991. JPRS-UPA–91–021, April 18, 1991.

139. "The USSR Economy in the First Half of 1991: USSR State Statistics Committee Announcement," *Ekonomika i zhizn*, July 1991. FBIS-SOV-91–147, July 31, 1991.

140. A. Yermishin, "Reliable Safeguarding of Freight," *Elektricheskaya I Teplovoznaya Tyaga*, July 1991. JPRS-UEA-91–042, November 20, 1991.

141. A. Sazhin, "Council Decides There Will Be No Hunger. What about Us?" *Pravda*, September 19, 1991. FBIS-SOV-91–187, September 26, 1991.

142. Radio Moscow World Service, November 14, 1991. FBIS-SOV-91–220, November 14, 1991.

143. Alexander Golov, "Can You Live Here and Not Break the Law?" *Independent Newspaper*, November 1991.

144. Vladimir Kostakov, "Super-Prohibitions and Super-Profits," *Kultura*, December 28, 1991. JPRS-UEA-02–002, January 17, 1992.

145. Radio Moscow World Service, January 28, 1992. FBIS-SOV-92–023, February 4, 1992.

146. "Traders Ready to Lower Prices," *Rossiyskaya gazeta*, January 11, 1992. FBIS-SOV-92–009, January 14, 1992.

147. Sergey Kornilov, "Press Conference," *Rossiyskaya gazeta*, February 24, 1992. FBIS-SOV-92–037, February 25, 1992.

148. ITAR-TASS, February 27, 1992. As reported by Alexander Rahr, "The KGB Survives under Yeltsin's Wing," *RFE/RL Research Report*, March 27, 1992.

149. "Our Correspondent . . . Homeless Black Sea Sailors Driven to Despair," *Krasnaya zvezda*, March 4, 1992. FBIS-SOV-92–046, March 9, 1992.

150. Sergey Panasenko, "Unless Theft and Corruption Are Stopped . . . ," *Rossiyskaya gazeta*, March 24, 1992. FBIS-SOV-92–059, March 26, 1992.

151. "Peasants Defend Themselves," *Izvestia*, April 15, 1992. FBIS-SOV-92–078, April 22, 1992.

152. Valery Ivanov, "25,000 People Are Missing," *Izvestia*, April 29, 1992. CDSP, May 27, 1992.

153. "Domestic Market," *Postfactum*, May 1, 1992. FBIS-SOV-92–086, May 4, 1992.

154. "Kyodo," *Interfax*, June 26, 1992. FBIS-SOV-92–125, June 29, 1992.

155. Ryzhkov, Congress Debates, *Izvestia*, December 14, 1989. CDSP, vol. 41, no. 51, 1990.

156. "The USSR Economy in 1990," *Ekonomika y zhizn*, January 1991. FBIS-SOV-91–023, February 4, 1991.

157. TASS, March 20, 1992. FBIS-SOV-92–056, March 23, 1992.

158. *Interfax*, April 30, 1992. FBIS-SOV-92–085, May 1, 1992.

159. Viktor Matkarov, ITAR-TASS, May 15, 1992. FBIS-SOV-92–096, May 18, 1992.

8

THE SOVIET MIND-SET: PUBLIC OPINIONS

A central assumption of this work is that aside from such uncontrollable forces as major natural calamities (e.g., a record drought) and invasions by foreign powers, people individually and collectively are the primary determinants of their fate. When examined alongside the realities that the members of society face in daily life, the following sampling of the mind-set of both the public opinion makers and, especially the people, provides valuable insight into the Soviet past, the present in the independent states, and what is likely to evolve in any foreseeable future.

AGRARIAN REFORM: PRIVATIZATION AND PEASANT ATTITUDES

From the beginning of the experiment in building communism, agriculture has been the major domestic economic problem area. Since the mid-1980s, that reality has been openly admitted by Gorbachev and numerous other internal commentators. Beyond serious shortfalls in the production of crops and livestock, other major problems include a primitive, wholly inadequate, and deteriorating rural transportation, storage, and processing infrastructure, as well as shortages of industrial inputs to the farms, all of which are major contributors to alarming levels of postharvest losses. Further, the dismantling of the old organization-management system has resulted in a breakdown in the distribution of materials and commodities.

In the name of agrarian reform, a move to privatization of farming has been promoted by numerous leaders and opinion makers as essential if the agriculture-food problem is to be resolved. As of the spring of 1992, however, the move to private farming is proceeding at a snail's pace and is meeting with considerable resistance, from both local officials and the peasants themselves.

March 1983

As early as 1983, there were reports of lease contracts adopted by peasant workers to go into private farming that had been abandoned later for the former guaranteed minimum wage system. For example, a "wealthy" Siberian farm abandoned the scheme, even after the workers' income had doubled as a result of their new efforts. Why? According to an *Izvestia* reporter, there was nothing in the shops to buy with their new earnings.[1]

December 1987

The rural sociologist Tatyana Zaslavskaya has stated in an interview that if the collective contract scheme is to be successful, production initiative must pass to the individual production groups. Unfortunately, as she observed, "[I]n seventy years of Soviet power, . . . sixty years . . . of state-run agriculture, generations have changed, and the people who today work in the kolkhozes and sovkhozes not only were never independent peasant farmers, but their parents were not independent peasants, and their grandparents even joined the kolkhozes." Thus Soviet peasants at the end of the 1980s, she added, lack the "psychological prerequisites" for perestroika to succeed. "I have been to many kolkhozes and talked to many people . . . those . . . who dream of working individually . . . just do not exist."[2]

March 1989

According to Gorbachev, in his major 1989 speech on agriculture: "Leasing is . . . received with caution by that part of collective farmers and workers who have lost, over many years, the habit of working conscientiously and got used to steady incomes irrespective of the end results."

A passage in Gorbachev's speech could portend the most important of all his agricultural reforms. He stated that restructuring agriculture requires "eliminating the existing administrative (departmental and territorial) system of management of agriculture and of the agrarian sector of the economy as a whole."

The kolkhozy and sovkhozy captured the Soviet Union's peasants in a position of working on the farms much like hired hands or, in Gorbachev's words, "day-labourers."

Addressing those who have called for abandoning the collective and state farms, Gorbachev said: "I believe that this viewpoint is both scientifically and practically ungrounded."[3]

"Why hasn't the high level of effectiveness of lease contracts become one of the main forces of the agricultural branch? On what level, where, is the greatest

Table 8.1
Press Support for Peasant Perestroika

	7/1/86 to 6/30/87		7/1/87 to 6/30/88		7/1/88 to 6/1/89	
	Positive	Negative	Positive	Negative	Positive	Negative
Family farm	17	0	10	4	2	3
Lease holding	1	0	9	4	13	30
Co-ops	0	0	2	3	7	13
Total:	18	0	21	11	22	46

Source: Alexandr Bekker, Moscow News, no. 28, 1989.

opposition to the development of lease relations? On the oblast level? Rayon? Enterprise?

"The answer turned out to be unanimous—on the level of the enterprise.

"It is becoming clear that today the administration is utilizing the contract more often than not to confuse the lessee, to invalidate the essence of the lease and to deprive the individual of incentives for labor productivity."[4]

June

Moscow News did a press survey of the changing views of the central press on leasing. It published a table (Table 8.1) reflecting that whereas the 1986–1987 articles reflected overwhelming support for the key elements of Gorbachev's rural reforms, by 1988–1989 there had been a complete reversal, with more than half of the commentaries being negative, including nearly a 3-to-1 rejection of the crucial lease-holding scheme.

A second table reporting survey results listed the nine specific criticisms found in the articles and the number of times they were repeated. At the top of the list was "price of product and wages," twenty-one times; second "lease requests denied and length of leases," eleven times; and third, "limited independence," ten times. Second from the bottom was "arson of farms and damage to equipment," three times.[5]

July

Often the farm directors violate the leases. "No peasant can be a true owner while being pressed by administrative regulations within which the kolkhozes and sovkhozes still operate."[6]

October

Former politburo member Igor Ligachev said, "I think that . . . kolkhozes and sovkhozes are and remain formations of the food fund. . . . [S]ome comrades . . . say the time has come to reorganize kolkhozes and sovkhozes and to transform them into small peasant, or as the say in the West, farming enterprises. Honestly speaking, I do not know what there is more of here—ignorance or political irresponsibility."[7]

"Over a period of sixty years, we have destroyed the social type of peasant and created something completely different. Initially, . . . he was a bonded worker with a plot of ground. But today he is a hired worker with a definite guaranteed wage. A peasant knows that, regardless of the results of his labor, he will receive his salary, any one of which will satisfy his minimum requirements. And the peasants do not wish to undertake the risk of receiving income based upon vague results of labor realized earlier. Studies [for example] conducted by my Siberian colleagues reveal that roughly [only] 20 percent of the peasants questioned by them are prepared to willingly undertake leases. . . .

"At the present time, the government assumes that the introduction of leasing at kolkhozes and sovkhozes constitutes radical changes. This is a myth. It is an illusion. The leasing of land and the economic independence of peasants at kolkhozes are impracticable. . . .

"Strong [collective] farms exist because of strong personalities and not because the kolkhoz system is good. But the fact of the matter is that not even the most eminent chairman is master of his own land. There is the raykom, oblispolkom, obkom and kraykom. There is always a needed element which can correct him in a timely manner. The land belongs not to him but rather to the state and unfortunately not everybody understands this fact. . . .

"The land is formally assigned to a kolkhoz, but only the state organs can establish the plan, when the planting and harvesting operations are to be carried out and the prices. For all practical purposes, a peasant is deprived completely of the opportunity of managing in an independent manner. . . . [T]he requirements for presenting economic independence to the peasants remain merely as unrealized slogans."[8]

"According to data from our surveys conducted in . . . [several oblasts], only 16 percent of the lessees polled entered into a lease on their own conviction. . . . According to data from sociologists in Belorussia, 72 percent of leasehold collectives in the republic were created at 'initiative from above.' Only 18 percent of those polled [in one oblast] turned out to be genuine leases. . . .

"About 70 percent of the kolkhoz farmers and sovkhoz workers think that a new 'dekulakization' is possible."[9]

" 'Indicators for the kolkhozy and sovkhozy of Piterskiy Rayon for . . . 1989?' The vertical columns list the farms, and the horizontal lines indicate deadlines for the procurement of hay, haylage, silage, fodder, threshing. . . . Some of the figures are circled in red pencil.

" 'Why those red circles? I am supposed to control,' V. Korolkov, the rayon party secretary, smiled and then explained: 'Here in that kolkhoz, all of a sudden milk production declined. One should telephone and find out what is happening. For example, if the tractor has broken down or the farm has remained without electricity, I must quickly inform the respective services.'

" 'Is there no one in the kolkhoz to do this?'

" 'There is, but my intervention greatly speeds up the discussions. Furthermore without the intervention of the raykom, the oblast services would make the kolkhoz wait. Naturally, I understand that these are not the proper methods. But what am I to do, just sit and look at higher production losses? . . .'

" 'Who in the rayon could make careless workers do that which they should? Only the party raykom. . . .'

" '[T]he brigade council does not even discuss any somewhat serious matter without "running it by" the party group in advance, and without the group's agreement. . . .'

" '[T]he people do not object to the direct intervention by the party committee and the party group in production matters. . . . [T]hey realize that is the only way one can get anything done.' ''[10]

"[A]s a rule, leasing subdivisions remain completely at the mercy of kolkhoz and sovkhoz offices, which very reluctantly give up the methods of management to which they are used.''[11]

"Often one hears that peasants do not want to lease land. . . . [T]hey have no faith in the future, in the fact that this is their enterprise and that no one will take it away from them or their children. Things were taken away at will in the past, after all!''[12]

November

"Unfortunately, one has to state that the gap between the 'master of the land' ideology and individual behavior not only persists but has become deeper.

"In 1986, 30 percent of sovkhoz workers and collective farms said they felt as masters of the land; in 1989, 48 percent of office workers, 16 percent of construction, shop and farm workers and 13 percent of industrial workers felt they were masters at their workplace. . . .

"[A] large share of rural workers do not find leasing attractive: only 25 percent expressed a desire to shift to this form of activity. . . .

"[T]o what extent in our country today are there greater obstructions to perestroika: in real life or in the mind? Perhaps . . . we should agree to consider as equally important the reorganization of the economy and the 'perestroika' of our own minds. . . .

"[What there is] bureaucratic centralism.''[13]

A collective farmer estimates that to set up a lease operation on 50–100 hectares, the cost for machinery, buildings and other capital expenses would "exceed 200,000" rubles.[14]

December

According to VASKhNIL president, academician A. Nikonov, "The lessee—in general, a diligent peasant—often is surrounded by a wall of envy and malice on account of his high earnings, while his labor is much more intensive."[15]

January 1990

"The recently published draft law, while establishing land as owned by collective and state farms, again disenfranchises the individual peasant. What will he be left with if he decides to leave the farm? At best he'll be given bad plots of land. That's why a peasant must know that the land of the collective farm has been formed by his will and it is his will, if he leaves the farm, to become the owner of a good plot of land.

"The mighty collective farms, the leaders of the collective farm system, don't risk anything."[16]

A farm wife wrote that the family gave up its highly productive private pig farm because "we cannot ram through the wall of bureaucrats, profiteers and grafters."[17]

"At thousands of collective and state farms living off state subsidies, the habit of living beyond their means for decades and producing less than they receive has led to the formation of the collective morality of an exploiter who lives off other people's labor. This is a harsh truth. But these tragedies have wiped the last greasepaint off the rosy assurances about the progressiveness of keeping leasing within the framework of the farms."[18]

At a conference of agriculturalists late in 1989, "newly emerged private farmers voiced this complaint at length from the speaker's platform. No one is paying attention to their troubles; they are not being given land and machines, every obstacle is being placed in their way so that the 'troublemakers do not corrupt honest kolkhoz members.' "[19]

February

A national poll of sovkhoz and kolkhoz workers revealed that only 27 percent "considered themselves supporters of leasing." Only 18 percent believed that the spreading of leasing would make the life of the people better.[20]

June

"Let the state build a decent farmhouse . . . provided with all utilities . . . a highly-mechanized cowbarn . . . rehabilitate the land . . . and build a hardtop road to the farmstead. Then the newly-created farm can be put up for competitive lease bidding, with subsequent transfer to possession for life with right of inheritance."[21]

July

Academician Vladimir Tikhonov said, "I believe, I am even convinced that unless there are radical changes in agriculture [real land reform] this year, real hunger awaits us next year. Just imagine, we have 220 million hectares of arable land and each year we purchase 40 million tonnes of grain, as much as 1.5 million tonnes of meat; we even buy potatoes although we grow six times more potatoes than the Americans. This is evidence of the fact that it is not nature that is to blame for the chronic depression, for the constant food crisis; economic conditions are to blame."[22]

"Our dear colleagues—manual and office workers, those engaged in intellectual pursuits and all residents of cities and worker settlements. We declare in a responsible manner that the principal cause of the crisis in agriculture lies not in the farms for organizing production nor with the peasants, but rather it has to do with the economic and social inequality of the peasants in society. The attitude towards the rural area as a type of internal colony, that existed throughout the years of industrialization, is still partially being retained today."[23]

"If economic relations do not change, if new incentives for peasant labor are not introduced, if the position of the peasants is not changed, if they do not become true masters of the land, then no investments are going to help. . . .

"[O]f course, we reject the demand for total decollectivization. . . .

"I will say frankly, the Law on Land is not working yet. . . .

"Comrades! In embarking on restructuring, we were clearly aware that no political, social or economic transformations would be possible without a revolution in people's minds, without spiritual rebirth and ideological renewal, in the broadest sense of the word."[24]

According to a poll of agricultural workers and leaders, "[K]olkhoz-sovkhoz production has become the 'sacred cow' of economic ideology. Its formula is as follows: public ownership unites people and is a socialist value, while private ownership to the contrary separates us and appears as an anti-value. . . .

"According to data obtained from our polls, the sensation of being an owner has been retained by only one out of every ten rural workers. In many individuals it has been replaced by the psychology of a day laborer, involving an entire series of deformation of economic and moral consciousness and behavior."[25]

August

According to a poll of the rural population in nineteen regions, "[T]he process of de-peasantization has crossed a critical line. Such is the opinion shared by 66 percent of the agricultural workers. If over the next few years a solution is not found for returning people to the land through the creation of interesting conditions for agricultural labor, then the food problem will assume the scale of a national catastrophe. . . . [Only] 6 percent of the respondents believe that 'none' of the peasants have lost interest in the land."[26]

"The legal construct of land possession that was adopted leaves virtually intact the existing land system. . . . [T]he law preserves the collective farms' and state farms' right to the permanent possession of land. . . . [Thus, the peasants] are defenseless against the high-handedness of the bureaucratic apparatus of collective farms and state farms."[27]

October

In an interview, Yuriy Chernychenko, USSR people's deputy, publicist, writer, and president of the new Russian Peasant Party, said, "[A]t present, collective farms are just a miserable fragment of the 'agroGULAG.' A hair cannot fall from the head of a cow without a resolution of the rayon party committee. . . . There are 230 million hectares of arable land in the USSR and all of it, to the last hectare, belongs to the CPSU."[28]

November

According to Ivan Silayev, chairman of the Russian SFSR Council of Ministers, "[T]he government considers it necessary to introduce a tax in kind in 1991 for all land users, with the exception of peasant farms and owners of personal orchards and vegetable gardens. . . . [I]t will not exceed 40 percent . . . [for most commodities. And state orders cannot] exceed 70 percent of total output."[29]

According to a survey of RSFSR kolkhoz and sovkhoz workers, "40 percent oppose private ownership of land. . . . Private ownership of land was advocated by 17 percent and 12 percent, respectively." Thirty-four percent and 42 percent, respectively, agreed that "in certain instances land should be sold or transferred to private ownership."[30]

December

The number of peasant farms "reached 29,500 as of 1 July" 1990.

Land reform will require ten to fifteen years, when "10 to 15 percent of the land now in use by kolkhozy and sovkhozy" will be privately cultivated.[31]

According to the new RSFSR land law, owners could not sell the land for ten years.[32]

The opening words of the RSFSR Congress's "resolution on the Program for Reviving the Russian Countryside and Developing the Agro-Industrial complex [were:] The Congress of the Russian SFSR People's Deputies affirms the diversity and equality of state, collective farm-cooperative, private and collective-shareholding forms of ownership and supports the development of all forms of farming: collective farms, state farms, peasant farms, and cooperatives and associations of peasant farms." The author points out, however, that out in the countryside, "many heads of Party committees, . . . still run the show in economic matters."[33]

A nationwide poll of kolkhoz and sovkhoz peasants and officials revealed that

"[T]he overwhelming majority think that land is the property of the whole people and cannot be under private ownership. Even among city dwellers 75 percent of those polled uphold this position. [A]mong kolkhoz members and sovkhoz workers, 83 percent and among managers and specialists, 88 percent [opposed private ownership].

"In all population groups (with the exception of workers at city enterprises) [only] from 13 to 19 percent give preference to individual farming . . . kolkhozy and sovkhozy should be the basic form. . . .

"Among kolkhoz members and sovkhoz workers . . . only 21 percent come out for the use of hired labor without any restrictions.''[34]

January 1991

In an interview, Vasiliy Starodubtsev, chairman of the USSR Peasants' Union, stated, ''[W]e did not find it possible to agree with the proposal to legalize private ownership of land for commodity production, or its sale and purchase. . . . It should be possible to buy and sell land that is allocated for dachas and private plots (in fact this is already done, only in veiled form).''[35]

"[L]and reform is the central link of all agrarian transformations. . . . Thus, the landowner, regardless of whether he is an independent peasant, cooperate, or sovkhoz, becomes the owner of the means of production. . . . [O]nly in such a situation can a normal market exist.''[36]

"[T]he Union republics are to introduce for 1991 state orders or other forms of obligatory deliveries of agricultural output to the state reserves, applicable to all landholders and land users producing agricultural output for the market. The output is to be paid for at state purchase prices.''[37] Anything left could be sold on the kolkhoz market.

February

"Has anything been done to reverse the tendency [for agricultural production to fall]? Nothing substantial. Has the land reform started? No. Instead of the reform, a referendum on private land ownership is to be held at the very time when agricultural work must be in full swing.''[38]

When a Dutch farmer, who spent most of 1990 on a Soviet farm near Moscow, was asked ''What's wrong with our agriculture?'' he answered, ''A high official tells farmers what to do, and they have to obey him.''[39]

March

In a representative poll of rural inhabitants, 71.6 percent of whom work on kolkhozy and sovkhozy, ''about 15 percent of respondents said they had . . . intentions [to leave the countryside] and 3.3 percent had already firmly decided to do so. . . . 9.9 percent of respondents want their children to stay and work on collective farms. 14.4 percent want to see them become independent farmers, and 22.2 percent recommend that their children leave the countryside and get a job in the city. . . . [For every one respondent who has faith in the Union Law on Land] four believe it is likely to be repealed. . . .

"The key obstacle to the development of the farmer movement is, in the respondents' view [to a poll of peasants], the lack of material-technical facilities—the difficulty in getting a loan, building facilities, buying equipment, etc. (50.1 percent), people's unpreparedness for independent farming (40.1 percent), impediments from collective farm administrations (25.9 percent)."[40]

May

According to a poll of collective and state farm workers in the RSFSR, the Ukraine, Belorussia, and Kazakhstan, "About 15 percent [intend to leave farming]. About 40 percent . . . want to work on the basis of a family contract, lease or another form of management, not leaving the kolkhoz (sovkhoz). A total of 39.6 percent of those polled will under no circumstances leave, because such work suits them fully."[41]

June

"As of 1 January 1991 there were 40,600 peasant farms to which were assigned about 700,000 hectares of land [17.2 hectares each]. . . ."

In a "Report of the Committee for Farm and Food Policy of the USSR Supreme Soviet: . . . According to figures as of 15 April 1991, 55,400 peasant farms have been created in the country, and 1,463,800 hectares of land have been transferred to their possession and use [26.4 ha. each]. . . ."

Given the various factors involved, "the committee calculated that, under optimum conditions over the next three to four years, private possession of the land—including private plots, could increase from nine million to 40–45 million hectares, which is 7–8 percent of all the farmland in the country."[42]

September

Izvestia reporters learned that in the Zvyalovo District local Soviet authorities have replaced the rayon party committees in running farm affairs.[43]

October

"President Mikhail Gorbachev is now conferring in Moscow with farmer representatives on ways to promote agrarian reform in the country. . . .

"Mr. Gorbachev admitted that the land reform had been grinding to a halt, with people in the rural areas obviously fearing to be left tête-à-tête with a free market. . . . He added that he no longer insisted on holding a national referendum on the private ownership of land, since it was a matter not to be decided by voting: the urban population might support the idea of private property and the rural residents reject it, or vice versa. The main thing was to ensure that the problem be decided not by the center but by the republics which would proceed from their specific living standards and economic practices, Gorbachev said."[44]

In an interview, "M. S. Gorbachev stressed that the agrarian economy is the most sensitive part of the whole state organism, and all future policy concerning the countryside should be structured with this in mind."[45]

"The life of private farmers in the Russian heartland is no sweeter: The agro-industrial monster is diligently stifling them. And the trail leads to the RSFSR Ministry of Agriculture and Food, where apparently the inveterate nomenklatura is running the show. The management system in the agro-industrial complex is still dictatorial. There is no sign of imminent land reform for this reason. Furthermore, ministerial officials have set traps for commercial structures. . . .

"In Russia as a whole the proportion of former party workers occupying local organs of power is between 30 and 90 percent."[46]

December

"Erich Liske, a private farmer from the north Russian city of Pskov, is suing the nearby collective farm for robbery. One morning he found out that all locks on his farm were broken and 140 calves and all farming vehicles stolen.

"The collective farm authorities admit their blame, claiming they could not accept that a nearby private farmer, called 'kulak' in Russia, could produce more than they did. And since they learned in school that the property of all kulaks was expropriated under the Bolshevik rule and the farmers were exiled to Siberia, they acted accordingly."[47]

According to President Yeltsin's December 26 land reform decree, "[M]embers of collective farms and workers on state-owned farms are given the right to leave them in order to create individual farms." The land will be transferred to former farm workers according to shares, by March 1, 1992. The new owners will have "the right to exchange their land and property shares, lease them or mortgage in banks for credits." The land can be sold if the proceeds are "invested into creating enterprises in rural areas." Prices for the land will be fixed by the government. Maximum size of plots are to be established by February 1, 1992. Land not transferred to individual former farmers will be sold, giving preference to such people as rural teachers.[48]

According to the Russian Federation ukase on agrarian reform, the kolkhoz and sovkhoz members have four choices: "The first is to change into an association of peasant farms. The second is to change into a joint stock company. The third is to change into a production cooperative with the share form of ownership. Finally, the fourth is to leave everything as it is."[49]

According to the Russian Federation minister of agriculture, "[M]andatory contracting volumes are being established for output [of all farmers]: 25 percent for farming; 40 percent for animal husbandry (except meat and milk); and 50 percent for meat and milk. What is fundamentally new is that the purchases will be made at market prices."[50]

"In the RSFSR at the beginning of November there were 34,700 private peasant farms. A total of 1.4 million hectares of land were granted to them. This averages 41 hectares per farm."[51]

January 1992

"According to the Russian government's decision all state and collective farms will be eliminated before January 1, 1993. Pending this state and collective farms will be reorganized into joint-stock societies, associations or cooperatives, depending on the farmers' wish, or divided into individual farms."[52]

"Russian Deputy Prime Minister Yegor Gaydar has refuted rumors to the effect that the Government plans in the next month or two to break up the collective and state farms. At a meeting with people's deputies he explained that it is just the process of transforming unprofitable farms which is to begin in two months' time: such farms make up 10 percent of the total number of collective and state farms."[53]

"Private ownership of land is being introduced in the Ukraine. A law on this was adopted at a plenary session of the Supreme Soviet today. The document states that land in the Republic may be owned collectively, privately, and by the state."[54]

March

"The current decline in agricultural production in Russia is caused by two important factors: decreased solvent demand for food products, and forced reorganization of collective and state-run farms. The real threat is that should the rate of declining production exceed 25 percent, the situation may become irreversible."

"The agricultural sector may lose its growth base . . . Agriculture is on the verge of bankruptcy."[55]

"At a meeting of the Russian Government . . . chaired by President Boris Yeltsin, a program of agrarian reform was discussed. . . . [T]he program will be spread over a three to four year period.

"The first step . . . is to privatize land, dissolving unprofitable farms, and transforming state and collective farms into commercial structures. The second level planned for 1993–4 is to form a new industrial and social infrastructure in agriculture. The third stage set for 1995 is the establishment of a market economy in the agrarian sector and attract foreign investment. . . .

"[C]urrently [there are] over 70 thousand working [private] farms in Russia. . . . [A]t the end of 1991 they supplied 1 percent of the agricultural products, by the end of 1992 they will supply 3.5–4 percent. The number of farms will grow by 10–12 thousand in the next two months."[56]

According to Russian Vice President A. Rutskoy, "Justified and serious concern is being caused by information from the provinces about attempts under the banner of privatization, auctioning, and encouraging private farming, to tear profitable farms apart and hand them out to people who often have no direct relationship with the land. . . . Take all possible measures to guarantee that . . . [the kolkhozy and sovkhozy] carry out sowing and harvesting work. If the need arises, submit proposals on measures in this direction which require intervention by the organs of supreme executive authority and the government."[57]

Vice President Aleksandr Rutskoy "thinks the transition to private farming in the countryside has nothing in common with a campaign to demolish the organized production of farm output in collective and state farms."[58]

According to Viktor N. Khlystun, Russian minister of agriculture, there is a limit set by the "acting constitution, which is a ten-year moratorium on buying and selling of land, I think that this moratorium blocks the formation of a normal land market and the formation of normal market relations."[59]

According to Viktor N. Khlystun, Russian Federation minister of agriculture, "Agrarian reform is proceeding with very great difficulties. Its implementation entails overcoming innumerable barriers—economic, sociopsychological, technological and others. We constantly come up against not only opposition but also distortion of its essence, deliberate misinterpretations discrediting its philosophy and the mechanism for carrying it out."[60]

According to Aleksandr Rutskoy, vice president of the Russian Federation, agrarian reform plans include "possibilities for the creation of centers (machine tractor stations) to provide private farms with technical servicing, fuel and lubricants."[61]

May

According to Viktor N. Khlystun, the Supreme Soviet deputies' "refusal to pass a law on selling land . . . [is primarily because] that land will be resold and then speculation will occur. He says that the state should regulate the process of selling and buying land. 'I think that congress's refusal to adopt a decision on the market circulation of land is a great mistake. This mistake will negatively affect the course of agrarian reform. I think that we should return to this issue, and the sooner the better,' he says."[62]

According to Russian Federation Vice President Aleksandr Rutskoy, "Deplorably, today we have to repeat that as a result of various inconsistent and insufficiently resourceful steps our agriculture again is held hostage of an economic experiment; the economic ties have been severed, inflation prevents us from conducting a realistic social policy in the sphere of agriculture, obstructing its technological revival."[63]

June

According to President Boris Yeltsin, there is "a most profound antagonism between individual farmers and members of collective farms. The latter earn two or three times less today."[64]

According to President Boris Yeltsin, " 'forced decollectivisation in agriculture' is inadmissable, he told a governmental meeting on Thursday."[65]

According to an adviser to President Boris Yeltsin, the president issued a decree creating the Land and Agribusiness Reform Center to be staffed by leading specialists "to encourage free enterprise in agriculture and related industries and solve personnel problems by attracting skilled specialists into agriculture."[66]

According to Russian Agricultural Minister Viktor N. Khlystun, "The financial status of private farmers is 'pitiful.' All this because parity of prices between industrial and agricultural output is still not being observed and equivalent exchange between the city and the countryside has been disrupted."[67]

According to members of the Russian Agrarian Union, agricultural "production is collapsing, the peasants are being impoverished, and agricultural areas are dying out, which leads to mass pauperization and starvation."[68]

VOX POPULI: POLLS AND OTHER INDICATORS

What was, and now is, the mind-set of the masses not in rural areas?

1987

A school teacher in Moldavia asked, "Do you think it is easy to wake up a nation . . . lulled to sleep for decades? Do you think it is easy to promote initiative when many people have to look up the meaning of this word in the dictionary?"[69]

October

In a national survey of workers and kolkhoz farmers, 73 percent of the respondents to a poll expressed doubt that improvement in their work would be reflected in higher wages.[70]

April 1988

According to TASS, a national poll taken in early 1988 revealed that 75 percent of the people interviewed felt that glasnost and democratization were necessary. Of course, a majority of any population is for changes that promise painless advances in welfare. When the respondents were asked about individual

Table 8.2
What Is Necessary to Combat Lines?

	For	Against
Distribute [scarce goods] to enterprises	36	46
Introduce [ration] coupons	29	54
Expand imports	79	11
Expand [private] cooperatives	39	38

Source: Gregoriy Pashkov, "With a New Deficit?" Nedelya, January 1-8, 1989. UPRS-UEA-89-012.

participation in making the changes, however, only 30 percent indicated a willingness to take an active role in the process.[71]

January 1989

A national poll was taken to learn popular attitudes about the vexing problem of lines, a major manifestation of Soviet consumer goods shortages (see Table 8.2). Lines in stores and at railroad and Aeroflot ticket windows were said to cause the greatest dissatisfaction.

When asked when the USSR will be able to eliminate lines, 0.3 percent said in one to two years, 33 percent said, "Never, we will not live that long." The remainder said four to nine years or not very soon.[72]

Public opinion sociologists polled 10,000 Leningrad citizens on their attitudes about perestroika, including "approximately 3,000 party activists. . . . For the majority of those who filled out the questionnaire (more than 90 percent), the present-day stage of social changes evokes—in addition to feelings of hope and optimism—unease and fears. . . . The survey also noted a confusion in our social awareness. The vast majority of the Leningraders acknowledged that they simply did not know what has to be done for perestroika. Alas, we continue to wait for instructions and explanations from above."[73]

April

In an anonymous poll of 13,000 people by sociologists of the CPSU Central Committee's Academy of Sciences, some of the questions and responses were as follows:

"Does restructuring interest you? . . . [O]nly every other person . . . answered yes it does. [Only] a quarter of those polled have become personally involved in restructuring. And three-fourths of them intend to keep on working in the old way.

"What about responsibility to society? According to the sociologists' data, this problem is of concern to only 28.6 percent of workers and 28.2 percent of executives. . . . Only 14.7 percent and 17.7 percent, respectively, of those polled are seriously interested in our social policy. . . . Only half of the respondents to the questionnaire are concerned about problems of morality, and a third about questions of family relations."[74]

May

At least as early as May 1989, Gorbachev was aware of the seriousness of the deteriorating public morale. In a speech to the Soviet Congress, he attempted to dispel the illusion that he was not aware of the mood of the people by saying: "I even know about the following instance: Veterans riding the last bus in Moscow carried with them some 'visual aids'—Brezhnev's portrait covered with medals and Gorbachev's portrait covered with ration coupons. *I know everything*."[75] (Emphasis added.)

October

According to an anonymous poll of 13,000 people by the CPSU Central Committee's Academy of Social Sciences, only "every other respondent" said perestroika "interested" them, and "three-fourths of them intend to keep on working in the old way."

In a survey of 2,462 Soviet people from seventeen provinces in sixteen republics, only 31 percent believed that the new parliament "will be able to alter the course of our history. . . . Half (52 percent) of the respondents take a doubtful view of this possibility. . . . [Nevertheless,] 66 percent of those responding to the questionnaire expressed support for M. S. Gorbachev."[76]

The following are findings of an in-depth poll of Muscovites on social tension: "Three quarters of the Moscow residents surveyed consider it a reality. More than 90 percent list conservative elements in the apparatus as the greatest danger for perestroika. . . . [For 64 percent believe] 'everything will sort itself out if there is a strong center . . . we need strict policies and discipline [70 percent]. . . . ' However, almost 90 percent think that the use of force against democracy is intolerable.

"[M]uscovites have a . . . less [than] positive view of our economics and nationality problems. Thus, more than two-thirds of Muscovites recognize the state of economy to be bad and only 6 percent good. . . .

"[Before] the first Congress of People's Deputies . . . 51 percent [of Muscovites polled] were confident of a solution of economic problems, whereas after only 32 percent were. And for nationality problems it was 55 and 27 percent, respectively."[77]

December

Deputy G. A. Arbatov said, "[T]he passions that are flaring up here [in the Congress debate are most troubling]. I can imagine what will happen in [Azerbaijan and Armenia] and Nagorno-Karabakh when all this is shown on television. I propose that the whole part of the debate involving Nagorno-Karabakh, Armenia and Azerbaijan not be shown on television. The same should be done in the future with respect to all nationality-related questions.''[78] The proposal passed 1,437 for, 443 against and 95 abstentions.

"Membership in the komsomol has dropped by one-fourth.''[79]

"A group of youngsters at a rally held this banner: 'Let's catch up and surpass Africa.' This may be their ironic way of stating the sad fact that the USSR economy is slipping to the level of a developing country.''[80]

January 1990

A survey of 922 Muscovites reveals the belief that perestroika is "correct" but 71 percent believe the "change should be faster." Moreover, 82 percent think that in the last three to four years, the Soviet economic position has become "worse." Only 53 percent reacted positively to the word *profit*, but only 38 percent to the word *capitalism*. Only 57 percent felt "it should be possible for individuals to set up and own enterprises in the Soviet Union. Do you think Gorbachev's policy will succeed during the next five years?" Yes 26 percent, more yes than no, 31 percent.[81]

According to a poll taken by the CPSU Central Committee's Academy of Social Sciences of 4,000 residents in the Tatar Autonomous Republic, Donetsk Province, and two provinces in the Russian Republic Non-Black-Earth Zone:

"Only 2 percent–4 percent think that living conditions in their district or borough will improve substantially in the years just ahead. . . .

"Insight into . . . the voters' general mood was provided by their answers to the question, 'What is the reason for our difficulties?' In first place (given by almost half of those polled) were reasons such as 'our people don't like to work and long ago forgot how.' [After that came] 'local leadership is to blame,' 'our old model of socialism is not appropriate to today's circumstances and you can't create a new model overnight,' and 'the central leadership is to blame.' Slightly less than a third answered: 'Saboteurs of restructuring are to blame.' ''[82]

In a poll of urban residents in several republics, only 13 percent expressed a desire "to have 'their own business' by opening or leasing small enterprises.''[83]

"Seventy percent of those polled associate the higher cost of living, cheaper goods being washed out of trade and finally, the sharp growth in crime with the appearance of the cooperatives.''[84]

According to a national poll, "only 14.7 percent of the population is positive toward cooperative and individual labor activity, 29.4 negative and 55.9 undecided or difficult to answer.''[85]

February

When 7,730 young people were asked in a national poll, "Toward what social system is humanity headed over the long term?" 8.4 percent replied communism,

13 percent capitalism, 48 percent a mixture of socialism and communism, and 31 percent "I do not know."[86]

In an Academy of Sciences poll of atheists who are teachers and specialists in the field of religion and atheism, 66 percent believe that the constitutional provision on protection of freedom of conscience is "unsatisfactory" and that until recently the rights of believers were being violated (56 percent).[87]

The trade unions are the "main opponents of the cooperatives. This hostility arises when people are told that cooperatives are nothing but a trick for making a profit at the expense of working people."[88]

A national poll on attitudes toward cooperatives revealed that "only 15 percent of the respondents had a positive attitude toward co-ops, 29 percent negative, 27 percent ambivalent and 13 percent indifferent. 56.2 percent believe their spread would mean more people earning excessive incomes."[89]

In December 1989, the All-Union Center for the Study of Public Opinion "carried out an opinion poll among 2,696 inhabitants of the country. Its selection fully mirrors the population's model. . . .

"[F]or as many as three-quarters of respondents, it is clear that our country mustn't be included among the advanced nations. . . .

"[O]nly 4 percent [saw the cause] in external enemies. . . .

"Sixty-seven percent . . . no longer believe in the possibility of building a society without hardships and suffering. . . .

"[Only 4 percent] voiced full confidence in the Party as being the spokesman for the people's interests. . . .

"[O]nly a quarter of the polled associate their hopes with the nascent democratic bodies of power. . . .

"[Only] twenty-six percent of the polled say that there must be no subjects closed for discussion. . . .

"Fifty-five percent agree to have smaller earnings in exchange for easier work or a guarantee of their condition's stability. And only 37 percent would like to earn well by working their hardest. Only 7.3 percent favor lifting all bans on enterprise and all 'ceilings' on wages, and 24 percent deem it necessary to revive independent farming. . . .

" 'What is your attitude towards people massing millions officially emerging in our country?'—38 percent negative since this money cannot be honestly earned,—40 percent negative even if it has been honestly earned. . . .

"[O]nly one in ten who work is proud of his workplace—enterprise, institution. Eighteen percent . . . feel like they are the masters in their home. . . .

"Fifty-two percent of the country's population consider themselves to be nonbelievers, with 20 percent flatly denying the existence of God and 28 percent being indifferent to the problems of religion; a mere 5 percent are actively involved in religious affairs. (By contrast, a mere 1.5 percent of people in the USA firmly declare a disbelief in God, 4 percent say that it's impossible to know anything about God's existence while 63 percent are unconditional believers). . . .

"Sixty-six percent of the polled have been baptized or taught in another way to believe in God, yet only 48 percent profess one or another religion and even less, 39 percent, want to teach their children to believe. . . . "

Summarizing the polls' findings related to what should be done about crime and lawlessness, the pollsters made the following conclusions: "These replies testify to the ruthlessness inherent in the mass consciousness and to its measure of authoritarianism. Whereas about half of the polled are flatly opposed to concentrating power in the hands of one person, a quarter assures that 'our people are in constant need of a strong hand,' and another 15 percent admit that this 'happens to be necessary in some situations. . . . ' "

What is the source of the hostile attitudes? "[A]lthough less than a tenth of respondents personally took part in any hostilities whatsoever, 55 percent happened to be 'under the tough leadership of a power-thirsty person,' 64 percent had to act obeying someone else's will, and 57 percent experienced injustice (a third—verbal insults, one in ten—assault and battery).

"Are you happy? . . . Seven percent . . . called themselves to be perfectly happy, and 39 percent said they were 'rather happy in general' (according to American data, the figures in the United States are 33 and 55 percent respectively). All in all, for 46 percent of Soviets the balance of joys and adversities is positive on the whole."[90]

March

According to a rayon party secretary, "Since in our country the party is a governing party and still handles all matters without exception, and since people do not sense any change for the better in their lives . . . , it is only natural that all the reproaches are leveled at the CPSU."[91]

April

According to a poll of Muscovites (Table 8.3), "[T]he ecological movement in the USSR is second only to the Church in enjoying the population's trust."

Another poll of Muscovites (Table 8.4) revealed that only 58 percent believe that the country should "go over to market relations." Moreover, when asked how such a change would affect various segments of society, they had great apprehension about its probable impact.

In a poll by the All-Union Center for the Study of Public Opinion (Table 8.5), the respondents were asked to appraise their leaders, look into the future, and indicate who is responsible for the crisis.

May

There was an unprecedented disruption of the 1990 May Day parade.

"In response [in a national poll] to the question, 'Is the living standard of the

Table 8.3
The Public's Trust and Concerns

	Trust completely	Trust	Not very much	Don't Trust
Church	17.5	46.8	24.1	4.8
Green movement	12.9	41.6	16.3	8.5
Armed forces	12.3	44.1	33.9	8.0
Judiciary	2.0	18.3	52.1	20.7
Government	4.0	24.3	42.1	22.5
CPSU (The Party)	5.4	33.4	37.0	17.3
Young Communist League	2.8	23.5	38.0	28.4
Trade unions	3.8	33.4	39.4	18.7
Militia	3.0	19.9	53.3	20.5

When polled concerning their major concerns:

	Very important	Important	Not very important	Altogether unimportant
Environmental pollution	74.4	23.7	1.4	0.4
Growing crime	71.8	22.9	3.6	1.2
Shortage of food products	69.4	25.0	4.4	1.2
Shortage of prime necessities	63.2	30.2	5.8	0.2
Threat of AIDS	60.8	23.5	7.2	7.2
Inter-ethnic conflicts	58.8	27.2	6.8	5.0
Alcoholism	43.3	28.0	43.3	10.9
Shortage of durables	41.0	45.	12.5	1.0
Anti-semitism	21.3	20.3	25.4	0.2

Source: A poll done by the Houston, United States based Institute of Sociological Research with the USSR Academy of Sciences. Moscow News, no. 22, 1990.

Table 8.4
Public Views on a Market Economy

How will a market economy affect the position of					
	Workers	Co-op members	Intellectuals	Pensioners	Managers
Better	16	53	18	6	26
No change	6	18	16	5	39
Worse	69	13	48	83	18
Undecided	9	16	18	6	18

Source: Moscow News, no. 20, 1990.

Table 8.5
Public Trust of the Leaders: The Future and the Crisis

To what extent do you trust the nation's leadership at present?

	January 1990	April 1990
Trust fully	12	16
Trust	53	43
Do not trust	22	29
Undecided	13	12

What changes in the country's political situation are the most likely in the coming year?

	January 1990	April 1990
Considerable improvement of the situation	10	6
Stabilization of the situation	13	14
Mounting difficulties	62	62
Economic disaster	11	14
No opinion	9	8

Today one often hears it said that the country is in a state of crisis. Who do you believe are primarily responsible for this?

The country's former leaders	37*
The present-day Party leadership	29
The CPSU as a whole	17
Ministries and government departments	12
The people as a whole	11
Ideologues of socialism	11
Ideologues of the `shadow economy'	7
Extremists and nationalists	6
Others	1
Hard to say	6

*Since the column adds up to more than 100, obviously some of the respondents felt the responsibility to indict more than just one group.

Source: <u>Moscow News</u>, no. 21, 1990.

Soviet people rising or falling?' 10 percent of those polled answered 'rising,' 22 percent 'not changing,' 67 percent 'falling.'

"Concerning the question of how the living standard will change in the next two to three years, 15 percent of the citizens answered that it will probably rise, 37 percent believed that the standard of living will remain the same and 46 percent that it will probably fall.

"The work of the USSR Supreme Soviet during the current year was characterized as 'very productive' by 1 percent of those polled, as 'rather productive' by 11 percent and as not very productive by 51 percent and as 'not productive' by 24 percent."[92]

Table 8.6
Who Is in Favor of a Market Economy?

		Proponents		Opponents
	Overall	In favor of rapid transit-ion	In favor of gradual transit-ion	
Directors of enterprises, organizations; mana-gerial staff	71	26	45	19
Specialists with higher education	68	26	42	23
White-collar workers	46	20	26	42
Skilled blue-collar workers	47	14	33	33
Unskilled blue-collar workers	30	18	12	6
Pensioners	38	8	30	34
Students	74	23	51	11

Source: "Otnoshenie naselenlya k perspektive perekhoda k runku," _Voprosy ekonomiki_, no. 7, 1990, p. 57, in Stephen K. Wegren, "Market Reform and Public Opinion," _Radio Liberty Report on the USSR_, November 30, 1990.

June

In a survey of Congress deputies (December 22, 1989, after the second Congress), only 44 percent felt that their hopes and expectations had been justified. A survey taken a month before revealed that only 37 percent wished to continue in the parliament. In the period between Congresses, while 75 percent felt the nation's international position had improved, 65 percent felt that the condition of the economy, standards of living, and so on had worsened.

The survey noted that only 41 percent said they "always" take into account their voters' views when voting in the Congress. "On the whole, the survey results show that the deputies feel fairly independent when voting."[93]

According to a report on an April 1990 survey of youth, "only 15 percent of Russian students think that Russia needs the Communist Party. . . .

"According to data from the Youth Institute [presented in the same report], nearly 20 percent of the young men and women want to leave [the USSR]."[94]

July

Table 8.6 reports the results of a survey of the attitudes toward moving to a market economy taken in four republics.

"According to the latest data collected by sociologists, people place the issue of privileges in fourth place in terms of the most significant problems troubling them; it comes after the growing shortage of goods, the inter-nationality conflicts, and the struggle against crime. . . .

Table 8.7
The CPSU: People's View

	Agree	Disagree	Hard to say
Do you agree that the CPSU must be made responsible for all of its errors over the 70 years of Soviet rule?	74	15	11
Do you agree with those who say the CPSU should be disbanded?	31	41	28
	Yes	No	Can't say
Would you like your children (grandchildren) to be members of the CPSU?	15	54	31
Are you satisfied with Mikhail Gorbachev's political report to the 28th CPSU Congress?	18	41	41
	Positive	Negative	Can't say
What is your attitude towards the growing criticism of Mikhail Gorbachev?	64	19	17
What is your attitude towards the growing criticism of the USSR government?	75	9	16
What is your attitude towards the growing criticism of the army?	63	20	17
What is your attitude towards the growing criticism of the KGB?	63	12	25

Source: A national poll conducted by the All-Union Center for the Study of Public Opinion, July 7-17, 1990, reported in Moscow News, no. 30, 1990.

"[I]f we do not liquidate the nomenclature's privileges, then, from one side [we will see] that social tension grows, and from the other side that the struggle to preserve one's own blessings will quickly consolidate the conservative forces in the apparatuses at all levels."[95]

According to a national survey, "[M]ost people oppose the proposed changes in state retail prices . . . only 10 percent of the respondents reacted positively to free-floating prices. . . .

"[S]even out of every 10 respondents . . . [expressed a belief] that transition to a market economy will worsen the material status of families."[96]

Table 8.7 reports findings of a poll of the "people's view of the CPSU."

Table 8.8
Social Barometer

Monuments to Lenin are being removed, on the decision of local Soviets, from city streets and squares in a number of places in the USSR. <u>Which</u> <u>of</u> <u>the</u> <u>following</u> <u>opinions</u> <u>do</u> <u>you</u> <u>share</u>?

This must be resolutely opposed	57
This must be allowed if local residents want it	33
Undecided	10

Lately, consumer items have been disappearing from the shelves. <u>What</u> <u>was</u> <u>the</u> <u>primary</u> <u>cause</u> <u>of</u> <u>the</u> <u>shortage</u> <u>of</u> <u>ciga-</u> <u>rettes,</u> <u>bread,</u> <u>etc.</u>?

The socialist planned economy	18
The so-called perestroika	12
Sabotage by perestroika's opponents	33
The mafia in the trade sector	36
Undecided	6

Source: Yuri Levada, "Social Barometer," (a September 1990 nation wide poll) reported in _Moscow News_, no 39, 1990.

August

"Sociologists cite a figure of up to two million . . . would leave the country if restrictions on emigration were lifted."[97]

September

"A total of 1.5 million Soviet citizens . . . have applied for emigration to the USA. . . . [The main reason is no longer political; it] is the fear of a crisis in the USSR, which threatens to develop into chaos."[98]

A September 1990 poll (Table 8.8) solicited views on retaining Lenin monuments and the "primary cause" of shortages.

According to polls reported in _Izvestia_, "In March 30 percent of those polled in a survey still believed in the possibilities of the Soviets [to solve the nation's problems], while in July that figure was only 11 percent."[99]

"In the opinion of 66 percent of economic experts surveyed . . . the economy is on the verge of collapse, and 30 percent feel that its position is difficult but still manageable. The same assessments were given by blue-collar workers, white-collar workers and collective farmers. . . . The situation at enterprises has worsened sharply: in 1989 this assessment was given by 9 percent of specialists, but now this figure is 67 percent. . . .

"The public's attitude toward the private sector is still unstable: In January 1990 the idea of developing that sector had the support of 59 percent, while in March this number was 57 percent and in May and June approximately one-half of those surveyed. . . .

"Forty-two percent of urban and rural residents alike were not opposed to the free sale of land (among CPSU members this figure was 38 percent, and among non-party members 55 percent). . . .

"Seventy-one percent of those surveyed feel that their officials are not concerned about 'simple' people. . . .

"[B]y June 1989 35 percent of working people, including 25 percent of CPSU members, said that they had lost hope in the party's ability to renew itself."[100]

October

As shown in Table 8.9, a nationwide poll by the All-Union Center for the Study of Public Opinion of 1,848 persons in seventeen regions of the country asked the people to look back at the October Revolution.

Table 8.9
Looking Back on the October Revolution

HEROES AND VILLAINS: WHICH OF THE FOLLOWING PERSONALITIES OF THE TIME OF THE REVOLUTION EVOKES IN YOU THE GREATEST* [in percentages]

SYMPATHY?		ANTIPATHY?
27	Bukharin	3
41	Dzerzhinsky	7
5	Kerensky	18
4	Kolchak	21
64	Lenin	8
10	Makhno	18
3	Milyukov	5
5	Nikholas II	10
7	Stalin	50
15	Trotsky	12
13	Hard to say	22

*[could choose more than one person]

Opinions differ as to how the October Revolution has affected the lives of our citizens. WHICH OPINION DO YOU ACCEPT?

22 it ushered in a new era in their history
23 it gave an impetus to their social and economic development
21 it arrested their development
16 it had disastrous effects for them
16 hard to say

PEOPLE AT A CROSSROADS

Imagine that the October Revolution is happening before your eyes. You would...

22 actively support the Bolsheviks

Table 8.9 (Continued)

```
21 cooperate with Bolsheviks in something
13 try to bide your time, taking no part in the events
 1 fight the Bolsheviks
10 emigrate
 2 something else
26 hard to say
```

THE CREATION OF THE EXTRAORDINARY COMMISSION AND ITS BEING GIVEN THE BROADEST RIGHTS

```
51 there was a need for this
23 this was unnecessary
23 hard to say
```

ESTIMATING THE LOSSES [CAUSED BY] THE DEPARTURE OF MANUFACTURERS AND ENTREPRENEURS FROM ECONOMIC LIFE?

```
69 a very considerable loss
15 not a very considerable loss
16 hard to say
```

Source: "The Russian Revolution: As Judged by Its Descendants," Moscow News, no. 44, 1990.

An August 1990 poll by the All-Union Center for the Study of Public Opinion (Table 8.10) solicited public views on secession.

Table 8.10
A Poll on Secession

	Approve of republics' secession	Against republics' secession	Hard to say
Ukrainians	55	26	19
Belorussians	42	41	17
Indigenous residents of Central Asia	24	54	22
Indigenous residents of the Baltic republics	91	1	8
Georgians	92	1	7
Russians in the Russian SFSR	44	41	15

Source: Yury Levada, "Social Barometer," Moscow News, October 14, 1990.

"[L]ast year, 2.5 million people [made short-term travel outside of the USSR]. . . . For purposes of comparison, in 1888 that number was 811,000 and in 1987, 254,000. . . .

Table 8.11
A New Coup, Hunger, and Solutions to the Crisis

Who is scaring who? Is there any danger of a coup: by the right-wing or conservative forces:

Yes	33
No	21
Hard to say	46

by the left-wing or radical forces:

Yes	17
No	27
Hard to say	56

Will we go hungry? Some people fear that a food shortage may strike the Soviet Union in coming months. Do you share this fear:

Yes	62
No	26
Not sure	12

What shall we do? What's the quickest way to correct the situation in the Soviet Union?

More powers for the Soviet president	9
The Ryzhkov-Abalkin economic program	3
The Shatalin-Yavlinsky economic program	15
New forces ready to use a "strong hand" and restore order	16
A federal government the public may trust	8
The republics taking over all power	25
Other remedies	2
Nothing can remedy the situation today	9
Hard to say	16

People could pick several answers for this last question. That is why the total exceeds 100 percent.

Source: Yuri Levada, "Social Barometer," Moscow News, No. 46, 1990.

"Recently departures of Soviet citizens for permanent residence abroad have increased significantly. Out of the 816,600 people who have left the Soviet Union in the postwar period, 344,000 left the country in the years 1988–1989."[101]

According to a national poll of those who "fully approve Gorbachev's activity," he received a 52 percent vote in December of 1989, which fell to 21 percent in October of 1990.[102]

A national poll conducted in October 1990 by the All-Union Center for the Study of Public Opinion (Table 8.11) asked questions about a new coup, hunger, and possible solutions to the economic crisis.

"A joke is even making the rounds: Nowadays, in order to quit the Party, you need recommendations from three non-Party people"[103]

November

In November, an all-Union and an all-Russian poll (Table 8.12) solicited views on the state of the economy, the political scene, and the attitudes of the respondents.

Table 8.12
Social Barometer: Learning to Be Patient

When do you believe the Soviet Union will extricate itself from the current crisis?*

During the coming year	1
In the next two or three years	8
In the next five or six years	15
By the year 2000	16
Even later	32
Never	12
Hard to say	16

What countries do you think we shall match, in terms of standard of living, in the year 2000?**

Most developed capitalist countries	1
Capitalist countries with average level of development	15
Developing countries	38
Least developed countries in Asia and Africa	20
Hard to say	26

What feelings do you experience first at the thought of the coming winter?

Confidence in tomorrow	3
Hope	15
Concern	61
Fear	16
Hard to say	5

How probable is it that in the course of this winter Mikhail Gorbachev will quit the post of president of the USSR?

Quite probable	10
Hardly probable	74
Hard to say	16

The "democrats" will take the country's power into their own hands?

Quite probable	13
Hardly probable	44
Hard to say	43

The military and the KGB will take the country's power into their own hands?

Quite probable	19
Hardly probable	49
Hard to say	32

Table 8.12 (Continued)

Will the following occur in the USSR, in your view, in the next six months?

Stabilization of the economic situation

Will commence	17
Will not commence	65
Hard to say	18

Mass famine?

Will commence	27
Will not commence	57
Hard to say	18

A lessening of consumer goods scarcities

Will commence	24
Will not commence	64
Hard to say	12

A wave of strikes

Will begin	58
Will not begin	20
Hard to say	22

The disintegration of the USSR

Will occur	44
Will not occur	34
Hard to say	22

*An opinion poll carried out by the Soviet Center for Public Opinion and Market Research (VCIOM) in November 1990 among 1,363 persons in twenty-one localities; replies are given in percentages.

**Beginning here, results are from the VCIOM's all-Russia poll in November among 1,354 persons in twenty localities.

Source: Professor Yuri Levada, "Social Barometer," <u>Moscow News</u>, no. 49, 1990.

December

" 'This place would really have been paradise,' quips Angela Shapiro, a Moscow housewife, 'if only the Bolsheviks had managed to create people who don't need to eat.' " [104]

January 1991

In January, Soviet citizens were asked to look back on 1990 (Table 8.13).

Table 8.13
Looking Back on 1990

An all-Union poll, December, 1990 asked: The year 1990 has drawn to a close. What has it been like for the Soviet Union in comparison with the previous year 1989?

88 harder than the previous year
 2 easier than the previous year
10 the same as the previous year

**Among the events of 1990, indicate those you consider to be the most important:

35 Boris Yeltsin's election as chairman of the Russian
   Federation's Supreme Soviet.
27 Germany's reunification
25 decision on the restoration of private land ownership in
   Russia
22 adoption of the Declaration on Sovereignty in Russia and
   other Union Republics
21 repeal of Article 6 of the USSR Constitution
19 the Persian Gulf crisis
15 Mikhail Gorbachev's election as USSR president
14 proclamation of Lithuania's independence and its consequences

**What do you think our country's inhabitants lacked in 1990 (give not more than three replies).

53 real power in the country
36 trust in the leadership
29 respect for our own history
26 political and other leaders
24 patience, endurance

*Who can be called the person of 1990? Give the names of three to five persons (in your republic, in the Soviet Union or abroad, men or women) who are worth of this title:

41 Yeltsin   3 Sobchak
22 Gorbachev   3 Nazarbayev
18 Thatcher   2 Prunskiene
 9 Bush   1 Hussein
 6 Kohl   1 Ryzhkov

[In answering this question, respondents did not choose the names from a list but submitted them themselves.]

*What feelings do you think have emerged and gained strength among the people around you during the past year? (give one or two answers)

42 fatigue, indifference
42 embitteredness, aggression
22 fear
20 frustration

Table 8.13 (Continued)

```
13 hope
 6 feeling of being free from lies
 5 pride for my people
 5 sense of human dignity
 4 don't know
```

If in 1985 you knew what the changes begun in the country at that time would bring about, would you have supported them or not?

```
33 would have supported these changes
33 would not have supported these changes
34 cannot say definitely
```

What would be your attitude towards the military taking power into their own hands and bringing about order in the country in the present-day situation.

```
22 positive
60 negative
18 don't know
```

*Items in which the respondents could select more than one; thus the total adds up to more than 100 percent.

**Items receiving less than 100% response not recorded here.

Source: Yuri Levada, "Social Barometer: Opinion Poll Findings (preliminary)," Moscow News, no. 1, 1991.

"When a year ago we asked people whether they had confidence in tomorrow, 62 percent answered negatively. But in September of this year [1990], only 1.5 percent still had confidence. Even in Moscow they numbered only 5 percent. And in many regions of the country, we could not find a single person who did not fear the future."[105]

Polls taken in 1986 "recorded women's active support for perestroika. . . . Five years have past. Just what sort of attitudes predominate among women today [as revealed in recent national polls]? Anxiety and tension (in one in two); uncertainty, disappointment (in one in four); and confusion, pessimism and depression (in one in ten). Less than one-third of those surveyed maintained faith and hope for a better future, and upbeat feelings. Tranquility and even enthusiasm were encountered in from 0.4 to 1.0 percent."[106]

February

A poll of 16,000 Communists as a nationwide sample and a poll of 1,831 former members of the party revealed the following:

"Seventy-four percent of the Communists polled declared their firm resolve to remain in the CPSU (last November the figure was 66 percent).

"Sixty-three percent think that the CPSU can lead our society out of its state of crisis, but only 38 percent adhere to this view without reservation. . . . Eighty percent believe the USSR must be preserved within its existing boundaries, 76 percent support having diverse forms of ownership and letting them all develop on an equal footing, and 65 percent favor the development of a multiparty system in the country. . . .

"Forty-six percent favor private ownership of land, while nearly the same number reject it.

"[H]ere is a sociological 'portrait' of those who have left the CPSU. Whereas in 1989, 35 percent of the total number who left the Party did so voluntarily, in 1990 the figure was 74 percent. The average age of the majority was thirty to fifty years, with over ten years in the Party. These people were mostly workers at industrial enterprises. A greater number of people left the Party for political reasons—due to lack of faith in the CPSU as the guiding force in society (26 percent), the absence of any real benefit from their participation in Party work (26 percent), or unwillingness to remain in the same ranks with unworthy people (25 percent). People also gave such reasons as disagreement with the policy of perestroika (17 percent), loss of faith in socialism (14 percent) and unwillingness to answer for the mistakes of the past (13 percent)."[107]

"In mid-January—at the height of the events in the Baltic—a regular telephone survey of Muscovites of a random representative sample . . . [of the city's population was surveyed] by the sociological group for the study of public opinion of the RSFSR Supreme Soviet.

"The survey showed [as compared to a year earlier]: the growing dissatisfaction of the population with the democrats, who have not been able to halt the deterioration of the situation in the country; a reduction in the ratings of all leading figures, including the recent idols; deep disappointment with the activity of the parties and movements that recently developed; appearance of a significant social basis for the possible establishment of an authoritarian regime."[108]

According to the same poll, whereas in August of 1990 49.7 percent of the respondents named Yeltsin and only 3.9 percent rated Gorbachev as the most respected authoritative political leader, in January 1991 Yeltsin's rating (still highest of all leaders) fell to 17.4 percent and no one named Gorbachev, who in the answer to another question was most often listed as the "least respected leader" (11.2 percent).

The same poll reported that whereas in November 1990, 20 percent agreed with the proposition "Should quickly establish order, having halted democracy and glasnost," as contrasted with "continue on the path of democracy and glasnost," 39 percent voted for establishing authoritarian order in January 1991.[109]

Table 8.14
What Is Perestroika?

An attempt to remain in power at the cost of a certain democratization of society, made by the ruling top level	18%
A word used to disguise the struggle for power being conducted within the country's top echelon	17%
An obsolete slogan which has outlived itself	14%
A revolutionary transformation of the country's society	10%
A renegation of socialist achievements	4%
Hard to define	29%

Source: "Politics," Moscow News, no. 12, 1991.

Table 8.15
Who Has the Most Power? The Mafia!

A a national poll by the All-Union Central Institute of Public Opinion asked: "Who now has the real power in the country?" The response was:

The USSR president	30%
Nobody	25%
Mafia and bosses of the shadow economy	42%
Difficult to give an answer	12%
The CPSU	12%
Army, military industrial complex, Supreme Soviet	8%
Council of Ministers	2%

Source: "Question: Who Has the Power?" Nezavismaya gazeta, March 9, 1991. JPRS-UPA-91-021, April 18, 1991.

March

Table 8.14 is a national poll on the people's view of perestroika.

As shown in Table 8.15, in 1990 the people believed that the mafia was the most powerful institution in the Soviet Union.

In November 1990, people cited as the most acute problems complicating their lives "the shortage and poor quality of food products (70 percent); the poor supply of manufactured goods (67 percent) and low incomes and high prices (61 percent). . . . "

"[When will the crisis end?] "Only 9 percent believe that this could take place in the next two to three years. Fifteen percent think it might occur within the next five to six years; 16 percent by the year 2,000 and 32 percent think it will come significantly later. Sixteen percent of the respondents were unable to give a definite answer, and 12 percent answered 'never. . . .'

"To summarize, the most important characteristics of current Soviet public opinion are as follows:

social pessimism: disappointment with the actual results of perestroika, and a loss of confidence in its rapid success;

frustration as manifested in deep concern over events taking place, alarm, weariness, a lack of confidence in the future, and the expectation of all sorts of disasters (inflation, monetary reform, economic catastrophe, nationwide famine and civil war);

suspicion and aggression as the reverse side of that alarm, widespread perceptions of 'plots of secret enemies' (of perestroika, democracy, the Russian people, the CPSU and so on), heightened attention is 'who is to blame,' and a desire to immediately punish the 'culprits';

a profound value and moral vacuum resulting from the collapse of communist ideology and the destruction of traditional Soviet values, such as the belief in Soviet society's 'great historical mission' in building communism; the grandeur, power and security of the Soviet 'empire,' and its economic and military power; heroic labor 'for the benefit of the motherland' and without regard for recompense; a constant readiness to work to accomplish great feats and to stoically endure daily hardship; scorn for material benefits, consumerism, and so forth;

a return to previously rejected religious and moral values, the growing authority of various religions, the attraction of all manner of mysterious phenomena and mysticism for a sizable number of people;

paternalism and egalitarianism that date back to our communal mentality; these traits flourished in the nutrient medium of 'real socialism' and are nourished today by people's poverty and depressed situation. Outspoken and aggressive envy of the status of any groups that are materially well off, and especially if they enjoy privileges. The view that people's material prosperity is a direct index of their dishonesty, in the form of involvement in the shadow economy, the appropriation of unearned income, and so on."[110]

April

Almost half a million people left the USSR in 1990, nearly twice as many as in 1989.[111]

"Our polls have demonstrated that 60 percent of people feel uncertainty about the future. Over 50 percent expect mass unemployment, 40 percent—famine, a third—the stoppage of railways. [When asked about their feelings:] First-mentioned were concern and uncertainty, with malice and aggressiveness coming second, and terror—third. . . .

"The gap between policy and social expectations is more dangerous today than ever before. It will only add to the radicalization of both right- and left-

Table 8.16
The Public's Trust in the Press

	Newspapers belonging to the CPSU	Newspapers of other parties, the independent press
Trust	24	29
Mistrust	41	21
Find it difficult to answer	35	49

We will compare the level of trust in the central press, radio television in January of last year (before the bloody events in Baku and the official lie about them), in October (on the eve of L. Kravchenko's arrival) and in March.

	January 1990	October 1991	March 1991
Fully trust	42	35	21
Completely mistrust	11	11	21

Source: Boris Dubin, "The Ostrich Pose, or The Results of Peace Making," Radical, May 3-9, 1991. JPRS-UPA-91-036, August 5, 1991.

wing forces in society. In the absence of a stable political centre the hopes of achieving consensus may be finally extinguished."[112]

May

"Data from public opinion surveys (carried out by the Center for the Study of Public Opinion of the USSR Academy of Sciences Institute of Sociology) . . . [reveal that] 27 percent of the population sees glasnost as a factor which plays a positive role in society. But 56 percent of those questioned noted that the effect of glasnost has been ambiguous. . . . [While] 9 percent . . . took note of its negative role. . . . 45 percent felt that glasnost must be developed only to certain limits . . . [and 28 percent] think that glasnost has gone too far. . . .

"Replies to a question about the objectivity of the mass media reveal that more than 80 percent of those questioned had encountered superficial analysis or distortions of various facts, events, and phenomena. Forty-eight percent of those people suggest that this happens 'often.' "[113]

A national poll (Table 8.16) asked the respondents to indicate which newspaper they trusted.

A March 1991 national study revealed that "22 percent of those questioned listen to foreign radios (according to their own testimony, 25 percent did this during the 70s and 80s), and 44 percent (as compared with 16 percent during the period of stagnation) have in recent years read literature which was previously banned."[114]

June

In a national poll concerning attitudes towards Jews: "Forty-four percent said that Jews are 'sly and hypocritical.' "[115]

August

On Monday, August 19, Radio Moscow announced that President Gorbachev had stepped down for reasons of "ill health." The coup leaders took over but by Thursday, August 22, they were deposed and Gorbachev returned to Moscow.

Responses to a national poll conducted by the All-Union Center for the Study of Public Opinion indicated that "[t]he KGB is trusted by 38 percent of those polled, and the army by 59 percent. The two bodies were equally trusted and distrusted by 17 and 18 percent respectively [i.e., the respondents were neutral]. The figures for those who do not trust them are 27 and 16 percent. The other people polled were 'don't knows.' "[116]

"A number of questions addressed by the National Public Opinion Studies Center to 3,106 respondents resembling Russia's population pattern last May concerned religion . . . :"

"Sixty-three percent said they have respect for and confidence in the Russian Orthodox Church. Seven percent said the Russian Orthodox Church must not be trusted. Thirty percent made no comment."[117]

On July 7–17, 1991 the Soviet Center for Public Opinion and Market Research randomly polled more than 2,000 people in thirty-three cities and seventeen rural districts of the country (Table 8.17).

In a poll by VCIOM (Soviet Center for Public Opinion and Market Research) 1,053 people in thirteen cities of Russia were asked "Do you agree that full-time students should be required to serve in the military? Yes 24 percent, No 68 percent, Don't Know 8 percent."[118]

In a poll conducted July 27–28 in thirteen cities of the Russian Federation, the respondents were asked "Do you support Russian Federation President Boris Yeltsin's Decree on Ending the Activities of Political Parties in State Bodies, Institutions and Organizations? The response was: Fully support 55 percent; Partly support 18 percent; Partly reject 6 percent; Fully reject 7 percent; and Don't know 14 percent."[119]

According to a poll taken in eighteen Russian regions, "In June [1991] 45.2 percent of Russians questioned wanted Gorbachev to resign (29.4 percent supported him). . . .

"On 21–23 August 61.2 percent of those polled [in Moscow] supported M. S. Gorbachev's return to the post of USSR president and only 19.7 percent demanded his resignation. . . .

"When asked in the same poll, who among major figures were they for or against, the response was "Yeltsin (91.1 percent for, 3.5 percent against). Let

Table 8.17
Social Barometer: Whose Interests Does the CPSU Express? (percentages)

```
      DOES THE CPSU ENJOY GREAT INFLUENCE IN THE CITY OR DISTRICT
WHERE YOU LIVE OR  DOESN'T IT HAVE GREAT INFLUENCE?

It has great influence                              24
Does not have great influence                       52
Hard to say                                         24

      IN WHOSE INTERESTS, DO YOU BELIEVE, DOES THE CPSU WORK
TODAY?

a) those of workers or the party and state apparat?

Of the workers                                      12
Of the party and state apparat                      67
Hard to say                                         21

b) those of progressive or conservative forces in society?

Of progressive forces                                8
Of conservative forces                              49
Hard to say                                         43

      WHAT KIND OF FUTURE WOULD YOU LIKE TO SEE FOR THE CPSU?
(give only one reply).

The return of the guiding and leading role in society
to the CPSU                                         11
CPSU turned into one of the parliamentary parties   31
Disband the CPSU                                    36
Hard to say                                         22
```

Source: "Social Barometer," Moscow News, no. 30, 1991.

us recall, incidentally, that at the elections 12 June Yeltsin became RSFSR President with 57.3 percent of the votes."[120]

"A sociological survey . . . provides evidence that about 30 percent of Soviet citizens favor the death penalty for homosexuals. Thirty percent said they were in favor of imprisonment for them, 30 percent were for forced medical treatment, and only 10 percent were in favor of their free existence."[121]

"[A] poll was conducted [a few days after the failed August coup] among a sample of 1,185 people representing the adult urban population of the RSFSR, the Ukraine, and Belorussia.

"The poll results are expressed as a percentage of those questioned.

1. In your opinion will Gorbachev manage to retain his position as a result of current events? (a) probably yes—27 percent . . . (b) probably no—61 percent . . . (c) unde-cided—12 percent. . . .

3. Who is the most popular politician at present? B. Yeltsin—74 percent, A. Sobchak—8 percent, A. Rutskoy—5 percent, M. Gorbachev—4 percent, G. Popov—4 percent."[122]

"BVA is one of the largest and most authoritative institutes in France for studying the market and public opinion. It is noted for its objectivity and rather accurate assessments. This is why the results of a survey conducted in Moscow by the BVA on August 26th are so interesting.

"So, do you have a good or bad opinion about Mikhail Gorbachev and Boris Yeltsin? (The answers are in percentages).

"Yeltsin: Good—74; Bad—7; Don't Know—19. Gorbachev: Good—22; Bad—35; Don't Know—43.

"Are you hopeful that Mikhail Gorbachev will be able to cope with the crisis in the USSR within the next few months?

"Yes—12; No—62; Don't Know—26.

"The same question about Boris Yeltsin:

"Yes—52; No—15; Don't Know—26.

"Who do you think is holding on to real power in our country?

"Mikhail Gorbachev—2; Boris Yeltsin—51; Both—29; Neither one—16; Don't Know—2.

"With regard to Mikhail Gorbachev's position during the state coup, with which of the following answers do you most agree?

"He prepared the coup—2; He was involved in it—15; He knew about it—44; He did not know about it at all—34; Don't know—5.

"Do you believe that another coup is possible?

"Yes—39; No—38; Don't Know—23.

"Are you for or against a total dissolution of the CPSU?

"For—76; Against—9; Don't Know—15."[123]

September

"In July, 1991, the National Public Opinion Studies Center (VCIOM) conducted a Union-wide poll . . . [on] whether fundamental economic perestroika was possible in the USSR without substantial aid from developed capitalist countries. . . .

"Thirty-nine percent of those questioned said [such] aid . . . was essential.

"The same proportion said we should . . . [be relying] on our own strengths and drawing on our own reserves. . . .

"Eight percent categorically opposed help from the West.

"Fourteen percent did not give a definite answer."[124]

The results of a poll (Table 8.18) taken in the Russian, Ukrainian, Belorussian, and Uzbek republics concerning the most popular political figures revealed that Boris Yeltsin was far out in front.

"[A] lightning poll of 177 members of the USSR Supreme Soviet and ninety USSR people's deputies, conducted 28 August . . . [revealed that] 74 percent of those polled confidently name the worsening economic situation as a factor which pushed the country toward the [August] putsch. . . .

"In a Moscow school there was an anonymous poll of girls in the tenth grade,

Table 8.18
Most Favored Political Leaders (percentages)

Yeltsin	45.5
Gorbachev	19
Sobchak	13
Bakatain and Yakovlev	3
Shevardnadze Nazabayev and Rutskoy	2

Source: "Moscow All-Union Radio Mayak Network," September 5, 1991. FBIS-SOV-91-173, September 6, 1991.

and around one-third of them replied that they wanted to become 'foreign currency prostitutes. . . . '

"[According to a national poll,] Just one-third of the population, . . . believes that our life will improve. What is there left for the other two-thirds?"[125]

"According to a [national] poll carried out by the National Public Opinion Studies Center (VCIOM), 71 percent of Soviet people are happy with their jobs. Twenty-two percent said they disliked their occupations. Seven percent found it hard to answer. Sixty-one percent regard themselves as medium-class specialists, 24 percent feel they are highly qualified, 6 percent estimated their skills as low, 9 percent failed to give a definite answer.

"The poll shows 45 percent of the respondents having a full chance to realize their professional potential, 39 percent—only part chance, 7 percent—no chance at all. A tenth of the respondents failed to answer."[126]

"*What Will Be the Fate of the Congress of People's Deputies?* [An] opinion poll by the National Public Opinion Studies Center on September 1 among 1071 persons from twelve cities of the Russian Federation shows that 41 percent consider the congress of USSR people's deputies should be dissolved and all powers be given to the republics. Thirty-six percent have an opposite opinion. The rest did not answer. . . .

"*Is Another Coup D'Etat Possible?* Thirty-seven percent of the respondents in the same poll believe another coup attempt is possible in the future. Forty percent rule out such a possibility. Twenty-three percent have no definite opinion.

"*What Do You Think about the CPSU?* Fifty-one percent said it should be banned. Thirty percent do not think so. Nineteen percent found it difficult to answer."[127]

According to a national poll, "Forty-one percent of the respondents said a Soviet citizen has too little freedom, 32 percent claimed that there was enough freedom, 13 percent said there was too much of it, and 14 percent did not know what to answer. . . .

"While seven Balts and Georgians out of every ten say there is too little freedom and very few people claim there is too much, Central Asians are quite different; only 28 percent of the Turkmen and Tadjiks and 36 percent of the

Uzbeks complained of restriction on freedom, and 20 percent of the Tadjiks say there is too much freedom and one out of three did not know what to answer. Interestingly, the Moldavans are not very freedom-minded either, judging by the poll, as only 20 percent say more freedom is needed and 27 percent say there is too much of it.''[128]

The findings of two all-Russian random opinion polls carried out, one in July and another in August 1991, provided a measure of the people's pulse (Table 8.19).

Table 8.19
Summer 1991: The Russian Pulse

The July poll

What feelings have been predominant among those around you in the past year?

Fatigue, indifference	48%
Brutality, aggressiveness	25%
Hope	25%
Confusion	19%
Despair	19%
Resentment	17%

Do you agree that during 74 years as a ruling party the communist party has finally discredited itself? (percentages)

	Agree	Disagree	Hard to say
All respondents	69	10	21
Subscribers to MN	80	11	9
Subscribers to Pravda	56	26	18

Do you agree that Russia's salvation will be a person able to lead people and bring order to the country? (percentages)

	Agree	Disagree	Hard to say
All respondents	70	12	18
Subscribers to MN	48	31	21
Subscribers to Pravda	68	17	15
Subscribers to Trud	78	8	14

If you knew in 1985 what the incipient changes would bring in the country would you have supported them? (percentages)

	Yes	No	Don't know
All respondents	23	52	25
Under 24 years	24	48	27
40-54	28	52	20
55 and older	16	59	25
Subscribers to MN	43	43	14
Subscribers to Pravda	21	49	30

Which of society's problems do you find most menacing? (VCIOM opinion poll, August 1991, 2021 persons)

Table 8.19 (Continued)

Growing prices	69%
Shortage of foodstuffs, goods	56%
Mounting crime	28%
Weakness of state authority	20%
State of the environment	19%
Threat of unemployment	18%
Crisis of morality, culture	16%
Ethnic conflicts	14%
Disintegration of the USSR	8%
Threat of a dictatorship	5%
Departure from the ideals of socialism	5%

Source: "Social Barometer," Moscow News, no. 38, September 1991.

"On September 14–15 the Moscow branch of the Soviet Center for Public Opinion and Market Research (VCIOM) randomly polled 2,302 people." The question was "If Lenin's body is buried, what should we do with the Mausoleum?" The answers were, "Leave it 66 percent. Remove it 20 percent. Don't know 14 percent."[129]

"On August 22 and [again] September 7, . . . the National Public Opinion Studies Center, polled Muscovites . . . asking . . . : 'Do you think the coup attempt was made by members of the Emergency Committee or by some other political forces behind them?' " The sum of answers exceed 100 percent because respondents were allowed to give several answers (Table 8.20).

Table 8.20
Muscovites Assess the August Coup

The coup attempt was made with support of (in percent)		
	August 22	September 7
Members of the Emergency Committee	19	21
KGB	24	15
Army, military industrial Complex	24	12
CPSU, Party apparatus	32	32
Gorbachev	7	8
Lukyanov	21	7
Others	16	12
Did not answer	15	19

Source: "Viewpoint: Who Masterminded the Coup?" Interfax, September 11, 1991. JPRS-UPA-91-041, September 18, 1991.

October

A national public opinion poll "showed that 35 percent [of the respondents] think the Union center is gone. Also 35 percent believe it still exists but under another name. The rest found it difficult to answer. . . .

"In the same poll the respondents were asked what, in their opinion, would the future of the CPSU be like. Thirty-one percent would welcome the transformation of the CPSU into an ordinary parliamentary party. Thirty percent favor its dissolution. Fourteen percent suggest that the CPSU should be deprived of its former rights. Ten percent want those rights to be restored. Fifteen percent did not answer."[130]

A poll in the Russian republic in 1989 revealed "a balance in Russia between those who completely trusted the organization [the CPSU] (23 percent) and those who completely distrusted it (24 percent). The rest were either 'don't knows' or neutral. As of today—September 1991—the former group has decreased by a factor of ten exactly: Only 2.3 percent continue to completely trust the CPSU while 65 percent refuse to."[131]

"DATA newsagency reports that four out of every ten people polled by the National Public Opinion Studies Center in September said they did not wholly trust the military, while 23 percent expressed complete confidence. Some 18 percent of those polled said they did not trust in the country's armed forces. Some 20 percent were unable to give a definite answer.

"The poll revealed the fact that confidence in the army is lowest in the Ukraine and highest in Russia—15 percent and 27 percent respectively, compared to the nationwide average of 23 percent. . . .

"Respondents to the same poll were asked to say how much they trust the KGB. In the opinion of 39 percent of the respondents, the KGB ought not to be trusted. Some 28 percent do not trust it, with reservations. Full confidence in the KGB was expressed by 8 percent. No definite opinion could be given by 25 percent.

"Greatest trust is enjoyed by the state security agency in Central Asia—13 percent of those polled (compared to 8 percent countrywide), while it is lowest in the Ukraine where the proportion of KGB supporters is one sixth that in Central Asia and one fourth the countrywide average."[132]

The responses to the VCIOM poll "taken among 2075 people from all over the Soviet Union" concerning attitudes towards four key politicians are presented in Table 8.21.

According to a national public opinion poll conducted August 19 to 21, while 46 percent of the population had hopes "for the country's better future, . . . Sixty-four percent of the respondents believe that worst times are still ahead."[133]

"[In] September the National Public Opinion Studies Center took [a representative] opinion poll in [Russia, the Ukraine, and Central Asia] asking . . . if they trust their republic supreme councils" (Table 8.22).

In a representative poll taken of adult urban residents in Russia, the Ukraine,

Table 8.21
The Standings of Four Key Politicians (percentages)

Politician	Entirely in favor	Not entirely in favor	Not at all in favor	Could not say
Gorbachev	15	42	31	12
Yeltsin	49	30	8	13
Silayev	35	20	9	36
Sobchak	37	23	1	29

Source: "Viewpoint," Interfax, October 14, 1991. FBIS-SOV-91, October 18, 1991.

Table 8.22
Public Trust in Supreme Soviets (percentages)

	Trust	Trust cautiously	Do not trust	Did not answer
Russia	31	35	14	20
Ukraine	15	53	22	10
Central Asia	42	27	17	14
Sample error is 3%				

Source: "Viewpoint: Are Republican Parliaments Trustworthy?" Interfax, October 28, 1991. FBIS-SOV-91-209, October 29, 1991.

and Belarus, the respondents were asked "What, in your opinion, is more necessary for our country now, democracy or 'a strong hand?' (a) democracy— 51 percent of those polled; (b) 'a strong hand'—35 percent of those polled; (c) I find it difficult to answer—14 percent."[134]

The results of a poll taken in the Ukraine after the August putsch revealed that "36 percent [of the respondents] believe in the capability of the current leadership of Ukraine to bring it out of the crisis; 47 percent do not think so, and 77 percent of Ukraine's population do not trust the leadership of the former [Soviet] union."[135]

A poll was taken October 5 and 6 in fifteen Russian cities. "Question: Do you think Russia's leaders can do something to lead the republic out the crisis soon? No 50 percent. Yes 28 percent. Don't know 22 percent."[136]

A random poll was taken October 12 and 13 in fourteen Russian cities. "Question: Do you think major armed conflicts between former Soviet Republics are possible in the next few years? Quite possible 32 percent. Possible 28 percent. Hardly possible 18 percent. Absolutely impossible 6 percent. Don't know 16 percent."[137]

November

Pravda received more than 20,000 responses to a poll conducted among its readers. "To the question: 'Are you confident of a happy future for your children?' the answers come out as follows:

"Yes, entirely—3 percent; more confident than not—12 percent; not confident rather than confident—25 percent; no, not confident—46 percent; don't know—10 percent."[138]

" 'It is quite likely there could be a revolt in December,' according to Major General Viktor Ivanenko, chairman of the Russian Soviet Federated Socialist Republic KGB. . . . [H]e said that 'there are some signs that people dissatisfied with the political line of the Russian leadership are getting restless.' "[139]

"A poll taken by the National Public Opinion Studies Center in October shows that the majority of the population of the country is not against allowing autonomous republics to withdraw from the Russian Federation. Fifty percent of those questioned replied that they supported the autonomous regions' attempts to become independent states.

"Twenty-four percent spoke out against granting . . . independence. Twenty-six percent did not give a specific answer. . . . [I]n the Ukraine . . . 52 percent were in favor of independence for the autonomous regions."[140]

"One of the objectives of a study conducted in October by the National Public Opinion Studies Center was to find out how the population felt about the agreement on an economic community, [a representative sample taken in Russia, the Ukraine and in Central Asia]. . . .

"The study revealed that 65 percent of respondents in Central Asia, and 52 percent and 36 percent respectively of those in Russia and the Ukraine believe that the agreement will help resolve the host of problems facing the republics."[141]

A representative poll taken in October in Russia, the Ukraine, and Central Asia asked, "Do you agree with the opinion that the suppression of the attempted state coup in August this year and the subsequent events lead to the possibility of effective reform in the republics? Thirty-seven percent replied in the negative. Thirty-two percent agreed. Thirty-one percent abstained."[142]

"During a traditional poll carried out by the National Public Opinion Studies Center in October, respondents were asked to assess the Soviet Union's economic, political, and interethnic prospects" (Table 8.23).

According to an *Izvestia* reporter, (as of November) the major reason that state orders for grain have been filled by only 51 percent is an unorganized, but nationwide, peasant strike manifested in withholding food from the cities and other food-deficit areas.[143]

A random poll taken October 19 and 20 in fourteen Russian cities asked "Do you think Boris Yeltsin should be given extraordinary powers to stage urgent economic reforms?" The answers were, "Yes 65 percent. No 25 percent. Don't know 12 percent."[144]

An opinion poll taken in thirteen Russian cities shows "that most Russians

Table 8.23
The People Look to the Future

	Expect improvement	Expect deterioration	No definite answer
In the economy	16	69	15
In politics	25	50	25
In inter-ethnic relations	23	55	22

Source: Interfax, November 13, 1991. FBIS-SOV-91-219, November 13, 1991.

are convinced that the USSR as a single state has completely disintegrated. . . .

"Sixty-three percent of those questioned said the Soviet Union no longer exists. One in five believes the USSR continues to exist. Seventeen percent are undecided. Margin of error—3 percent."[145]

A representative poll of Muscovites asked the following question: "They say that free prices will fill shop shelves with goods and foodstuffs. . . . Do you want free prices to be introduced? Yes 35 percent, No 50 percent, Don't know 15 percent."[146]

A poll taken in thirteen Russian cities in November asked "Are you willing to tighten your belt in the hope that Russia's radical economic reforms will succeed in a year's time?" The answers were, "Yes 43 percent, No 42 percent, Don't Know 15 percent."[147]

In 1990 and 1991, the Times Mirror Center for the People and the Press conducted a massive study of political attitudes and values all across Europe. Table 8.24 presents the responses to one of the questions in the poll: Is it the responsibility of the state (in the United States, asked the government) to take care of very poor people who can't take care of themselves?

The participants in a nationwide poll were asked "if they would support slogans announced by the State of Emergency Committee now: preservation of the Union, restoration of law and order in the country, etc." Forty-one percent said yes, 41 percent said no, and 18 had no opinion.[148]

A VCIOM poll revealed that "44 percent of Russians, 24 percent of those living in Central Asia and 19 percent of Ukrainians think that either this winter or spring their republics will be hit by economic catastrophe and mass disorder. . . . 49 percent of Central Asian inhabitants, 44 percent of Ukrainians and 31 percent of Russians did not agree with this claim."[149] The rest had no answer.

December

"[A] November 9–10 opinion poll taken by the National Public Opinion Studies Center among 1002 people in thirteen Russian cities showed that 72

Table 8.24
Is the State Responsible for the Poor?

	Percentages saying they completely agree
US	23
Germany (West)	45
Germany (All)	50
Poland	56
Hungary	58
UK	62
France	62
Germany (East)	64
Czechoslovakia	66
Italy	66
Lithuania	68
Ukraine	69
Russia	70
Spain	71
Bulgaria	71

Source: "How Americans and Europeans Diverge," The Christian
Science Monitor, November 22, 1991.

percent of respondents believe Soviet President Mikhail Gorbachev has lost power. Fourteen percent are sure that he still controls the situation. The rest are undecided.

"Another survey taken by the center on November 9–19 in Russia, Ukraine, Belorussia, Lithuania, Georgia, Azerbaijan, Kazakhstan, Uzbekistan and Tajikistan found that 56 percent predict Gorbachev's disappearance from the political arena. Nineteen percent think he has not exhausted his political capabilities. Twenty-five percent found it difficult to answer."[150]

A poll taken in thirteen Russian cities by the Soviet Center for Public Opinion and Market Research on November 16 and 17 asked "Do you think autonomies should have the right of secession from Russia? No 64 percent, Yes 28 percent, Don't know 12 percent."[151]

A poll taken in fourteen Russian cities by the Soviet Center for Public Opinion and Market Research on November 23 and 24 asked "Would you be prepared to open a bank account in the near future and start your own business? No 64 percent, Yes 20 percent, Don't know 16 percent."[152]

"MN Express Poll. Question: 'Is Russia supposed to uphold the rights of Russians alone, or the rights of all citizens of Russia irrespective of nationality?' All citizens of Russia 73 percent. Russians alone 23 percent. No opinion 4 percent."[153]

In a poll taken December 8 and 9 in thirteen Russian cities, the respondents were asked "How do you feel about the outcome of the Ukrainian independence referendum? I have a great concern 58 percent, I support it 20 percent, I have no opinion 16 percent, I don't know the outcome 6 percent."[154]

"The results of sociological research carried out by the All-Union Center for the Study of Public Opinion in November this year show that 44 percent of

Table 8.25
Pravda **Readers Assess 1991 (percentages)**

Year of great positive changes	0
Year of positive changes	0
Normal year	1
Year of negative changes	29
Year of extremely negative changes	51
Other	19

Source: Vyacheslav Gerasimov, "Results of Poll of Readers. Time of Mistakes and Seeing the Light," Pravda, January 3, 1992. FBIS-SOV-92-005, January 8, 1992.

Russians, 24 percent of people living in Central Asia, and 19 percent of Ukrainians believe that economic catastrophe and mass riots await their republics this winter or next spring."[155]

January 1992

"[J]udging by the polls of recent months, the majority of our people believe that the worst times are still to come (the view of 79 percent of Russia's inhabitants polled in November). . . .

"In November, . . . over 50 percent of the former Union's population expected no improvements in political life, over 60 percent in interethnic relations, and 75 percent in the economy."[156]

"According to the latest VCIOM polls (December 15–16, covering 1,004 persons in the cities of Russia), 64 percent approve of the Commonwealths' establishment."[157]

In a poll taken in fifteen Russian cities, the question was "Will the army come out in support of a policy of strength in the near future? Yes 34 percent, No 41 percent, Don't know 23 percent."[158]

"A public opinion poll conducted by the Japanese economic newspaper *Nihon Keizai* showed that [in all of the former Soviet Republics] the prime concerns . . . [are] the increase in prices (81 percent), the shortage of food and basic consumer goods (77 percent) and the soaring crime rate (52 percent) rather than the danger of a new coup or a dictatorship (5 and 5.1 percent respectively). . . .

"The poll showed that many elements of reforms, proposed by Boris Yeltsin, enjoy the support of Russian residents. . . . [However], the move to introduce free market prices was approved by only 25.9 percent of the Russian participants in the survey and 56 percent were against."[159]

In December of 1991, *Pravda* readers were asked to assess the year's events (Table 8.25).

In a public opinion poll taken in St. Petersburg, 40 percent of the respondents "approve of Yeltsin's activity on the whole. . . . Thirty-four percent of those questioned disapprove of his policy. . . . Twenty-six percent of respondents were undecided.''[160]

"The republican social protection coalition, which includes the overwhelming majority of parties, public organization and movements, noted at its meeting that the liberalization of prices has placed the population of Kazakhstan in intolerable conditions, fraught with a social explosion.''[161]

"[O]n January 25–26 the National Public Opinion Studies Center took an opinion poll among 1020 respondents in thirteen Russian cities which showed that 45 percent believe only state control over prices and distribution of goods and resources can save the Russian economy.

"Thirty-six percent think that full freedom of entrepreneurship is the only way out. Twenty percent were undecided. Margin of error—3 percent.''[162]

"The threat of popular unrest is growing.'' According to a poll of Muscovites,'' 45 percent of the population will support actions against the economic policy of the government, while 43 percent will refrain from such actions.''[163]

According to a poll, "43 percent of the Muscovites . . . 'doubt the ability of the present Russian Government to extricate the republic from the crisis.' [Only] 31 percent of the capital's residents still have faith in the Russian Government.''[164]

"According to the [Russian] National Public Opinion Center, in large cities one in three supports price liberalization, in small towns—one in four, in villages—only 16 percent while more than two thirds are against it.''[165]

"As the results of a poll ordered by the Russian National Bank show, 66 percent of the respondents feel that the transition to a market economy must be continued. Only 18 percent spoke for giving up the reforms [even though they believe price increases] have already assumed a disastrous scale.''[166]

"According to the results of a poll conducted in Moscow this January by the Institute of Sociology together with the Moscow Sociological Agency, almost 32.8 percent of Muscovites . . . expressed their full confidence in Boris Yeltsin.

"14.1 percent of citizens spoke strongly against the Russian president, and 7.9 percent were less negative.''[167]

The results of a *Moscow News* express poll were as follows:

"The Russian Government gives its assurance that there will be no monetary reform in the near future. Do you believe this or not? Yes—20 percent. No—62 percent. Hard to say—18 percent.''[168]

"[J]udging by public opinion polls the people's indignation is not aimed as yet against the president of Russia.

"According to the results of the poll carried out by the RSFSR Supreme Soviet press center for the study of public opinion [as heard], 43 percent out of 1,200 people polled from various regions of Russia support Yeltsin's policies. About 19 percent of those polled expressed a negative attitude toward the activities of the president.''[169]

An express poll taken January 4–5 in thirteen Russian cities asked ''Are you afraid of losing your job in 1992? Afraid 30 percent. Have no work 23 percent. Hard to say 5 percent. Not afraid 40 percent. Already unemployed 2 percent."[170]

An express poll taken January 11–12 in thirteen Russian cities asked "If spontaneous mass action breaks out in your city or district against the leadership of Russia, will you be among the opponents or supporters of the leadership, or would you prefer not to interfere? Among the supporters of the leadership 16 percent. Hard to say 12 percent. Would not interfere 42 percent. Among the opponents of the leadership 17 percent. Such action is impossible 13 percent."[171]

Summarizing the results of an all-Russia opinion poll on attitudes toward democracy, Professor Boris Grushin of the Service for the Study of Public Opinion stated that the findings reveal that "more than half the population has no real conception of what democracy is.

"The key element of democracy [for the respondents] is rigid control, order and the absence of conflict. . . . It is a myth that democracy has completely triumphed in the hearts of the former Soviet people. This view is held by only 3 percent of Russia's population."[172]

According to a poll of military officers in the Moscow military district, "Fifty-six percent of respondents said that officers' money allowances provide for very low living standards. Forty-four percent . . . said that such allowances are insufficient altogether. Seventy-five percent of respondents are dissatisfied with their housing. Fifty percent are dissatisfied with the quality of health service. Eighty-two percent feel a lack of social security."[173]

February

According to a representative poll taken in Russia, the Ukraine, and Kazakhstan only "28 percent of the respondents in Kazakhstan, 8 percent in Russia, and 7 percent in Ukraine predict a deeper integration and stronger ties between the CIS states."[174]

According to a Georgian public opinion poll, 64.8 percent of the respondents said things will be better in 1992 than in 1991, 44.6 percent "believe that at the moment developments in Georgia proceed in the right direction, 29.5 percent of respondents have a different view."[175]

"Are you ready to join the march against price increases? Four out of ten people surveyed in Kazakhstan, 39 percent of the Russians, and one third of Ukrainians answered 'Yes.' "[176]

In a poll taken by the Institute for the Sociology of Parliamentarianism on January 2, 53 percent of the respondents said they "believe in the success of Yeltsin's economic policy." In response to the same question on February 6, 42 percent were positive.[177]

According to a poll of Muscovites, 43 percent "do not trust a single one of the Russian politicians."[178] The poll also reported that "[t]he number of people

Table 8.26
Muscovites on Solving the Economic Crisis

```
    Do you think that the present introduction of free prices
will help extricate the country from the crisis?

                        January   February

No, or more likely no      47        45
Yes, or more likely yes    31        32
Hard to say                22        23

    Is Russian Government activity helping to extricate the
country from the crisis?

                        January   February

No, or more likely no      43        45
Yes, or more likely yes    26        22
Hard to say                31        33

    Is the activity of the Russian president helping to extri-
cate the country from the crisis?

                        January   February

No, or more likely no      32        36
Yes, or more likely yes    44        42
Hard to say                24        22"
```

Source: Oleg Savelyev, "People Still Have Faith For the Time
Being," Kuranty February 20, 1992. FBIS-SOV-92-035, February 21,
1992.

who believe that the Commonwealth is collapsing rose from 24 percent on 2 February to 43 percent on 13 February.''

A Moscow ''street poll'' was taken on January 18 and February 15. Each time the same questions concerning solving the economic crisis were asked (Table 8.26).

March

A citizen of Archangel, Russia, told a Western reporter the following joke: ''Here we have two paths to development: reality and fantasy. . . . Reality would be if Martians come down and did everything for us, . . . Fantasy would be if we managed to do everything ourselves.''[179]

''According to the results of a survey conducted by the National Public Opinion Studies Center (VCIOM) from February 8–18, 52 percent of Russians, 53 percent of Kazakhs, and 44 percent of Ukrainians prefer an economic system based on private ownership and market mechanisms. . . .

''Sixty-one percent of Russians, 59 percent of Ukrainians and Kazakhs are certain the Communist Party will never again be a force to be reckoned with.''[180]

Table 8.27
The Public's Political and Economic Expectations (percentages)

	IN POLITICS		
	Russia	Ukraine	Kazakhstan
Improvement	27	37	52
Worsening	56	45	39
	IN ECONOMY		
Improvement	22	28	46
Worsening	68	59	45
The rest were undecided.			

Source: Interfax, February 28, 1992. FBIS-SOV-92-040, February 28, 1992.

In a January poll 65 percent of Muscovites said they were "without any hope" that conditions would improve. Response to a February poll was 61 percent.[181]

In response to a poll concerning how Muscovites "are personally managing to resolve your material problems," 43 percent said "Have reduced all possible expenditure"; 27 percent, "Are not eating as well."[182]

According to a poll in twenty-five Belarus localities, "43 percent of people favor immediate privatization, and only fifteen people out of 908 respondents categorically opposed it."[183]

According to a Belarus poll, 61 percent of the respondents were against "withdrawal from the CIS." Only 15.7 percent were for withdrawal.[184]

In a poll taken in Russia, the Ukraine, and Kazakhstan, the respondents were asked what do they expect in the political and economic spheres (Table 8.27).

In a random poll taken January 25–26 in thirteen Russian cities, the respondents were asked "Do you support appeals for antiprice rise strikes? Do not support 43 percent. Support 25 percent. Ready to join 20 percent. Hard to say 12 percent."[185]

March

In a poll taken in several of the republics in January, "[t]he respondents were asked how they assess the economic situation in their republics today" (Table 8.28).

According to a poll taken among officers and warrant officers in ten military garrisons in the Russian Federation, "[O]nly 17 percent of those polled support the government's activity, whereas 56 percent do not approve of it. . . . Ninety percent of those polled note a fall in living standard compared with last year. . . . A total of 84 percent of the servicemen share the view that social tension is growing in society, and they do not rule out the possibility of spontaneous mass actions in this connection. . . .

Table 8.28
Republic Citizens Appraise Economic Situation (percentages)

	Good	Bad	Critical
Russia	1	41	53
Ukraine	1	40	56
Belarus	1	52	45
Estonia	1	46	48
Georgia	1	39	60
Kazakhstan	9	57	29
Uzbekistan	5	57	31

How have your family's living standards changed lately?

	Improved	Remained the same	Worsened
Russia	11	16	70
Ukraine	11	19	67
Belarus	3	23	71
Estonia	19	17	62
Georgia	23	43	33
Kazakhstan	8	17	72
Uzbekistan	10	24	63

Source: "Viewpoint," Interfax, March 5, 1992. FBIS-SOV-92-044, March 5, 1992.

"According to the majority of cadre service personnel (76 percent) the division of the Armed Forces could lead to the emergence of conflicts between the armed forces of the independent Commonwealth states. . . .

"The poll showed that the army is still pinning hopes on the wisdom of politicians, does not want to participate in political battles, and is convinced that, without society's assistance, the Armed Forces are not in a position to cope with their problems."[186]

According to a poll taken in March in Moscow and Kiev, "The number of people dissatisfied with life has increased from 65 to 69 percent over the past two weeks. . . . Thirty-three to thirty-four percent of people believe that it is 'impossible to endure' the present prices."[187] Those Muscovites who view Yeltsin as "unequivocally positive" fell from 42 percent to 34 percent in two weeks time.

A poll taken in the Russian Federation asked "If you were faced with the choice again today, which decision would you make: 'Yes' to [saving] the Union or 'No' to the Union? 'Yes' to the union—70.5 percent. 'No' to the Union—22 percent. Other opinion—2.8 percent. Hard to say—4.9 percent."[188]

"An opinion poll taken by the Russian parliamentary subcommittee on public opinion studies show that 60 percent of respondents are angry with reform while 18 percent are satisfied with its first results."[189]

"[A]n elderly woman teacher . . . swears that she would better starve to death than go and peddle cooperative merchandise."[190]

Public opinion polls conducted by the Institute of Socio-Political Studies "indicate that every fifth person in the Russian Federation would want to emigrate."[191]

According to a poll of Muscovites, "The number of people dissatisfied with their present life noticeably increased in the first three weeks of March: 68 percent on 5 March; 69 percent on 12 March; and 73 percent on 19 March."[192]

April

"After the Russian law on entry and departure became effective soon, up to two million people are likely to leave the country in search of work abroad. Aleksandr Baburov, a leading specialist of the Russian Labor and Employment Ministry, told ITAR-TASS on Wednesday."[193]

According to a poll taken by the Social Studies Center of Latvia, 58 percent of the Latvians polled and 56 percent of the people of other nationalities said that the Supreme Council of Latvia "takes the interests of the people into account to a rather small extent."[194] Only 21 percent of the Latvians and 13 percent of the people of other nationalities believe that the Council members "act chiefly in the interests of the people."

" 'Over a million Jews in CIS countries are in various states of readiness to emigrate to Israel' declared Simha Dinitz, chairman of the Jewish Agency, on his return to Tel Aviv on Sunday [19 April]." He said leaders of the Russian Federation 'are seriously concerned about increasing anti-Semitism in Russia."[195]

"The number of servicemen who deserted their units without permission is estimated at tens of thousands."[196]

June

The support of Muscovites for Yeltsin has been decreasing, as measured by an Institute of Sociology of Parliamentarianism poll. Table 8.29 reveals how Muscovites defined their attitudes toward both the president and the Communist party.

"The situation that has taken shape around real power in Moscow is becoming increasingly intolerable and explosive. In the opinion of 62 percent of those [Muscovites] polled either there is no boss in Moscow at all or it is the mafia that rules. In the opinion of the majority (62 percent), bribery in Moscow has increased over the past year. . . . " In the same poll 70 percent of Muscovites expressed dissatisfaction with life.[197]

ELITE VIEWS: POLITICIANS, INTELLECTUALS, AND JOURNALISTS

1987

In his book, Gorbachev wrote, "[E]verything depends upon the people." He continued, "A drastic change must be made in social and political thought."

Table 8.29
Muscovites Rate Yeltsin and the Party

```
        Support for Yeltsin

                                      Percentage of those polled

Very positive, and active supporter              2
Positive                                        28
With some positive interest                     15
Indifferent                                      5
With some suspicion                             22
Negative                                        16
Sharply negative, an active opponent             1
Hard to say                                     11
```

In the same poll the Muscovites were asked would you personally like the communists to return to power in Russia?

```
                    Percentage of those polled

Yes                      12
No                       59
All the same to me       11
Hard to say              18
```

Source: Nugzar Betaneli, "Can Communists Return to Power?" *Izvestia*, June 9, 1992. FBIS-SOV-92-114, June 12, 1992.

And again, "One more conclusion—the most important one I would say—is that we should rely on the initiative and creativity of the masses; on the active participation of the widest sections of the population in the implementation of the reforms planned."[198]

April 1988

"[There are quite a few] obstacles ahead [to perestroika] from mines laid by the past."[199]

May

In a speech to the CPSU Central Committee on "Socialism through Democratization," Gorbachev said, "[T]he key to everything is democratization. . . . Therefore, the aim of perestroika is mobilization of the human potential."[200]

July

"The economist and first deputy chief editor of . . . *Kommunist*, Otto Latsis, recently said that the wage-leveling mentality is 'the main danger' to economic reform in the Soviet Union. 'The most dangerous thing of all, is that over the years this way of thinking has affected literally everybody. People don't want more themselves, and they don't want others to want more.' ''[201]

August

"For years we were called on to think alike. Now that thinking alike has ceased to be considered an invariable virtue, you would think that a wide diversity of viewpoints would readily manifest itself. Yet, that hasn't happened. In fact, an extremely narrow range of views keeps getting repeated. . . .

"An 'enemy of restructuring,' a 'foe of restructuring' or an 'opponent of restructuring'—regardless of our intentions in attaching such labels, can we possibly forget how other labels, such as 'enemy of the people,' were once used? As long as people writing in the press continue to regard their opponents as enemies who must be exposed, there will be no liberation of thought. . . .

"[As the writer Yu. Burtin asked]: 'How many generations would it take just to repair, in some way, the damage from all that slaughter of the past few decades, to restore what had been accumulated over centuries? . . . '

"Unfortunately, it is this form of national self-awareness [lack of self-criticism] that often manifests itself today. Today the myth of the enemy of the people is being replaced by the myth of the enemy of the nation, which may lead to equally destructive consequences. . . .

"Historically, liberalism lost out in our country. The people preferred the idea of social justice to the idea of personal freedom. In general, liberalism frequently loses out in history, since it does not turn into a faith, into a mono-idea that is capable of capturing the enthusiasm of the masses. . . .

"Liberalism is despised by the conservatives, who stand guard over 'ideological purity' (and personal privileges). And the representatives of national radicalism have very little trust in the values of freedom, although their criticism of a number of moss-grown dogmas has objectively served to expand freedom's boundaries. One would think that those who have risen up against the retrogrades in the name of democratization and shaken the edifice of Stalinism would value the ideas of liberalism. But they, too, as I have tried to show, have relatively little respect for freedom of thought. . . .

"The demand of freedom for oneself presupposes the recognition of freedom for others. If we do not recognize intellectual freedom as a principal value (and codify the right to it in law), we will not become an open society. So far, we are just at the beginning of the path toward one.''[202]

October

"If we ponder over the crux of the matter, a serious deformation of the basic principle of socialism 'from each according to his ability to each according to his labor' has occurred. Following this, many concepts have also been distorted: What seems socially just, often is not such in practice, and vice versa. . . .

"We do not tire of talking about the high social protection of the Soviet people and, for example, the absence of unemployment. Meanwhile, unemployment has already become chronic in a number of the country's regions. At times representatives of some professions remain without jobs even in big cities for a long time.

"Wage leveling is one of the most profound reasons for social injustice in Soviet society. It has impregnated all the cells of society and has become deeply rooted in the mass consciousness. For decades we had a lenient attitude toward loafers and clods and redistributed in their favor what sloggers earned. . . .

"Today we accept as proper the fact that in our country a skilled, semiskilled, and even unskilled worker often earns more than a talented engineer, a nurse (not working to her full capacity and receiving several wages), more than an experienced physician, and a yardman more than a mature architect, a jurist, and so forth. . . .

"A great deal was born as a result of the doctrinaire approach to our ideological legacy and the attempts to squeeze vital contradictory life into the Procrustean bed of a dogmatically understood doctrinaire. . . .

"What to do with people who are unable and do not want to work at full capacity? What to do with 5 million alcoholics? What to do with undisguised loafers? . . .

"[T]he redistribution of the national product in the interest of drunkards, loafers, habitual hack workers, and so forth is the grossest violation of the socialist principle of distribution according to labor."[203]

December

Although some authoritarian systems have evolved into democracies, "[t]here has been no example in history of a totalitarian political system peacefully developing into democratic system. . . . I think that our country is now going through a period of transition from totalitarianism to authoritarianism. . . . But the road to this [a democratic society] won't be easy and we are just at its beginning."[204]

April 1989

"We cannot help but see that . . . uneasiness is growing in society. People are reacting badly to shortages, to the waiting in lines that take up time, and frankly, are humiliating to people. People perceive this situation as a gap between word and deed, as a discrepancy between promises and the real changes in life."[205]

June

According to one Ukrainian Congress deputy, "individualism, which by the very recent standard of our society was a curse, a danger and a disease, has suddenly become an unbearable cross. . . .

"As far as I know, one of the main problems in creating a law-based state is equalizing state and individual rights. . . .

"For me personally, perestroika is an attempt to become free of the dictatorship of the collective . . . free . . . of the tyranny of collectivism. . . .

"Let me remind you that it was Stalinist mythology that deified such collectivist concepts as class, party, state and revolutionary legality. . . .

"The drama of perestroika processes stems primarily from the need to attain spiritual autonomy.

"Such autonomy attracts and frightens at the same time. I remember the time when I was discharged from the army. It was the moment of happiness and horror. I was happy because I no longer had to march in a file and terrified because I would have to choose my own path in life and be responsible for every step I would take.

"It was a fear of civilian life. I had a shameful desire (which I was unwilling to admit even to myself), to sign up for an extra tour of duty.

"The dismay and troubles we now see and feel with our skin stem from the desire for, and fear of, general decollectivization and doubt whether or not we could become individuals.

"It is understandable that many want to sign up for an extra tour, especially those who cannot do anything except issue or obey orders.

"Nationalism both of a street and an office variety, crude as well as intellectual, is a form of extra tour of duty at the Administrative Command System."[206]

"I am pained by ration coupons in the seventy-second year of Soviet power, I am pained by the breakdown of the economy, by the ravaged countryside, by the sometimes barbarous relations between nationalities, by the rivers without fish and by the cities with chemical smog. . . .

"But what hurts the most is that you older comrades, our fathers and grandfathers, haven't left us young people any acceptable ideals on which we can build our life, toward which we can strive, for which we can fight and which we can instill in young people."[207]

August

"Under present-day conditions centralism is more important since the CPSU as a united all-Union political organization, acts as a major factor for the consolidation of all society. The obvious collapse of public order in the country, disorganization, irresponsibility and a noticeable lack of discipline in all its manifestations cannot be overcome by democratic measures alone, measures of centralism, inseparably linked with them are also needed."[208]

The thoughts of the speakers at the Central Committee Plenum can be summed up in saying that "the Party continues to live according to the standards and principles laid by Stalin. . . . [T]he present day Communist is a conformist, an executor not inclined to independent thinking and work, incapable of an initiative, a deed, civic bravery. As a result, the Party has become a hostage of its own system. . . .

"[B]ureaucracy is a class preventing our movement towards socialism, but to overthrow the power of bureaucracy a social revolution is needed, and it is the Communist Party which must lead this revolution . . . to the victory of socialism.

"Popular early in this century was the following cynical political maxim: if a country is in a crisis it is necessary to start war. Today it would be like this: if it is in a crisis, start a revolution."[209]

The Supreme Soviet "drafts do not change anything radically, because the state monopoly remains unshakeable. . . .

"Yesterday's ministerial functions are being built into the laws of tomorrow. If anything is capable of wrecking our ship, its the loading of the cargo of the command system in the democratic cabins. . . .

"I'm convinced that state bureaucratism is invincible while it reigns supreme in the Party. It is the conservatives in the Party who hinder the dismantling of the command system, the soil which grows only high-ranking weeds. The CPSU must purge itself of the eternally 'leading,' incompetent comrades, and restructure itself democratically."[210]

September

"One esteemed deputy put it bluntly. The cooperatives, he said, are the cancerous tumor of the people. . . . The following simple thought could also be heard at the session: 'There were no cooperatives before, and there was something in the shops then. Now there is nothing at all.' . . . Apart from shortages, the growth of cooperatives has raised the number of divorces, increased the accident rate on railroads, and brought AIDS into the country. They say that the ozone hole is also due to them. . . .

"[One deputy said:] '[T]he government, I believe, is embarking upon a road to cut down the co-op movement whose development it had engendered.

" 'I think this can be proved by the fact that cooperatives are being placed under the rule of the local authorities. The unjust (compared with that for state enterprises) tax rate—double taxation—will also hold co-op growth in check. No real equality of ownership is envisaged, equality in supplies is illusory too.' "[211]

November

In establishing markets, "the people are not prepared to abandon equalization all of a sudden although many of them are displeased with it. We shall need a rather lengthy period of psychological adaptation."[212]

"The home is a place inside which one can take off the entire burdens of the day, one can relax and rest and gather strength for the next day. . . .

"Khrushchev inherited a frightened and disciplined society, whereas Gorbachev inherited a corrupted one. . . .

"It seems to me that all of us are now like the person who is forced to look the terrible truth in the eyes every day. Unaccustomed to this, the terrible truth angers him, makes him indignant, and triggers his protest. . . .

"Our main trouble today is division. There are those on the left and those on the right. There is no golden middle. This is horrible! . . .

"[I]n the past a psychological stereotype appeared and strengthened: 'I would rather die than let *him* live better than *I* do.' The fact that *he* was more talented and that *he* could invent something for the general good, something which no one else could do, was unimportant. . . .

"Wise men have claimed that no socioeconomic system can die before having exhausted all of its possibilities. In Russia capitalism died one could say in childhood. Was this a violation of the laws of history? I do not know."[213]

December

"The CPSU, while continuing to be the guarantor of political and social stability in the country, has in fact taken up a defensive, conciliatory position. It is not making sufficient efforts to consolidate society or its own ranks; step by step, it is yielding to the bloc of separatists and 'left radicals' are prepared to dismember the USSR and sell off our national wealth to Western 'Partners.'

"It is difficult to cite any other period in our Homeland's past when our national dignity and our national pride were reviled with frank sadism.

"The rubbing of 'blank spots' in our history until they become black holes, is aimed at instilling a persistent inferiority complex in Russians and all Soviet people. . . .

"Bureaucrats, both central and local, and corrupted elements are heightening social tension. Crime has spilled out into the streets and permeates the sphere of production and distribution. It now threatens the safety of every person and is giving rise to an atmosphere of fear in society. . . .

"*The fatherland is in danger!* That is the sober and honest conclusion to be drawn from an analysis of what is going on."[214]

"There are universal shortages because, given the conditions that the worker has been placed in, he cannot and does not want to do highly productive work. First of all the individual is alienated from the means of production in our country, and from the results of his labor. Second, a great deal in labor depends on factors of a spiritual and moral nature, not just on forms of ownership."[215]

January 1990

A key block to perestroika lies in the people. They "believe in a state society, not a civil society, and it is so difficult to change these views."[216]

"[T]he state . . . , we have been told from infancy, provides clothing, shoes, education, employment, food and housing. . . . Lack of money was sanctified and the cult of equalization and asceticism promoted for many generations. People have lost their ability to do something about their own plight."[217]

February

In a speech to the February 1990 Central Committee Plenum, Central Committee member and Ambassador to Poland V. I. Brovikov said:

"[R]estructuring . . . in less than five years has plunged the country into the abyss of a crisis and has brought it to a point at which we have come face to face with a rampage of anarchy, the degradation of the economy, the grimace of general ruin and a decline in morals. In this situation, to claim that the people are 'for' all this, that it pleases them is politically indecent, to say the least. The people are against this, and they are saying so more and more loudly."[218]

"There is said to be a co-op 'lobby' headed by Academician V. Tikhonov [president of the Union of Co-ops] and People's Deputy A. Sobchak, . . . which led to rumors that they were financially influenced by them."[219]

April

According to politburo member A. N. Yakovlev, "A 'communism,' deduced from the vulgar 'from each according to his abilities, to each according to his needs,' [is] utopian."[220]

In an interview, Leonid Abalkin, vice chairman of the Council of Ministers of the USSR said, in regard to successful change to a market economy: "We have to overcome the ossified stereotypes of whole generations! Shaping a new mentality, getting rid of dogmas—these are the all-important and most difficult aims."[221]

According to a doctor of philosophy and leading scientific associate of the Academy of Sciences: "[M]any people . . . who, in their youth, were not affected by the Stalinist repressive machinery, have found themselves alienated from the past, having grown up in an atmosphere of thoughtless placidity and blind reliance on the infallibility of the leaders. . . .

"[Because of the command system] the working people became alienated also from the means of production and the distribution of the products of their labor as well as real power in their own enterprises. . . .

"[W]e have actually not become accustomed to and still cannot live under conditions governed by broad democracy and glasnost. We have no experience in true democratic management."[222]

May

"[A] plan has been drawn up at the Komsomol and was recently sent to the national government. It is the state and namely the state that must assume the obligation to guarantee young people a place to work under all circumstances. . . .

"The USSR needs 'modernization,' especially, the development of political culture, of a 'culture of citizenship,' and of the masses' active participation in political and economic decisions [which] plays a decisive role in solving the consensus problem. . . .

"Our middle class is very small, no more than 20–30 percent of the population, or by some estimates, no more than 15 percent. It is weak and, in terms of its professional make-up a large share of it consists of workers who are not highly skilled (for instance, highly paid workers in especially difficult and dangerous industries) and are not related directly to economic activity (the administrative-party apparatus). Moreover, the privileged strata of our society ever more 're-produce' themselves in the next generation, making these strata ever more 'closed.' All this means that in practice the middle class has ceased to perform its basic social function—to accept the most active people, to create a possibility for social advancement and vertical mobility."[223]

July

Dr. Yurii Skubko, founding member of the Democratic Union, said in an interview, "[W]e have moved towards recognizing perestroika as an attempt to save the doomed, unproductive, and ineffective system of Communist totalitarianism. It is simply a transition [from totalitarian] to authoritarian rule, with all the people in the nomenklatura still retaining their position and powers of decision making. . . .

"Perestroika has come to its logical end. Perestroika was an attempt to modernize the existing system. Everything that it could do has been done. We have come to the moment of collapse of the whole system. We must now disband the basic structures that are holding together this system. . . .

"He [Gorbachev] has brought into his Presidential Council two fascists [Veniamin] Yaring [cochairman of the United Russian Worker's Front] and [Valentin] Rasputin [a secretary of the Union of Writers], who is a gifted writer but is also one of the ideologists of the 'Pamyat' society.[224]

August

"According to the Shchit [Shield] union, the army has a plan for taking control of the country region by region."[225]

September

"A two-fold collapse of the center has occurred. The center has slipped as a result of the organizational legalization of rightist and leftist forces. . . . The USSR's political center has been drained of viability, too. . . .

"Our attempts to create all state institutions from scratch on a contractual basis are attempts to put into effect yet another grandiose utopia [like communism], something that will lead to a situation in which society finds itself without an organizing core. . . .

"God grant our people's elected representatives and the country's reformist leadership the wisdom to see the abyss toward which we are rushing at full steam before we fall into it."[226]

"As soon as we pronounce the word privatization, we immediately hear: you want to engender private business, capitalism. But I think that privatization, as it is generally understood, is a change of the owner. In the context of our economy, this means that we transfer the rights of ownership from the state to collectives, to the people, or to individuals. . . . We do not pursue the aim of eliminating state property, but of putting an end to the all-out depersonalization of property which has torn man away from property, pushed him away, and killed his interest in work. This is the real situation in our country, or specific feature. . . .

"The shaping up of a market economy will take five to ten years."[227]

October

Gorbachev: "I decisively reject attempts to equate the movement toward a market with a restoration of capitalism."[228]

"Leonid Albalkin expressed the view that . . . creating an effective economy will take no less than a decade and perhaps the life of a whole generation."[229]

"The main reason behind my leaving the Party . . . has to do with the fact that the country was inevitably sinking into, and is finally in, an economic crisis. The fundamental cause of this crisis is the system of Party-state monopolies. . . .

"The state is powerless since political power is in the hands of the Party apparat. . . . I think that the twenty-eighth Congress showed the party's unwillingness to relinquish its political control over society. . . .

"Today terror does not come in the form of physical destruction. Instead it shows itself in the drowning out of anybody who thinks differently. This is just another kind of terror. . . .

"[N]o one presented any constructive programs at the Congresses. Gorbachev himself adopted a very cautious, weak, and, I would say cowardly position of neutral, general support for economic reforms."[230]

November

"[S]ociety has entered a very risky phase of development. In essence we have a threefold crisis of power. First the process of peeling the Party skin off state mechanisms is proceeding slowly and painfully. . . . Second, . . . political institutions created after restructuring began are also in a state of crisis. Third, . . . a crisis of the Soviets as a system of power has begun and is deepening. . . .

"Gorbachev deserves a monument. He deserves it if only for facilitating the communist empire's disintegration. . . . Our country is being liberated from ideological slavery. . . . [H]owever there is still an enormous section of the population for whom slavery is natural. Alas, seventy years of unprecedented, cruel social experiment really did succeed in developing a new genus of person: Homo-Sovieticus."[231]

"The social ideal of Marxism, which was utopian but attractive to the lumpenized masses, and what seemed to be amazingly simple methods for realizing that ideal by means of the forcible redistribution of power and wealth according to the well-known formula 'he who has nothing will become everything' fell upon exceptionally fertile Russian soil. The expectation of a miracle is a feature of our national character. . . .

"Unfortunately, it must be said that dead dogmas still have us by the throat."[232]

Speaking on the occasion of the seventy-third anniversary of the 1917 revolution, Gorbachev said: "[O]ur October Revolution [was] the greatest revolution of the Twentieth Century, unequaled in scope and impact on people's destiny. The values that the socialist revolution brought the masses of the people are everlasting."[233]

December

V. A. Kryuchkov (KGB head) says Radio Liberty is a key arm of the CIA working to subvert the USSR and the NTS (National Labor Alliance, *Narodno-trudovoi soyuz*), the "chief unifier of anti-socialist forces" is "generously financed" by the CIA.[234]

" 'He [Gorbachev] doesn't want to give Russia to the Russians, he wants to hold it for himself,' Yeltsin told a news conference. 'Gorbachev was a communist, is a communist, and will always be a communist.' "[235]

According to a Soviet historian, "Stalinism created a mentality of slavishness among the Soviet people and deep rooted beliefs in conservatism and authoritarianism, an intolerance of pluralism and compromise persist. Thus, the Soviet Union is 'Europe's sick man.' "[236]

July 1991

According to Aleksandr Yakovlev, "The ideology that has ruled in our country has taught us to mistrust each other, to suspect each other, and, on occasions to inform on each other." In order to live in a truly lawful, democratic society, Soviet people must adopt an entirely different morality, he added.[237]

August

In explaining his resignation as Gorbachev's chief adviser, Aleksandr Yakovlev said: "I . . . lost . . . faith . . . in societal improvement and party reform. . . . At the twenty-eighth party congress I said that unless we become younger and renew ourselves, we will be left on the sidelines. . . .

"I am increasingly convinced that our tragedy results from Marxist dogmas. Stalin implemented in a freaky manner what was inherent to Marxism. . . .

"I have read a lot about Marx's and Engel's derisive attitude to peasants. They wrote so much about class struggle and violence. Imagine—total harmony can only be achieved through a class struggle. First one class eliminates another and then there is total harmony. Evolutionary maximalism, the dictatorship of the proletariat based on violence—these are horrible things. . . .

"This is how I began to reject Marxism as a guide to action, and realized socialism's defeat."[238]

September

In an article warning of the threat of a rise of "neo-Bolshevism," academician S. Shatalin warned, "People! Let us refute F. Bacon's famous words: 'It is the ape's resemblance to man that disgusts.' Neo-Bolshevism's resemblance to democracy is particularly disgusting. Neo-Bolshevism must not prevail. We must forget the physical and moral guillotine forever."[239]

On September 17 the Extraordinary Twenty-second YCL Congress met, declaring that it is disbanding.[240]

October

A *Komsomolskaya pravda* commentator and press secretary to Yeltsin gained entry to the top secret documents in the CPSU Central Committee. Citing from the documents he found, he wrote: "[I]t was he [Lenin] who conceived the following idea (and I quote from genuine archive sources); ' . . . to try to punish Latvia and Estland militarily (for example, "on the shoulders" of Balkhovich move the border somewhere by a verst, say, and hang 100–1000 of their officials and rich men). . . . '

" 'In the guise of greens (we will blame it all on them later) go in 10–20 versts and hang some kulaks, priests, and landowners. The prize: 100,000 rubles for each hanged man.' "[241]

"According to the analysis, carried out by the control department of the Russian president's administration, more than 70 percent of the regions, territories, autonomous republics and districts did not support the Russian leadership during the August [coup] events. They sided overtly or covertly with the State of Emergency Committee. Some of them preferred to wait-and-see or not to disclose their real stand," Valeriy Kachurin writes in the newspaper [*Rabochaya tribuna*].[242]

In an interview, Gorbachev said: "[O]ur [Soviet] people are linked by the same historical destiny. . . . We have inherited an unprecedentedly dense network of mutual relationships and we must remain together and continue to advance in close ranks.

"There are people in Russia, including within Boris Yeltsin's entourage, who believe it necessary to secede, like the other republics and live as an autonomous entity. Yet another intellectual utopia, and one of the most dangerous! Russia will not be able to leave by itself. Perhaps in a few years. . . . But today such isolationist plans are too dangerous. For the other republics, including the Ukraine, isolationism is a catastrophe."[243]

"Commenting on the consequences of Marxism in the USSR, Aleksandr Yakovlev said, in part: 'At the end of the day Marxism has brought us to the abyss, to backwardness and extirpation of one's conscience.' In his view, by attaching itself to Marxist teaching, Bolshevist Communism lost out in its dispute with history because of the sins originally implanted in its genes. The first sin was the sacrifice of the actual living person to an abstract one, of the individual to the community, and of life to a master plan. The second sin was the sacrifice of morals."[244]

November

"In an interview for . . . *Stern* [Hamburg] magazine Gorbachev said: 'If we don't get the social and economic situation under control, if food becomes even more scarce, the bitterness among the people will increase further. And this bitterness could culminate in a violent revolt. . . .' The crisis can only be got under control, 'if now, in addition to all the supply difficulties, the union does not fall apart.' Gorbachev added: 'We are standing on a precipice. Worse still we can even see down into the abyss.' "[245]

On November 6, 1991, Russian President Boris Yeltsin issued a decree "[t]o put a stop to the activities in the RSFSR of the CPSU, the RSFSR Communist Party, and to dissolve their organizational structures."[246]

"On 12 November, the organizing committee of the founding congress of the All-Union Communist Party, Bolshevik [Vsesoyuznaya Kommunisticheskaya Partiya—VKPB] distributed the party's manifesto, endorsed by the delegates to the founding forum held in St. Petersburg on 7–8 November. The manifesto proclaims the founding of the VKPB as the true heir to the cause of Lenin and as the party that will continue it on the contemporary stage. . . .

"Nina Andreyeva, former leader of the Society for Leninism and Communist Ideals, became general secretary of the VKPB."[247]

December

In a television interview, sometime-presidential adviser Alexandr Yakovlev stated:

"We have created a society that has the mentality of the lumpen. The lumpen only waits for other people to stuff something into his mouth, even if it is nothing but a beggar's pittance, as long as he has to do nothing in return. The most important thing for the lumpen is that he does not have to work. . . .

"Look, we are all a product of these old structures. . . . The old ways are in the genes of even the most democratic and progressive new leadership forces. They are used to ordering others around, they are used to permitting or prohibiting things. . . . In our minds, we are still the Bolsheviks of yesterday. The human psyche cannot be changed overnight. That takes time. . . .

"Why is our agriculture unproductive? It is unproductive because half of all those we are employed in a kolkhoz are in the administration. They are all chiefs and hardly any of them really works."[248]

January 1992

Providing excerpts from his new book, sometime-Gorbachev adviser Aleksandr Yakovlev wrote:

"A new nomenklatura is in the making. The same people, having failed to pay the bills presented to some of the electorate and to others by parliament, are going round the circle, changing their official positions. Old games are being played again by the old rules in Staraya Ploshchad (Old Square), in the former building of the CPSU Central Committee which now houses Russia's government."[249]

"History does not repeat itself, of course, but in some respects present-day Russia still looks like the Weimar Republic of 1932."[250]

According to Tatyana Koryagina, Russian deputy, "I am enormously disappointed by Yeltsin and by his government, which only consists of words and not deeds. Yeltsin has become a dangerous figure—above all, on those days when he dedicates himself almost exclusively to alcohol. He is unpredictable and capable of anything if he sees his power in danger."[251]

According to Aleksandr Rutskoy, vice president of the Russian Federation, "I do criticize the state of affairs here. Because what's happening in Russian politics and economics these days doesn't have much to do either with democracy or with market reforms."[252]

According to Russian Federation Vice President A. Rutskoy, "Now we have anarchy instead of democracy. It is impossible to make a transition from dictatorship to democracy bypassing the process of firm authority, the power of the law. Therefore, we are now in the most vulgar, banal dictatorship—the dictatorship of the street and that of street leaders. . . .

"We do not have a real power today. Power is where the laws are observed. Everybody disregards them these days."[253]

February

In an interview for Tokyo Television, former Soviet president Mikhail Gorbachev said, "I think Yeltsin has used populist methods to reach the position he is now. . . . '' Looking back to his final months in office he observed: ''Some people said: Gorbachev is trying to preserve the bureaucratic center. Yeltsin skillfully used this and dealt us a great blow. They started malicious gossip for political struggle and won.''[254]

The following is from an interview with former Soviet Foreign Minister Eduard Shevardnadze. ''[Shevardnadze] The danger [of upheaval] persists, and it might even be greater than before the coup last August. Developments are taking place against an unfavorable background; economic crisis, high social tension, poor living conditions. . . .

''[Interviewer] Where does the potential danger come from? From the nationalist on the right wing, or from the communists?

''[Shevardnadze] I do not differentiate between those two groups because in this situation, they may and will join forces.''[255]

'' 'I believe that a thorough, well-planned and comprehensive preparation for counterrevolution is occurring in this country,' Academician [economics] Shatalin said. He also named the 'two main forces preparing the attack.' One of those forces, according to him, is 'communist fundamentalism, the worst of the former CPSU.' The second force is Russian fascism, against which Shatalin had warned at the CPSU Central Committee Plenum back in February of 1990.''[256]

March

According to studies done by the Russian Supreme Soviet Subcommittee on Political Reform and ''experts from the 'RF-Politika' analytical center:

''A system of 'nomenklatura enclaves' inherited from Soviet times is actively forming and consolidating itself politically. . . . In actual fact it [the party nomenklatura] has moved into the structures of state power in the so-called center and at local levels. . . . [W]hen we analyze the data, we are forced to note with great regret that in the majority of regions, and in the center as well, the party-state nomenklatura constitute up to 70–80 percent, and in some regions, even more. . . . Yes, the nomenklatura era is probably over, but the nomenklatura system remains. . . .

''V. Varov: 'I wish to stress once again: In the final analysis, it is not a question of specific individuals. The issue is the system of activity of the power structure, sabotage. Sabotage, customary in the hinterland, is unfortunately being carried out rather intensively also in Moscow, St. Petersburg, and Yekaterinburg, where actual party bosses hold up to 30 percent of power, and if we are talking about the party nomenklatura—a figure of 80 percent again.' ''[257]

''The deregulation of fuel prices is 'heart failure and death for the country, but since nations don't die, the government will,' St. Petersburg Mayor Anatoliy Sobchak said in a news conference.''[258]

''In an interview with *The Washington Post*, . . . former Soviet President Mikhail Gorbachev . . . likened the atmosphere in the country to 'an insane asylum.' ''[259]

April

In an interview, former Soviet Prime Minister Nikolay Ryzhkov said the following about Gorbachev's leadership: "I did indeed sense that he had no clear line of where to go, that he was tossing about from the left to the right bank."[260]

May

President Yeltsin held a press conference in which he addressed charges about his problem with alcohol. He said he was "ashamed of those who raised such matters," asserting that the charges came from his political enemies.[261]

The author of an article in *Sovetskaya Rossiaya* argued that Yeltsin's drinking is a "threat" to security, stating: "Personal life is something completely different from alcoholic addiction in someone who is in charge of the 'nuclear briefcase.' "[262]

"On 15 May Russian People's Deputy V. B. Isakov stated during discussion of the agenda in parliament that President Yeltsin had again not been sober at the meeting with the CIS countries' leaders in Tashkent, and that it was time that this stopped. . . . The risk is not that presidents drink like all normal people; a risk occurs if they go to work in this state."[263]

"President Islam Karimov emphasized that the economy of sovereign Uzbekistan is completely relinquishing the shackels of ideology."[264]

"Lithuanian parliamentary speaker Vytautas Landsbergis hinted on Tuesday [26 May] he may resign if attempts to restore the old regime go on in the republican parliament.

" 'Either the creeping coup is stopped, or I am out,' he told a parliamentary session.

"The 'creeping coup in the Lithuanian parliament,' according to Landsbergis, is organized by the Democratic Labour Party of Lithuania and associated political forces, which 'strive to restore the old regime.' "[265]

"Barely had the brash and uninspiring Sixth Congress of Russian People's Deputies begun to fade in the memory when Boris Yeltsin decided to rekindle the emotions that had raged at and around it. During his tour of the Federation's north he suggested that it would not be a bad idea to 'disperse' the Congress."[266]

June

"Former Soviet Communist Party General Secretary Mikhail Gorbachev was expelled from the party last Saturday [13 June] for 'the ruination of the party and the state and betrayal of the interests of working people,' a resolution adopted at a meeting of members of the Communist Party Central Committee said."[267]

"[A]t an expanded session of the Officers Meetings' Coordinating Council of the CIS Joint Armed Forces the chairman of the council . . . said that 76 percent of the Russian officers consider that a civil war is inevitable or possible. 'The separation of armed forces' is the main cause which can lead to an armed conflict.''[268]

''President Snegur today told the Moldovan parliament, . . . that Russia has unleashed war against Moldova. 'We have to call a spade a spade—we are at war with Russia,' the Moldovan president stressed.''[269]

July

An interviewer asked, ''Boris Nikolayevich, we have been educated, we are instructed, we have the consciousness that authority is always personified. There was Khrushchev's authority, there was Brezhnev's authority, and the period of Yeltsin's authority. Tell us, are you ready to assume responsibility for everything in Russia from the central structures down to, say desolate rural settlements, rural soviets? . . .

Yeltsin answered, ''In the first place the president is responsible for everything. I do not reject this responsibility.''[270]

NOTES

1. *Izvestia*, March 28, 1983.

2. Bohdan Nahaylo, ''Interview with Tatyana Zaslavskaya,'' *Radio Free Europe: Radio Liberty*, RL 365/87.

3. Mikhail Gorbachev, *On the Agrarian Policy of the CPSU in the Present Conditions*, (Moscow: Novosti Press Agency, 1989), p. 25. Report . . . at the Plenary Meeting of the CPSU in the Central Committee, March 15–16, 1989.)

4. I. Yelistratove, ''Leasing through the Eyes of the People's Control Committee,'' *Sovetskaya rossiaya*, March 14, 1989. KPRS-UEA-89–018, June 26, 1989. A study by the RSFSR KNK (People's Control Committee).

5. Alexander Bekker, *Moscow News*, no. 28, 1989.

6. V. Nefedov, ''Development of Leasing,'' *Kommunist*, July 1989. JPRS-UKO-89–016, September 21, 1989.

7. V. Krestyaninov, ''Leasing: Why Are We Hesitating?'' *Agitator*, October 1989. JPRS-UPA-09–001.

8. ''Vladimir Tikhonov: Land for the Peasants,'' *Yunost*, October 1989. JPRS-UPA-90–001.

9. A. Moregachev, ''Does the Peasant Need Emancipation,'' *Sel'skaya zhizn*, October 12, 1989. JPRS-UEA-90–001. Interview with the director of the Institute for Socioeconomic Problems in the Agroindustrial Complex, USSR Academy of Sciences.

10. Aleksandr Iosifvich Leshchevskiy, ''Let Us Not Substitute Interest for Control,'' *Kommunist*, October 1989. JPRS-UKO-89–021, December 11, 1989.

11. V. Nefedov, ''In the Vise of the 'Coverage,' '' *Sovetskaya rossiaya*, October 18, 1989. JRPS-UEA-89–040, December 20, 1989.

12. ''Kalinin Conference on Labor, Leasing,'' *Sotsialisticheskiy trud*, October 1989. JPRS-UEA-90–002, January 30, 1990.

13. ''Socialist Idea and Social Creativity,'' *Kommunist*, November 1989. JPRS-UKO-90–002.

14. N. Avdeyev, "Do Not Call Me to the Homestead," *Pravda*, November 13, 1989. JPRS-UEA-89–041, December 21, 1989.

15. A. Nikonov, *Ekonomicheskaya gazeta*, December 1989. JPRS-UEA-90–010, March 21, 1990.

16. Vladimir Tikhonov, "Farmers Ought to Own Land," *Moscow News*, no. 2, 1990.

17. "The Admissions of a Farmer Who Gave Up," *Moscow News*, no. 2, 1990.

18. *Izvestia*, January 5, 1990.

19. Kapitolina Kozhevnikova, "There is a Peasant in Russia," *Literaturnaya gazeta*, March 12, 1990, JPRS-UEA-90–011, April 2, 1990.

20. N. N. Alekseyenko, "From Alienation to Hope," *Stepnyye prostory*, February 1990. JPRS-UEA-90–018, May 25, 1990.

21. *Sel'skaya zhizn*, June 12, 1990. JRPS-UEA-90–022, July 24, 1990.

22. "Economist-Deputies on Radical Economic Reform," *Voprosy ekonomiki*, no. 9, 1989. *The Soviet Review*, July-August 1990.

23. "Appeal by the Constituent Congress of the USSR Peasant Union to Kolkhoz Members, Manual and Office Workers, the Intelligentsia and to All Soviet People," *Sel'skaya zhizn*, July 1, 1990. JPRS-UEA-90–036, October 30, 1990.

24. "Gorbachev's Political Report to the 28th CPSU Congress," *Pravda*, July 3, 1990. CDSP, August 2, 1990.

25. V. Boykov, "Agrarian Policy: Land and Emancipation," *Izvestia*, July 7, 1990. JPRS-UEA-90–039, November 23, 1990.

26. V. Boykov and A. Kolesnikov, "What Do the Peasants Think about the Land Question?" *Selskaya zhizn*, August 15, 1990. JPRS-UEA-90–039, November 23, 1990.

27. G. Bystrov, "Give the Peasant Land and Freedom," *Izvestia*, August 26, 1990. CDSP, September 26, 1990.

28. Vitaliy Korniyenko, "Party of the Peasant House," *Molod Ukrayiny*, October 25, 1990. JPRS-UEA-91–004, January 23, 1991.

29. I. Abakumov, V. Kurasov, and M. Petrov, "Who Will Feed Russia, and How?" *Izvestia*, November 28, 1990. CDSP, January 9, 1991.

30. "What People Are Talking About: Enough Shows, Give Us Bread!" *Pravda*, November 27, 1990. CDSP, January 9, 1991.

31. V. G. Pinegin, " 'Course of Perestroika' rubric: 'How to Carry Out Land Reform?' " *Zemledeliye*, December 1990. JPRS-UEA-91–011.

32. I. Abakumov, V. Gavrichkin, and M. Petrov, "Land Was Made the Property of Those Who Work It," *Izvestia*, December 4, 1990. CDSP, January 9, 1991.

33. V. Gavrichkin, "On Subjects of the Day: The Laws Provide Guarantees, But What About People?" *Izvestia*, December 6, 1990. CDSP, January 9, 1991.

34. O. Sepanenko, "Not to Cook Pancakes," *Pravda*, December 4, 1990. JPRS-UEA-91–011. [Interview with Doctor of Economic Sciences A. Shutkov, VASKHNIL official.]

35. L. Savchenko, "We Recognize Only Parliamentary Forms of Struggle," *Zemlya i lyudi*, January 18, 1991. JPRS-UEA-91–024, May 17, 1991.

36. V. Shaykin and S. Kostornoy, "Land Reform and APK Development," *Selskaya zhizn*, January 26, 1991. JPRS-UEA-91–012, March 17, 1991.

37. "On Urgent Measures to Improve the Food Situation" (Presidential Decree, January 10, 1991), *Izvestia*, January 10, 1991. CDSP, vol. 43, no. 2, 1991.

38. Andrei Sizov, "Smaller Harvests Greater Imports for 1991," *Moscow News*, no. 8, 1991.

39. "Dutch Farmers Make Points on Soviet Farm," *Moscow News*, no. 8, 1991.

40. Liliya Babayeva, "Land: Why No Takers?' *Moscow News*, no. 11, 1991.

41. L. V. Babayeva, "Who Will Do the Feeding?" *Ekonomika I Organizatsiya Promyshlennogo Proizvodstava (EKO)*, May 1991. JPRS-UEA-91–044, December 6, 1991.

42. "On Realization of the Bases of Legislation of the USSR and the Union Republics on Land and on Progress in Land Reform," *Delovoy mir*, June 22, 1991. [Translation source misplaced.]

43. V. Konovalov and A. Abirov, "Yelatov to Yeltsin: It's Time to Put an End to Soviets," *Izvestia*, September 28, 1991. CDSP, November 6, 1991.

44. *Interfax*, October 4, 1991. FBIS-SOV-91–194, October 7, 1991.

45. M. Silanovich, "The Rural Economy: Many Structures—Many Ways," *Selskaya zhizn*, October 23, 1991. FBIS-SOV-91–205, October 23, 1991.

46. S. Razin, "But There Is a Long Way to Go . . . ," *Komsomolskaya pravda*, October 19, 1991. JPRS-UEA-91–041, November 25, 1991.

47. "They Come to Steal," TASS, December 6, 1991. FBIS-SOV-91–238, December 11, 1991.

48. *Postfactum*, December 28, 1991. [Translation source misplaced.]

49. *Sel'skaya zhizn*, January 7, 1992. JPRS-UEA-92–002, January 17, 1992. Interview with Viktor Nikolayevich Khlystun, Russian Federation minister of agriculture.

50. *Izvestia*, December 31, 1991. JPRS-UEA-92–002, January 17, 1992. Interview with Viktor Nikolayevich Khlystun.

51. N. Petrov, "Private Farms," *Ekonomika i zhizn*, December 1991. JPRS-UEA-92–002, January 17, 1992.

52. *Interfax*, January 4, 1992.

53. Moscow Radio Rossii, January 22, 1992. FBIS-SOV-92–015, January 23, 1992.

54. Moscow Mayak Radio Network, January 30, 1992. FBIS-SOV-92–021, January 31, 1992.

55. "Interfax Business Report," *Interfax*, March 9, 1992. FBIS-SOV-92–049, March 12, 1992.

56. *Interfax*, March 19, 1992. FBIS-SOV-92–055, March 20, 1992.

57. "Government Telegram," *Sel'skaya zhizn*, March 27, 1992. FBIS-SOV–92–060, March 27, 1992.

58. "Politics," *Postfactum*, March 20, 1992. FBIS-SOV-92–057, March 24, 1992.

59. Moscow Central Television, March 24, 1992. FBIS-SOV-92–059, March 26, 1992.

60. Moscow Radio Rossii, April 7, 1991. FBIS-SOV-92–070-S, April 10, 1992.

61. Aleksandr Rutskoy, "The Agro-Industrial Reform: What Should It Be Like," *Sel'skaya zhizn*, April 15, 1992. CDSP, June 3, 1992.

62. Moscow Russian Television Network, May 9, 1992. FBIS-SOV-92–093, May 13, 1992.

63. Vyacheslav Terekhov, "Exclusive Interview with Vice Premier Aleksandr Rutskoy," *Interfax*, May 15, 1992. FBIS-SOV-92–096, May 18, 1992.

64. "Vesti," Moscow Russian Television, June 4, 1992. FBIS-SOV-92–109, June 5, 1992.

65. Ivan Novikov and Genadiy Talalayev, ITAR-TASS, June 4, 1992. FBIS-SOV-92–109, June 5, 1992.

66. "Presidential Bulletin," *Interfax*, June 5, 1992. FBIS-SOV-92–112, June 10, 1992.

67. "Government Adopts Additional Measures," *Rossiyskaya gazeta*, June 9, 1992. FBIS-SOV-92–113, June 11, 1992.

68. Moscow Programma Radio Odin Network, June 3, 1992. FBIS-SOV-92–113, June 11, 1992.

69. Mikhail Gorbachev, *Perestroika: New Thinking for Our Country and the World* (New York: Harper and Row, 1987), p. 76.

70. *Agitator*, October 1987. [Translation source misplaced.]

71. Radio Free Europe: Radio Liberty, April 29, 1988. RL 186/88.

72. Gregoriy Pashkov, "With a New Deficit?" *Nedelya*, January 1–8, 1989. UPRS-UEA-89–012.

73. Yuriy Pompeyev, "The Party of Hope: A Commentator's Reflections," *Leningradskaya pravda*, January 7, 1989. JPRS-UPA-89–024.

74. L. Ponomarev and V. Shinka, "There's Happiness and There's Happiness," *Pravda*, April 5, 1989. CDSP, vol. 41, no. 14, 1989.

75. Mikhail Gorbachev, "May 25, 1989 Speech to the Soviet Congress of Deputies," *Pravda*, May 25, 1989.

76. *Argumenty i fakty*, October 21–27. 1989. CDSP, vol. 41, no. 46, 1989.

77. A. Demidov, "We Think the Way We Live: Muscovites' Opinion: The Sociopolitical Aspect," *Moskovskaya pravda*, October 6, 1989. JPRS-UPA-90–003.

78. "Second Congress Debates," *Izvestia*, December 14, 1989. CDSP, vol. 41, no. 50, 1989.

79. *Molodezh Estonii*, December 12, 1989. JPRS-UPA-90–018, April 4, 1990.

80. Anatoly Druzenko, "Still No Freedom of Information?" *Moscow News*, no. 51, 1989.

81. "MN's Sociological Service," *Moscow News*, no. 2, 1990.

82. V. Komarovsky and V. Kornyak, *Izvestia*, January 20, 1990. CDSP, vol. 42, no. 5, 1990.

83. V. Kosmarskiy, *Rabochaya tribuna*, January 13, 1990. JPRS-UEA-90–010, March 21, 1990.

84. "Are Business and Law Compatible?" *Moskovskaya pravda*, January 7, 1990. JPRS-UEA-90–010, March 21, 1990.

85. A. Glushetskiy, "Viewpoint: Are Cooperative Incomes Too High?" *Ekonomika i zhizn*, January 1990. JPRA-UEA-90–013, April 12, 1990.

86. Marina Mulina, "Do Young People Believe in Socialism?" *Sobesednik*, February 1990. JPRS-UPA-90–025, May 8, 1990.

87. *Argumenty i fakty*, February 10–16, 1990. JPRS-UPA-90–018, April 4, 1990.

88. "Under Threat," *Moscow News*, no. 6, 1990. Conversation between Professor Andrei Orlov, vice chairman of the State Commission of the USSR Council of Ministers on Economic Reform; Lev Baranov, department head of the USSR Procurator's Office, which supervises the fulfillment of legislation in economic activity, and state legal adviser second class; and Viktor Loshak, deputy editor-in-chief of *Moscow News*.

89. "Attitude of the Population to Cooperative and Individual Labor Activities," *Kommersant*, February 1990. JPRS-UEA-90–018, May 25, 1990.

90. "Homo-Sovieticus: A Rough Sketch," *Moscow News*, no. 11, 1990.

91. T. Yakhlakova, "The Party: Does It Guide? Direct? Struggle?" *Sovetskaya kultura*, March 10, 1990. JPRS-UPA-90–024, May 8, 1990.

92. Aleksandra Kiseleva, "Did Anyone Call a Sociologist," *Poisk*, 25–31 May, 1990. JPRS-UPA-90–044, July 26, 1990.

93. *Kommunist*, June 1990. JPRS-UKO-90–005, April 16, 1990.

94. A. Mutazayev and T. Piskaryeva, "Youth: the Search for a Place in Perestroika," *Pravda*, June 27, 1990. JPRS-UPA-90–048, August 16, 1990.

95. Vladislav Starchevsky, "They Will Fight for Their Privileges," *Nedelya*, July 2–8, 1990. JPRS-UPA-90–058, October 9, 1990. An interview with Ella A. Pamfilova, a member of the Supreme Soviet of the USSR, the secretary of the commission concerning privileges.

96. V. Kirichenko, "People and Prices," *Pravitelstvennyy vestnik* July 1990. JPRS-UEA-90–028, August 15, 1990.

97. Sergey Zaytsev, "Emigration: A Policy of Prohibition Is Unacceptable," *Leningradskaya pravda*, August 15, 1990. JPRS-UPA-90–060, October 31, 1990.

98. Gleb Pyanykh, Dmitry Didorov, and Ann Niva, *Moscow News*, no. 34, 1990.

99. L. Shevstova, "Crisis of Power—Why It Arose and How to Get out of It," *Izvestia*, September 17, 1990. CDSP, October 31, 1990.

100. Vladimir Boykov and Zhan Toshchenko, "In the Mirror of Sociological: So As Not to Be Like Jourdain," *Partiynaya zhizn*, September 1990. JPRS-UPA-90–069, December 14, 1990.

101. "Exit and Entry: How It Will Work," *Sovetskaya kultura*, September 8, 1990. JPRS-UPA-90–060, October 31, 1990.

102. "What Can Gorbachev Count On?" *Moscow News*, no. 45, 1990.

103. Ruben Safarov, "Will the CPSU Survive?" *Pravda*, October 8, 1990. CDSP, vol. 42, no. 39, 1990.

104. Peter Gumbel, "Soviet Ingenuity Is Filling the Food Gap," *The Wall Street Journal*, December 7, 1990.

105. Tatyana Zaslavskaya on a national poll as cited by Richard Pipes, *Foreign Affairs*, vol. 70, no. 1, 1991. *Komsomolskaia pravda*, October 30, 1990.

106. Professor Galina Sillaste, "The Propaganda of Fatalism," *Pravda*, January 5, 1991. JPRS-UPA-91–008, January 5, 1991.

107. "It's Psychologically Tough for Communists These Days," *Pravda*, February 26, 1991. CDSP, March 27, 1991.

108. Leontiy Byzoyev, "Democracy Is Losing Popularity: A Shift of Public Opinion in Moscow," *Nezavismaya gazeta*, February 16, 1991. [Translation source misplaced.]

109. Ibid.

110. T. Zaslavskaya, *Poisk*, March 22–28, 1991. JPRS-UPA-91–033, July 2, 1991.

111. "Weekly Record of Events," *Report on the USSR*, April 26, 1991.

112. Tatyana Zaslavskaya, "When the 'Powers that Be' Err," *Moscow News*, no. 13, April 91.

113. Viktor Britvin, "Glasnost: Where Is the Threshold and Where Is the Flaw?" *Radical*, May 3–9, 1991. JPRS-UPA-91–036, August 5, 1991.

114. Boris Dubin, "The Ostrich Pose, or the Results of Peace Making," *Radical*, May 3–9, 1991. JPRS-UPA-91–036, August 5, 1991.

115. "Viewpoint," *Interfax*, June 19, 1991. FBIS-SOV-91–125, June 28, 1991.

116. "Believe Comrade!" *Komsomolskaya pravda*, August 6, 1991. FBIS-SOV-91–152, August 7, 1991.

117. *Interfax*, August 7, 1991. FBIS-SOV-91–152, August 7, 1991.

118. "Should Students be Called up for Military Service?" *Moscow News*, August 11–18, 1991.

119. "Russia: Party Membership No Longer Relevant," *Moscow News*, August 4–11, 1991.

120. Ye. Dobrynina, "Since the Putsch Gorbachev's Popularity Has Risen 31.8 Percent," *Komsomolskaya pravda*," August 27, 1991. FBIS-SOV-91–168, August 29, 1991.

121. V. Gushchin and V. Buldakov, "Sex, AIDS . . . and Human Rights," *Argumenty i fakty*, August 1991. JPRS-UPA-91–038, August 26, 1991.

122. "Sociologists: Who Is Who," *Izvestia*, August 31, 1991. JPRS-UPA-91–039, September 4, 1991.

123. N. Dolgopolov, "Frenchmen Are Looking for the One Who Is Best," *Komsomolskaya pravda*, August 29, 1991. JPRS-UPA-91–042, October 7, 1991.

124. "Should We Accept Western Help?" *Interfax*, September 6, 1991. FBIS-SOV–91–173, September 6, 1991.

125. Ye. Sorokin, "Our Commentary," *Pravda*, September 14, 1991. JPRS-SOV-91–183, September 20, 1991.

126. *Interfax*, September 24, 1991. FBIS-SOV-91–185, September 24, 1991.

127. "What Will Be the Fate of the Congress of People's Deputies?" *Interfax*, September 4, 1991. JPRS-UPA-91–039, September 4, 1991.

128. "Viewpoint," *Interfax*, September 7, 1991. JPRS-UPA-91–040, September 13, 1991.

129. *Moscow News*, Number Thirty-nine, September 29–October 6, 1991.

130. "Viewpoint," *Interfax*, October 9, 1991. FBIS-SOV-91, October 9, 1991.

131. Aleksey Levinson, "CPSU Completely Trusted by 2.3 Percent of Population," *Izvestia*, October 2, 1991. FBIS-SOV-91–198, October 11, 1991.

132. "Do the People Have Confidence in the Country's Armed Forces," *Interfax*, October 11, 1991. FBIS-SOV-91–198, October 11, 1991.

133. "Viewpoint," *Interfax*, October 21, 1991. FBIS-SOV-91–203. October 21, 1991.

134. *Interfax*, October 26, 1991. FBIS-SOV-91–208, October 28, 1991.

135. Kiev Radio, October 24, 1991. FBIS-SOV-91–207, October 25, 1991.

136. *Moscow News*, October 13–20, 1991.

137. *Moscow News*, October 20–27, 1991.

138. V. Gerasimov, "Mirrored by the Poll; What Is the Future," *Pravda*, October 25, 1991. FBIS-SOV-91–2115, November 6, 1991.

139. TASS, November 5, 1991. FBIS-SOV-91–214, November 5, 1991.

140. *Interfax*, November 1, 1991. FBIS-SOV-91–213, November 4, 1991.

141. "Outlook for Agreement on Economic Community," *Interfax*, November 6, 1991. JPRS-SOV-91–217, November 8, 1991.

142. *Interfax*, November 12, 1991. FBIS-SOV-91–219, November 13, 1991.

143. V. Konovalov, "Undeclared Strike of Peasants of All Republics," *Izvestia*, November 7, 1991. FBIS-SOV-91–219, November 13, 1991.

144. *Moscow News*, October 27–November 3, 1991.

145. "Viewpoint," *Interfax*, November 14, 1991. FBIS-SOV-91–220, November 14, 1991.

146. "Free Prices Feared," *Moscow News*, November 3–10, 1991.

147. *Moscow News*, November 17–24, 1991.

148. *Interfax*, November 9, 1991. FBIS-SOV-91–221, November 15, 1991.

149. *Interfax*, November 27, 1991. FBIS-SOV-91–229, November 27, 1991.

150. "Viewpoint," *Interfax*, December 4, 1991. FBIS-SOV-91–233, December 4, 1991.

151. *Moscow News*, November 24–December 1, 1991.

152. *Moscow News*, December 1–8, 1991.

153. *Moscow News*, December 8–15, 1991.

154. *Moscow News*, December 15–22, 1991.

155. Tatyana Yarygina, "What People Really Think on Their Way to a Market System," *Izvestia*, December 7, 1991. JPRS-UEA-92–001, January 3, 1992.

156. "Social Barometer," *Moscow News*, December 29, 1991–January 5, 1992.

157. "Social Barometer," *Moscow News*, December 29, 1991–January 5, 1992.

158. *Moscow News*, December 22–29, 1991.

159. Vladimir Solntsev, TASS, January 4, 1992. FBIS-SOV-92–004, January 7, 1992.

160. *Interfax*, January 15, 1992. FBIS-SOV-92–011, January 16, 1992.

161. Alma-Ata Kazakh Radio Network, January 12, 1992. FBIS-SOV-92–011, January 16, 1992.

162. "Viewpoint," *Interfax*, January 29, 1992. FBIS-SOV-92–019, January 29, 1992.

163. Moscow Russian Television Network, January 25, 1992. FBIS-SOV-92–021, January 31, 1992.

164. "This Is What Muscovites Think," *Rossiyskaya gazeta*, January 30, 1992. FBIS-SOV-92–021, January 31, 1992.

165. "Viewpoint," *Interfax*, January 30, 1992. FBIS-SOV-92–020, January 30, 1992.

166. Radio Moscow, January 30, 1992. FBIS-SOV-92–020, January 30, 1992.

167. Tamara Ivanova, TASS, January 28, 1992. FBIS-SOV–022, February 3, 1992.

168. "MN Express Poll," *Moskovskiye Novosti*, January 1992. FBIS-SOV-92–020, January 30, 1992.

169. "Novosti," Moscow Teleradiokompaniya Ostankino, January 31, 1992. FBIS-SOV-92–020, January 30, 1992.

170. *Moscow News*, January 12–19, 1992.

171. *Moscow News*, January 19–26, 1992.

172. Alexander Rubtsov, "Democracy as Understood in Modern Russia," *Moscow News*, January 26–February 2, 1992.

173. *Interfax*, January 31, 1992. FBIS-SOV-92–023, February 4, 1992.

174. "Viewpoint: Does the CIS Have a Future?" *Interfax*, February 3, 1992. FBIS-SOV-022, February 3, 1992.

175. *Interfax*, February 5, 1992. FBIS-SOV-92–025, February 6, 1992.

176. *Interfax*, February 11, 1992. FBIS-SOV-92–029, February 12, 1992.

177. Moscow Teleradiokompaniya Ostankino, February 9, 1992. FBIS-SOV-92–029, February 12, 1992.

178. Nugar Betaneli, "Favorable Changes in People's State of Mind," *Izvestia*, February 18, 1992. FBIS-SOV-92–035, February 21, 1992.

179. Justin Burke, "Western Food Shipments Buy Time for Reformers in Russian Cities," *The Christian Science Monitor*, March 2, 1992.

180. "Viewpoint," *Interfax*, February 25, 1992. FBIS-SOV-92–037, February 25, 1992.

181. Nikolay Kuznetsov, "They Will Not Be Taking to the Barricades," *Kuranty*, February 25, 1992. FBIS-SOV-92–038, February 26, 1992.

182. Nugzar Betaneli, "Mirror of February Sentiments," *Izvestia*, February 25, 1992. FBIS-SOV-92–039, February 27, 1992.

183. Moscow Radio Rossii Network, February 23, 1992. FBIS-SOV-92–039, February 27, 1992.

184. "One-Line Cables," *Krasnaya zvezda*, February 21, 1992. FBIS-SOV-92–039, February 27, 1992.

185. "Express Poll," *Moscow News*, February 2–9, 1992.

186. "Report by Colonel F. Markarov . . . , Data from the Latest Sociological Research in the Armed Forces," *Krasnaya zvezda*, March 6, 1992. FBIS-SOV-92–048, March 11, 1992.

187. Nugzar Betaneli, "Identical Sentiments in Russian and Ukrainian Capitals," *Izvestia*, March 17, 1992. FBIS-SOV-92–053, March 18, 1992.

188. A. Khlopyev, " 'Yes!' to Union: Russians Confirm Their Choice of 17 March Last Year," *Sovetskaya rossiya*, March 19, 1992. FBIS-SOV-92–055, March 20, 1992.

189. *Interfax*, March 18, 1992. FBIS-SOV-92–055, March 20, 1992.

190. Lyudimila Saraskina, "Capitalism Is for the People to Choose," *Moscow News Fax Digest*, March 24, 1992. FBIS-SOV-92–060, March 27, 1992.

191. *Interfax*, March 26, 1992. FBIS-SOV-92–060, March 27, 1992.

192. Nugzar Betaneli, "Voters Propose Their Own Agenda for the Congress," *Izvestia*, March 24, 1992. FBIS-SOV-92–063, April 1, 1992.

193. ITAR-TASS, April 7, 1992. FBIS-SOV-92–070, April 10, 1992.

194. Riga Radio Network, April 15, 1992. FBIS-SOV-92–077, April 21, 1992.

195. ITAR-TASS, April 20, 1992. FBIS-SOV-92–078, April 22, 1992.

196. "Novosti," Moscow Teleradiokompaniya Ostankino, April 24, 1992. FBIS-SOV-92–087, May 5, 1992.

197. Nugzar Betaneli, "Half of Muscovites Assess Economic Situation as Grave, but Bearable," *Izvestia*, June 23, 1992. FBIS-SOV-92–124, June 26, 1992.

198. Mikhail Gorbachev, *Perestroika: New Thinking for Our Country and the World*, pp. 44, 48, 76.

199. *Pravda*, April 5, 1988.

200. *Pravda*, May 11, 1988.

201. "Stochki zreniya dela," *Nedelya*, no. 27, 1988, pp. 6–7. As cited in RL460/88, October 10, 1988.

202. A. Latynina, "The Tolling of the Bell Is not Prayer," *Novy mir*, August 1988. CDSP, January 4, 1989.

203. Aleksey Kiva, "Wage Leveling," *Sovetskaya kultura*, October 1988. JPRS-UEA-89–003.

204. A. Migranyan, "Is It Easy to Become Europe?" *Century and Peace*, December 1988. JPRS-UPA-89–015.

205. "M. S. Gorbachev's Closing Remarks at the Plenary Session of the CPSU Central Committee on April 25, 1989," *Pravda*, April 27, 1989. CDSP, June 7, 1989.

206. Yu. Bogomolov, "A Film for Every Day," *Literaturnaya gazeta*, June 14, 1989. JPRS-UPA-89–047, July 27, 1989.

207. Congress speech by S. V. Chervonopisky, first secretary of the Cherkassy City ZUCL Committee, Ukraine Republic, *Izvestia*, June 3, 1989.

208. "Both Democracy and Centralism," *Moscow News*, no. 42, 1989. Interview with Leon Onikov, official of the CPSU Central Committee executive secretariat.

209. Leonid Ionin, "Party Reform Is Urgent," *Moscow News*, no. 42, 1989.

210. Mikhail Poltorain, People's Deputy of the USSR, "Who's Sewing a Trench Coat for Perestroika?" *Moscow News*, no. 42, 1989.

211. "Cooperatives, Law and Emotions," *Moscow News*, no. 41, 1989.

212. *Kommunist*, November 1989. JPRS-UKO-90–002. Conversation with the director of USSR Gosplan Scientific Research Economics Institute.

213. Viktor Sergeyevich Rozov, writer and playwright, "Negating Negation," *Kommunist*, November 1989. JPRS-UKO-90–002.

214. "For a Policy of National Accord and Russian Rebirth," *Literaturnaya Rossia*, December 29, 1989, pp. 2–3. CDSP, vol. 42, no. 1, 1990.

215. "Second Congress Debates," *Izvestia*, December 17, 1989. CDSP, vol. 42, no. 1, 1990.

216. Fyodor Buriatsky, chairman of the Subcommittee on Humanitarian, Scientific and Cultural Cooperation of the Supreme Soviet Committee on International Affairs, *Meeting Report Kennan Institute for Advanced Russian Studies*, January 1990.

217. A. Manilova, "Social Accounting: Does Everyone Poor Mean Everyone Equal?" *Leningradskaya pravda*, January 23, 1990. JPRS-UEA-90–013, April 12, 1990.

218. *Pravda*, February 7, 1990. CDSP, vol. 42, no. 16, 1990.

219. *Sovetskaya rossiya*, February 25, 1990. JPRS-UEA-90–011, April 2, 1990.

220. Aleksandr Nikolayevich Yakovlev, *Kommunist*, February 22, 1990. JPRS-UKO-90–007, April 18, 1990.

221. "What Hinders Reform?" *The Literary Gazette International*, April 1990.

222. V. Leybin, "The Problem of Alienation through the Lens of Perestroika," *Kommunist*, April 1990. JPRS-UKO-90–009, June 19, 1990.

223. N. Naumova, "The Transitional Period: World Experience and Our Problems," *Kommunist*, May 1990. JPRS-UKO-90–011, August 1, 1990.

224. Michael McFaul, "The Last Hurrah for the CPSU," Radio Liberty Report on the USSR, July 27, 1990.

225. Andrei Nuikin, "Military Coup in the USSR?" *Moscow News*, no. 37, 1990.

226. A. Migranyan, historian, "Social Forecast: An Indissoluble Union?—On the Prospects of the Soviet State System," *Izvestia*, September 20, 1990. CDSP, October 31, 1990.

227. "Mikhail Gorbachev's Speech at the Session of the USSR Supreme Soviet," *Pravda*, September 22, 1990. *Reprints from the Soviet Press*, December 15, 1990.

228. "M. S. Gorbachev's Concluding Remarks at the Plenary Session of the CPSU Central Committee," *Pravda*, October 11, 1990. CDSP, vol. 42, no. 42, 1990.

229. V. Dolganov and A. Stepovoi, "Izvestia Parliamentary Correspondents Report from the Kremlin," *Izvestia*, October 19, 1990. CDSP, vol. 42, no. 42, 1990.

230. Vladimir Tikhonov, "I'm Leaving the Party: Why?" *The Literary Gazette International*, October 1990.

231. "To Our Readers," *The Literary Gazette International*, November 1990.

232. Aleksei Kiva, doctor of history, "October in the Mirror of Utopias and Anti-Utopias," *Izvestia*, November 5, 1990. CDSP, vol. 42, no. 44, 1990.

233. TASS, November 8, 1990. [Translation source misplaced.]

234. "The Fourth Congress of USSR People's Deputies," *Izvestia*, December 24, 1990. CDSP, vol. 43, no. 2, 1991.

235. Justin Burke, "Gorbachev Shifts to the Right," *The Christian Science Monitor*, December 6, 1990.

236. Andrei Giachev, "Will the West Save Us from Ourselves," *Moscow News*, December 1990.

237. Alexander Yakovlev, Central television, "TSN," July 27, 1991; *Report on the USSR*, August 9, 1991.

238. Tamara Zamyatina, TASS, August 2, 1991. FBIS-SOV-91–150, August 5, 1991.

239. Academician S. Shatalin, "Infantile Disorder of Leftism, or Why Society Is Threatened by Neo-Bolshevism," *Komsomolskaya pravda*, September 20, 1991. FBIS-SOV-91–189, September 30, 1991.

240. "The Final and Decisive Congress of the All-Union Lenin Young Communist League," *Nezavisimaya gazeta*, September 28, 1991. CDSP, October 30, 1991.

241. Pavel Voshchatov, "Land of Commandments: CPSU Short Course in Top-Secret Documents," *Komsomolskaya pravda*, October 2, 1991. FBIS-SOV-91–195, October 8, 1991.

242. TASS, October 30, 1991. JPRS-SOV-91–211, October 31, 1991.

243. "I Shall Bear My Burden to the End," *Le Figaro*, October 28, 1991. FBIS-SOV-91–210, October 30, 1991.

244. Nikolay Stepanchenko, "International Service," TASS, October 3, 1991. JPRS-UPA-91–043, October 18, 1991.

245. *Berlin, ADN*, November 18, 1991. FBIS-SOV-91–223, November 19, 1991.

246. "On the Activities of the CPSU and Russian Soviet Federated Socialist Republic Communist Party," TASS, November 6, 1991. FBIS-SOV-91–216, November 1991.

247. Moscow Radio Rossii Network, November 9, 1991. FBIS-SOV-91–219, November 13, 1991.

248. Vienna ORD Television Network, December 3, 1991. FBIS-SOV-91–234, December 5, 1991.

249. Alexandr Yakovlev, "Seven Ds or How Many Steps We Must Make into the Future," *Moscow News*, January 5–12, 1992.

250. Dmitry Kazutin, "What I Have Read, Heard or Seen," *Moscow News*, January 5–12, 1992.

251. Christel Vollmer, "Yeltsin's Adviser: Missiles Will Fly Soon," *Bild Am Sonntag*, January 12, 1992. FBIS-SOV-92–010, January 15, 1992.

252. "Nation and Society," *Interfax*, January 17, 1992. FBIS-SOV-92–012, January 17, 1992.

253. *Argumenty i fakty*, January 1992. FBIS-SOV-92–015, January 23, 1992.

254. Tokyo NHK General Television Network, February 10, 1992. FBIS-SOV-92–029, February 12, 1992.

255. Mainz ZDF Television Network, February 11, 1992. FBIS-SOV-92–029, February 12, 1992.

256. Dmitry Kazutin, "What I Have Read, Heard or Seen," *Moscow News*, February 16–23, 1992.

257. Robert Minasov, "The Nomenklatura Prepares to Take Revenge," *Rossiyskaya gazeta*, March 4, 1992. FBIS-SOV-92–048, March 11, 1992.

258. *Interfax*, March 18, 1992. FBIS-SOV-92–054, March 19, 1992.

259. TASS, March 24, 1992. FBIS-SOV-92–058, March 25, 1992.

260. Moscow Russian Television Network, April 19. FBIS-SOV-92–078, April 22, 1992.

261. *Interfax*, May 15, 1992. FBIS-SOV-92–099, May 21, 1992.

262. Vladimir Isakov, "Parliamentary Diary: Historical Suicide," *Sovietskaya rossiaya*, May 19, 1992. FBIS-SOV-92–099, May 21, 1992.

263. L. Nikitinskiy, "To the President's Health! Why Rumors of 'Regime Violation' by Russian Leader Are Turning into Parliamentary Scandal," *Komsomolskaya pravda*, May 19, 1992. FBIS-SOV-92–099, May 21, 1992.

264. "Presidential Bulletin," *Interfax*, May 20, 1992. FBIS-SOV-92–103, May 28, 1992.

265. Kazis Uscila, ITAR-TASS, May 26, 1992. FBIS-SOV-92–103, May 28, 1992.

266. Nikolay Andreyev, "The Russian President Is Constant in His Unpredictability," *Izvestia*, May 7, 1992. FBIS-SOV-92–092, May 12, 1992.

267. ITAR-TASS, June 15, 1992. FBIS-SOV-92–116, June 16, 1992.

268. "Kyodo," *Interfax*, June 17, 1992. FBIS-SOV-92–119, June 19, 1992.

269. Valeriy Demidetskiy, ITAR-TASS, June 22, 1992. JPRS-SOV-92–120, June 22, 1992.

270. Moscow Russian Television Network, July 15, 1992. FBIS-SOV-92–137, July 16, 1992.

SUGGESTED READINGS

Aslund, Anders. *Gorbachev's Struggle for Economic Reform*. Ithaca, New York: Cornell University Press, 1989.

Brada, Joseph S., and Karl-Eugen Wadekin, eds. *Socialist Agriculture in Transition*. Boulder, Colo.: Westview Press, 1987.

Breslauer, George W., ed. *Can Gorbachev's Reforms Succeed?* Berkeley, Calif.: Berkeley-Stanford Program in Soviet Studies, Center for Slavic and East European Studies, 1990.

Bronfenbrenner, Eurie. *Two Worlds of Childhood: U.S. and U.S.S.R.* New York: Russell Sage Foundation and Basic Books, 1970.

Duncan, E. R., ed. *Dimensions of World Food Problems*. Ames: The Iowa State University Press, 1978.

Jasny, Naum. *The Socialized Agriculture of the USSR*. Stanford, Calif.: Stanford University Press, 1946.

Fainsod, Merle. *How Russia Is Ruled*. Cambridge: Harvard University Press, 1952.

Glasnost Examined: Inside the USSR. Washington, D.C.: World Media Association, 1988.

Gorbachev, Mikhail S. *On the Agrarian Policy of the CPSU in the Present Conditions* (Report . . . at the Plenary Meeting of the CPSU Central Committee, March 15–16, 1989). Moscow: Novosti Press Agency, 1989.

Gorbachev, Mikhail S. *Perestroika: New Thinking for Our Country and the World*. New York: Harper and Row Publishers, 1987.

Hammer, Darrell P. *The USSR The Politics of Oligarchy*. Boulder, Col.: Westview Press, 1990.

Kelley, Donald R., and Shannon G. Davis, eds. *The Sons of Sergei: Khrushchev and Gorbachev as Reformers*. New York: Praeger, 1992.

Laird, Roy D., and Edward Crowley, eds. *Soviet Agriculture: The Permanent Crisis*. New York: Praeger, 1965.

Laird, Roy D., and Betty A. Laird. *A Soviet Lexicon*. Lexington, Mass.: Lexington Books, 1988.

Laird, Roy D., and Betty A. Laird. *Soviet Communism and Agrarian Revolution*. Harmondsworth, England: Penguin Books, 1970.

MaCauley, Martin, ed. *Gorbachev and Perestroika*. London: Macmillan Press, 1990.

MacIver, Robert M. *The Web of Government*. New York: Macmillan, 1948.

Mitrany, David. *Marx against the Peasant*. Chapel Hill, N.C.: The University of North Carolina Press, 1951.

Nove, Alec. *Glasnost in Action*. Boston: Unwin Hyman, 1990.

Popper, K. R. *The Open Society and Its Enemies—The High Tide of Prophecy: Hegel, Marx and the Aftermath*, vol. 2. London: George Routledge and Sons, 1947.

Pryor, Frederic L. *The Red and the Green: The Rise and Fall of Collectivized Agriculture in Marxist Regimes*. Princeton, N.J.: Princeton University Press, 1992.

Rahr, Alexander. *A Biographical Directory of 100 Leading Soviet Officials*. Boulder, Colo.: Westview Press, 1990.

Tilly Charles. *From Mobilization to Revolution*. Reading, Mass.: Addison-Wesley, 1978.

INDEX

About the Author

ROY D. LAIRD is Professor Emeritus of Political Science, Russian and East European Studies at the University of Kansas. Most of the fifteen books and monographs that he has authored or co-authored, edited or co-edited have dealt with Soviet and East European domestic affairs, especially agricultural and peasant affairs. He organized the first International Conference on Soviet and East European Agriculture, which was held at the University of Kansas in 1962. Over the years Laird's work has been supported by such institutions as the Rockefeller Foundation, National Science Foundation, Ford Foundation and the Hays-Fulbright program. His most recent book, with Betty A. Laird, is *A Soviet Lexicon: Important Terms, Concepts, and Phrases.*